Strike from the Sea

Strike from the Sea

A Survey of British Naval Air Operations, 1909-69

Robert Jackson

Arthur Barker Limited   5 Winsley Street London W1

SBN 213 00158 6

Printed in Great Britain by
Willmer Brothers Limited, Birkenhead

Contents

'*It is not the beginning of any great matter, but the continuing of the same until it be thoroughly finished which yieldeth the true glory.*'

— from Drake's Prayer, used in the Royal Navy's Commissioning Ceremony.

List of Illustrations

Introduction

To compress the story of sixty years of British Naval Aviation into sixty thousand words or so has been no easy task. Of necessity, much has had to be left out. The task has been made no less difficult by the fact that much of the information on the Fleet Air Arm's operations since 1945 is still classified; it will be some time yet before the full story of the Royal Navy's airmen over Suez, for example, can be told.

In the past half-century, all things have changed in the Royal Navy except two: tradition and courage. This is primarily a story of men, and of courage; courage that has called for the same qualities of will and mind whether it involved a suicidal attack on an enemy battle fleet or a desperate attempt by a young pilot to save his friend's life in a crippled aircraft over the Indian Ocean, a quarter of a century later.

The story of the Fleet Air Arm in its early days was one of too little – too late. Of men flung into combat and sacrificed because the aircraft they flew were outdated and outclassed, of the policy-makers turning a blind eye to what was going on in the world around them and refusing to learn past lessons.

Let us fervently hope that those early sacrifices never have to be repeated for the same reasons: because there is too little, and it is too late.

I have received assistance from many quarters in the preparation of this book, but I should like to thank the following in particular for their help:

John Gladish, who flew Camels with the RFC and RAF during the First World War, and who commanded the Fleet Air Arm Photographic Squadron as a Lieutenant-Commander

I

RNVR in the Second; Commander Shrives, Naval Air Command PRO, RNAS Lee-on-Solent; J. D. Brown, Esq., of MoD (Admiralty) Historical Branch, author of *Carrier Operations in World War Two* (Ian Allen); Frank Yeoman, who knows more about Sopwith Camels than anyone else I have met; and, last but far from least, John McVittie, who flew Swordfish on escort duties in both hemispheres.

Prologue: So Great a Prize

It was bitterly cold in the Sopwith Camel's tiny, cramped cockpit. Rivulets of moisture streamed from Lieutenant Stuart Culley's eyes and froze on his cheeks. He had found it impossible to wear his goggles; a film of frost misted them over within seconds. His hand on the stick felt numb and lifeless. The cold had brought with it a strange sense of detachment; even the full-powered roar of the oil-spitting Bentley B.R.1 rotary had become nothing more than a kind of dull, heavy silence.

Only one thing had any reality; the great, silvery cigar that hung in the sky beyond the whirling arc of the Camel's propeller, the elongated shape of Zeppelin L.53, towards which the little fighter had been clawing its way for the past forty minutes as it cruised serenely at twenty thousand feet.

It was 09.30 hours on 11 August 1918. The previous evening, the Harwich Light Cruiser Force had put to sea and set course towards the Heligoland Bight, where it was to conduct a 'special operation'. The force consisted of four light cruisers and eight destroyers, accompanied by six flying-boats. The light cruisers carried six coastal motor-boats, whose task was to range the coastal waters of the Bight at high speed and make torpedo attacks on any enemy shipping they ran into. The whole force was under the command of Vice-Admiral Sir Reginald Tyrwhitt, supervising the operation from his flagship, the cruiser *Curacao*.

There was, however, another purpose behind the Harwich Force's penetration into enemy waters – a purpose centred upon a weird-looking contraption towed behind one of the destroyers, HMS *Redoubt*. It was a lighter, with its top boarded over to make a platform of sorts; and perched precariously on the plat-

3

form, lashed by the spray as the lighter bounced around in *Redoubt's* wake, was a Sopwith Camel.

The idea was simple enough. During previous operations, the Harwich Force had been considerably hampered by the presence of Zeppelins, prowling backwards and forwards over the warships at heights of up to twenty thousand feet – where they were safe from naval gunfire and from interception by the float planes that the Force carried with it. The nearest British land base was Harwich, and no aircraft existed that possessed a four-hundred-mile radius of action coupled with the ability to outclimb and outfight the airships. The logical step, therefore, was to convey fighter aircraft to a point where they would stand a reasonable chance of coming to grips with the enemy – hence the lighter-borne Camel.

In the early hours of 11 August, the ships of the Harwich Force began to transmit a series of fake wireless signals with the object of advertising their presence to the enemy. Admiral Tyrwhitt was confident that it would be enough to lure the Zeppelins into the air in the morning – and the Camel's pilot would have the chance they were all waiting for.

The pilot in question, Lieutenant Culley, was feeling anything but confident. He had gained a fair amount of experience in flying off a pitching deck at Rosyth, where he had taken part in trials on the aircraft-carrier *Nairana* – but the *Nairana* was a far different proposition from a thirty-foot lighter. So far, only two attempts had been made to fly off a lighter; the first had ended in disaster when the Camel, piloted by Lt.-Colonel C. R. Samson, failed to attain flying speed and nose-dived over the front of the platform into the sea. Samson struggled out of the cockpit under water to find the lighter right above him; somehow, he had managed to claw his way from underneath it and had surfaced just in time. The second test, made by Culley himself, had been a success – but only just. There were still a lot of snags – and there had been time to iron out only one or two before the Harwich Force sailed on 10 August.

The cruisers hove-to off the island of Terschelling at 05.30 hours and lowered their six motor-boats into the water. Half-an-hour later, the little craft moved off at high speed towards the mouth of the River Ems. An attempt was made to launch three flying-boats which, like Culley's Camel, had been towed with the Force on lighters – but there was a long swell, no wind, and the aircraft were too heavily laden with fuel and ammunition to take off under these conditions. The other three flying-boats, covering the Force from their base at Great Yarmouth, had not yet arrived on the scene. When they did, at 07.30, they were immediately ordered to patrol the enemy coast and search for the six motor-boats, which were by that time overdue. As a matter of fact, the boats had run into serious trouble. Since 07.30 they had been continually harassed by well-directed air attacks made by seaplanes of the German Naval Air Squadrons at Borkum and Norderney. Three boats were bombed and set on fire for the loss of one seaplane; three more came under heavy fire from the shore and ran aground.

The three Felixstowe F.2A flying-boats from Great Yarmouth, meanwhile, had failed to locate the motor-boats – but shortly after eight o'clock the leader of the formation, Major Robert Leckie, spotted a Zeppelin approaching from the north-east at fifteen thousand feet. Not wishing to break wireless silence, he turned back and warned the Harwich Force of the airship's presence by visual signals. By similar means, he was informed that the Camel was being prepared for take-off; a minute later he was ordered to return to base and did so somewhat reluctantly, as his patrol was not even half over.

The L.53 was sighted by the warships at 08.25, several miles away to the north-east. Admiral Tyrwhitt immediately brought the flotilla round in a wide turn and ordered the destroyers to lay a smoke screen, hoping to lure the airship further out to sea. The L.53's commander, Korvettenkapitän Proelss, fell for the bait. He turned and followed the warships cautiously, slipping in and out of tufts of scattered cloud. Far below, one of the warships – HMS *Redoubt* – turned into the wind and increased her speed to thirty knots. On the lighter behind her, Culley's ground crew clung grimly to the Camel's wings and tried to keep their footing on the slippery platform. There were no hand-rails;

one slip would be enough to send a man hurtling overboard.

08.55 hours. Already soaked to the skin, eighteen-year-old Culley sat hunched in the cockpit, trying to escape the worst of the flying spray, and gave a signal. Teetering to keep his balance, a mechanic swung the Camel's propeller; his was the worst job of all, for in addition to the risk of falling overboard he would be chewed to pieces by the whirling blades if he should happen to stumble forward.

To everyone's surprise, the one hundred and fifty hp Bentley burst into life at the first turn, blinding the men on the wings with fierce slipstream. One of them indicated that the shackles fastening the aircraft to the platform had been undone, and Culley opened the throttle. Another signal, and the crew slid off the wings and threw themselves flat on the sodden deck.

Free from any restriction, the Camel's tail came up immediately as Culley held the stick neutral. The thirty-knot wind did the rest; after a run of only five feet, the little fighter lurched into the air. For a long moment it hung there, apparently motionless, a few feet above the heaving sea – and then a cheer went up as it slowly began to gather speed.

With the sun behind him, Culley started the long climb towards the enemy. The Zeppelin had been clearly visible when he took off, but now he lost sight of it. As he climbed higher, he seemed to be heading into an opaque void; the effect of bright sunlight reflected on a thin haze. There was, however, one consolation; if he couldn't see the enemy, it was unlikely that the enemy would be able to see him.

The minutes ticked by with painful slowness. As he climbed on, a film of ice began to form on his drenched clothing. In spite of his thick flying combination, the chill ate through to the bone.

At 09.15 the Camel suddenly burst out of the white murk – and Culley sighted the airship again, above him and to port. The distance between the two narrowed gradually, but at this height the Camel's rate of climb was painfully slow. Five minutes later, the Zeppelin turned back towards the German coast, climbing as it did so; the crew had at last woken up and spotted the fighter rising to intercept. By 09.30 the Zeppelin was at nineteen thousand feet and the Camel some three hundred feet lower, and Culley knew that if he was going to have any chance of success the attack would have to be made now; another couple of minutes, and the Camel would have reached its ceiling. Its twenty-eight-foot wings were already beginning to vibrate as the machine approached the stall.

The vast bulk of the airship seemed to fill the whole of the sky above him, and the Camel shuddered as he opened fire with the first of his two Lewis guns. After firing only fifteen rounds, it jammed. Desperately, he hauled back the stick into the pit of his stomach and opened up with his second Lewis, pouring a double charger of ammunition into the Zeppelin's envelope. A second later, the Camel fell away in a vicious stall-turn to the right.

The controls responded once more as the speed increased and Culley eased the fighter out of its dive. Looking over his shoulder, he felt wild elation as he saw a dull red glow starting to spread along the side of the L.53. He pushed the stick hard over and dived out of the way as the airship began to fall slowly, feeling the heat as it dropped past him. Seconds later, the Zeppelin was a fiery torch, burning from stem to stern as it fell vertically towards the sea three miles below. A tiny figure dropped away from the blazing bulk, tumbling over and over, its clothing alight. Fascinated, Culley watched as the burning mass plunged into the haze below, staining the sky with a great question-mark of smoke.

Far below, a great cheer went up from the warships of the Harwich Force as the men saw the smouldering mass of girders and fabric that had been the L.53 tumble out of the murk and smack into the sea in a cloud of steam. Then, as the minutes went by, their elation changed to anxiety as Culley's aircraft failed to appear.

Above the haze, Culley was in trouble. For a start, he was uncertain of his position. After cruising around for several minutes in a vain attempt to locate the British flotilla, he flew to the Dutch coast and turned south until he sighted Texel. Turning out to sea again, he went down to six thousand feet, flying on a northerly heading towards the Terschelling Bank. But there was still no sign of the ships; patchy cloud hid the water. Then suddenly, the Camel's engine spluttered and died as the main fuel tank ran dry. Culley rapidly switched to the reserve tank and the motor at once burst into powerful life again – but the secondary tank held only enough petrol for a further twenty minutes' flying. If he failed to sight the ships within the next couple of minutes, he would not have enough fuel to reach the Dutch coast again.

Looking down through a gap in the clouds, he spotted a Dutch fishing boat and decided to land in the sea beside it. Throttling back, he glided down – and then, emerging into a clear patch, he saw two destroyers. Close behind them came the whole flotilla.

Out of sheer relief, Culley looped and rolled his fighter over the warships for several minutes; then he curved down to make a perfect landing in the water ahead of HMS *Redoubt*. An hour later, with Culley safely aboard the destroyer and the Camel hoisted on to the lighter, the warships turned and set course for Harwich.

It was the second time in history that an enemy aircraft had been destroyed by a fighter launched from a vessel at sea. Almost exactly a year earlier, on 21 August 1917, Zeppelin L.23 had been shot down in flames off Lodbjerg, Denmark, by Flight Sub-Lieutenant B. A. Smart, flying a Sopwith Pup launched from a platform on HMS *Yarmouth*. Smart had come down in the sea and had been picked up by the destroyer HMS *Prince*, but the Pup had been wrecked. On the other hand, Culley's action – for which he was later awarded the DSO – was significant because it marked the first time that a fighter and its pilot had been safely recovered after being launched by, and successfully providing air protection for, a Naval force engaged in an operation against the enemy. It would be nearly a quarter of a century before Culley's exploit would be repeated, on a far greater scale, in European waters.

And on that August day half-a-century ago, as the Harwich Force turned for home, Admiral Tyrwhitt made a curious signal to the flotilla. It read: 'Flag. General. Attention is drawn to hymn number 224, verse 7.'

When the sailors turned up the reference in their hymn books, they understood. For verse 7 of hymn 224 ran:

'Oh happy band of pilgrims,
Look upwards to the skies,
Where such a light affliction
Shall win you such a prize.'

1 The Navy Grows Wings

In March 1907, Wilbur and Orville Wright offered to sell the patents of their flying machine to the British Admiralty. The offer was turned down because, as a senior Naval officer recorded at the time, it was not felt that the employment of flying machines by the Royal Navy would serve any practical purpose during the foreseeable future.

The Admiralty could not really be blamed for any lack of foresight; in common with most government bodies throughout the world, it simply held the opinion that the aeroplane was a toy, an ingenious plaything that still had to prove that it might have some practical value. It was only when Blériot made his famous hop across the Channel – and that was still two years in the future – that influential people in Britain and elsewhere began to wake up to the fact that flying, other than as a new sport for the adventurous and foolhardy, might have a serious future.

Airships, as opposed to heavier-than-air machines, were an entirely different proposition. For some time, the Admiralty had been following airship development in Germany with considerable interest – and it was no longer possible to ignore the enthusiasm with which flying was being greeted in that country. In July 1908 the Director of Naval Ordnance, Captain R. H. S. Bacon, DSO, proposed that the firm of Vickers Sons and Maxim should be approached with a view to submitting a design for a rigid-type airship for use by the Royal Navy – and the proposals were supported by Admiral Sir John Fisher and the Admiralty Board. The proposals were duly passed on for consideration by the Imperial Defence Committee, who reported – six months later, in January 1909 – that although they did not consider the country to be in any danger of hostile air attack, they

11

felt that the only way the Royal Navy could investigate the potential of airships was by using them itself. Accordingly, £35,000 was set aside in the Naval Estimates of 1909–10 for the building of a Naval airship.

Vickers Sons and Maxim's tender was finally accepted on 7 May 1909, and construction of the airship – known as Rigid Naval Airship No. 1, or more popularly as the 'Mayfly' – began almost immediately at Barrow-in-Furness. A special unit under Captain Murray Sueter was formed at the Admiralty to liaise with the makers during the building of the craft.

Captain Sueter was also a member of the Advisory Committee for Aeronautics, which had been appointed by the Government a month earlier under the presidency of Lord Rayleigh. There were ten members in all, drawn from every organization in Britain that showed an active interest in aviation. It was this Committee that paved the way for the formation, three years later, of the Royal Flying Corps and the Naval Air Service.

By the end of 1910, however, with the 'Mayfly' rapidly nearing completion, the Admiralty – although its interest in heavier-than-air machines was slowly awakening and although applications had been requested from Naval officers who were interested in learning to fly – still showed no inclination to buy any aircraft of its own to train a cadre of qualified Naval pilots. Across the Channel, the French Navy was quicker off the mark; in September 1910 it had purchased its first aircraft, a Farman, and seven officers were in the process of learning to fly it. An even more significant step towards the future of Naval aviation had been taken in the United States in November, when Eugene Ely – a pilot working for Glenn Curtiss – has succeeded in flying a fifty hp Curtiss biplane from a fifty-seven-foot platform mounted on the light cruiser USS *Birmingham*. In spite of hitting the sea seconds after take-off, he stayed in the air and landed safely ashore. Two months later, in January 1911, he landed successfully on a one hundred-and-two-foot platform on the cruiser *Pennsylvania* and took off again forty-five minutes later. He received a nice letter from the US Navy Department, congratulating him on his exploit – but that was all. Ely never lived to see the birth of the aircraft-carrier; he was killed in a flying accident soon after his history-making feat.

It was in February 1911 that British Naval aviation finally started to get off the ground – and it had a strange beginning. One of the pioneers of the Royal Aero Club, Frank K. McClean, offered the Admiralty the use – completely free of charge – of two of his own Gnome-engined Short biplanes for training purposes. Another pioneer airman, George Cockburn, volunteered to act as flying instructor. Training was to take place at Eastchurch on the Isle of Sheppey, which was used by members of the Royal Aero Club.

The Admiralty, hardly surprisingly, snapped up the offer. Out of the two hundred Naval officers who applied, four were selected; they were Lieutenants C. R. Samson, A. M. Longmore and R. Gregory of the Royal Navy, together with Lieutenant G. V. Wildman Lushington, an Officer of Marines. The latter went sick early in March and his place was taken by Lieutenant E. L. Gerrard of the Royal Marine Light Infantry. Samson and Longmore were the first to qualify for their pilot's certificates on 24 April, and they were followed by the other two officers on 1 May. All four took part in a flypast when Prince Louis of Battenberg, commanding the Reserve Fleet at Sheerness, visited Eastchurch on 11 May.

In addition to the two original Short biplanes, McClean loaned four more later in 1911; all but one, Short No. 36, which was eventually returned to its owner, were subsequently bought by the Admiralty.

In August 1911, while the training of more Naval pilots went on at a slow but steady rate, a long-awaited event took place: the launching of the 'Mayfly' at Barrow. The triumph, however, was short-lived. On 24 September she broke her back while being manhandled into her shed during a high wind and was completely wrecked. As a result, the Admiralty – in the face of considerable opposition – decide to abandon rigid airships and concentrate on the development of aircraft.

In October 1911, a small permanent staff of twelve naval ratings was attached to Eastchurch – and the first naval air station in Britain was in the making. The following month, Commander Oliver Schwann – who had been a member of the special unit attached to Vickers Ltd to liaise on the building of the ill-fated 'Mayfly', and who had become passionately interested in the possibility of flying an aircraft off the sea with the aid of floats – achieved his ambition by making a short hop in an Avro biplane equipped with floats. He crashed at the end of it; but the aircraft was not badly damaged and made several more trials early the following year, piloted by the aircraft engineer and designer. S. V. Sippe.

Meanwhile, alarm was steadily growing in Government circles over Britain's lack of military aircraft, compared with France and Germany. On 18 November 1911, the Prime Minister – Mr Asquith – sent a memorandum to the Imperial Defence Committee in which he asked them to 'consider the future development of aerial navigation for both Naval and Military purposes, the means which might be taken to secure to this country an efficient Air Service, and also whether steps should be taken to form a corps of aviators for Naval and Military purposes, or otherwise to co-ordinate the study of aviation in the Navy and Army'. The Imperial Defence Committee passed on the request to its technical sub-committee, whose recommendations – submitted in February 1912 – were to lead directly to the formation of the Naval and Military Wings of the Royal Flying Corps two months later.

While the Defence Committee was laying the foundations of British military aviation, a handful of naval pilots continued to experiment with new ideas and techniques. Foremost among them was Lieutenant Samson; in December 1911 he succeeded in flying Short biplane S.38, with special flotation bags attached to her wheel-skids, off a platform built over the bows of HMS *Africa* in Sheerness Harbour and in landing safely on the sea. Also in December, for the first time, the task of the Navy's airmen in time of war was clearly defined. Their primary role was to be one of reconnaissance, but they would also be required to search for enemy submarines, to locate minefields and to act as spotters for naval guns. With remarkable foresight, the task included the ability to 'ascend from a floating base' – a glimpse of the aircraft-carriers of the future.

On 13 April 1912, the Royal Flying Corps was constituted by Royal Warrant. Captain Murray Sueter was appointed to command the Naval Wing; his opposite number in command of the Military Wing being Captain F. H. Sykes. Two months later, on 19 June, a Central Flying School was formed at Upavon in Wiltshire, with Captain Godfrey Paine, CB, MVO, as its Commandant. Although Upavon was to take over all basic flying training, Eastchurch – now under Commander Samson – was to continue as an advanced flying school and an experimental unit.

On 8 May 1912, the new Naval Wing was given an opportunity to show its paces at a review of the fleet held at Weymouth. Commander Samson provided the highlight of the naval air demonstration by taking off from the foredeck of HMS *Hibernia* in a modified Short S.27 as the warship steamed into the wind at ten knots – the first time a British aircraft had taken off from a moving ship.

In July, Captain Sueter and the Director of the Royal Aircraft Factory, Mervyn O' Gorman, visited France, Austria and Germany to gather information on the state of airship development in those countries – and they came back seriously perturbed by what they had seen. In their report to the Imperial Defence Committee, they stated that Germany's latest Zeppelins were not only capable of ranging over vast areas of the North Sea, but also of reaching the coast of Britain without refuelling. In addition, they were also equipped to carry bombs. As a result of this report, it was decided to set up a chain of air stations to defend Britain's east coast. Initially, there would be nine; at Berwick, Newcastle, Cleethorpes, Cromer, Harwich, Dover, Portsmouth, Plymouth and the Lizard. These would be followed by seven more, at Scapa Flow, Aberdeen, Cromarty, the Clyde, Filey, Weymouth and Pembroke. At the same time, the duties of the Naval Wing were expanded to include the prevention of attacks on warships, dockyards and other vital targets by hostile aircraft and airships.

It was on 11 December 1912 that the Naval Wing suffered its first fatal flying accident. It happened when Lieutenant Wilfred

Parke, an experienced naval pilot, was flying a Handley Page Type F monoplane from Hendon to Oxford. The engine began to misfire and Parke made the mistake of turning downwind – with the result that the motor stalled and the aircraft dived into the ground. Both Parke and his passenger, Arkell Hardwick – Handley Page's chief pilot – were killed.

By the end of the year, Britain's first seaplane station – the Isle of Grain – had been commissioned. Also by this time, twenty-two officers and petty officers had qualified as pilots; and a further thirty had completed their basic flying training at Upavon. At the beginning of 1913 the Naval Wing had a total of sixteen aircraft on its inventory; eight biplanes, five monoplanes and three seaplanes. It had also acquired a small non-rigid airship known as Naval Airship No. 2 and built by T. E. Willows.

On 7 May 1913, the old cruiser HMS *Hermes* was commissioned as the headquarters ship of the Naval Wing. She was fitted with a trackway on her forecastle from which an eighty hp Caudron amphibian made several trial flights during the spring of that year. Later, she was equipped with three Short S.41 'Folder' twin-float biplanes, which were housed in a canvas hanger. These modified versions of the basic S.41 had wings that folded backwards along the fuselage for easy stowage – a significant development in the design of naval aircraft.

In July 1913, for the first time, aircraft were used by the Royal Navy in conjunction with surface vessels during a series of fleet manoeuvres. A total of 351 ships of all types took part, divided into two opposing forces known as Red and Blue. Blue was the strongest force, consisting of 239 warships to Red's 112. The seaplane-carrier *Hermes* also formed part of Red force. The ratio between the two fleets, in fact, was an almost exact reproduction of the ratio existing at the time between the Royal Navy and the Imperial German Navy.

When 'war' was declared at four o'clock in the afternoon of 23 July, part of the Blue fleet was on station off the Scottish coast near Rosyth; the remainder, apart from a small force of destroyers and cruisers, was in position off the Outer Hebrides. Their object was to bring Red's forces to action wherever pos-

sible, to forestall any possible invasion by the latter of Blue's
coast.

In addition to the *Hermes,* which carried two Short S.41s,
Red force also had the air station at Great Yarmouth with its
complement of four aircraft: another Short S.41, equipped with
W/T (great strides in the development of which had been made
during trials in May); two Farman MF.7's newly acquired from
France; and a Borel seaplane. Blue force had a similar number
of aircraft divided between the air stations at Leven and
Cromarty.

In the early hours of 24 July the *Hermes* left Great Yarmouth
Roads and anchored to the north of Spurn Point. That afternoon, one of her Short seaplanes was lowered into the water and
the pilot managed to take off uneventfully, in spite of a heavy
swell. His orders were to patrol to the north, but a few minutes
after take-off a thick fog began to descend and he was forced to
return. However, the first air patrol of the 'war' had been made
– and throughout it, the crew of the Short had been in constant
touch with the *Hermes* by wireless.

After hoisting the seaplane on board, the *Hermes* returned to
Great Yarmouth where she took on a third aircraft, a Caudron
floatplane, before putting to sea again. Two patrols had meanwhile been flown that day by the Yarmouth-based aircraft; one
of them, a Farman MF.7, returned with a report of two submarines off Cromer.

Unlike the Red machines, Blue force's aircraft were not
equipped with W/T. Flying began on the second day of the
manoeuvres, with a ninety-minute patrol over the Firth of Forth
by Leven's Short seaplane. No 'enemy' craft were sighted and
the aircraft returned to base. That same day, the Borel seaplane
from Great Yarmouth located the two submarines that the
Farman had spotted the day before; the pilot swooped down and
took their numbers, which he reported on landing.

More submarines were sighted on the morning of the 26th,
and that afternoon the Red aircraft suffered their first 'loss' when
Yarmouth's Short seaplane made an emergency landing near
Winterton and was captured, together with its crew, by Blue

forces. The first phase of the manoeuvres ended on the 27th; the last patrol was made from Yarmouth by the Borel seaplane in blinding rain, but in spite of the conditions the pilot sighted and reported a submarine.

The re-opening of 'hostilities' on 31 July found all Great Yarmouth's aircraft unserviceable from a variety of causes. Two machines – the Farman and the Short, which had been sportingly returned by the other side – were nevertheless airworthy by the following morning and two patrols were flown, both aircraft sighting Blue warships. That same morning, a Short seaplane from the *Hermes* failed to return from a patrol; a search was started, but both the crew – Commander Samson and Lieutenant Fitzmaurice – and the aircraft later turned up safe and sound, having been fished out of the sea after an engine failure by the German steamer *Clara Mennig*.

The incident caused some amusement, not to mention considerable embarrassment, and it was on that note that the manoeuvres ended. The Naval Wing had learned a number of useful lessons, not the least of which was the value of aircraft fitted with W/T equipment. The work done by the *Hermes* had proved the value of the seaplane-carrier; and, perhaps most important of all, the manoeuvres had shown that the success of naval air operations in time of war would depend on complete co-operation between land-based and seaborne aircraft. Another thing that the manoeuvres had done was to dispel the myth that the strength of the Royal Navy alone made Britain's shores invulnerable to hostile attack; the aura of false security had been torn aside once and for all.

In the autumn of 1913 the Navy issued specifications for three new types of aircraft following a recommendation made by the First Lord of the Admiralty, Winston Churchill. The first was for a 'fighting seaplane', to be based on a ship; the second for a reconnaissance seaplane to act as a spotter for the fleet; and the third envisaged a land-based fighter aircraft for home defence. The Naval Wing had a requirement for twenty-five of the first type, twenty of the second and fifteen of the third.

Meanwhile, experiments with aircraft armament were being

carried out under the direction of Lieutenant R. H. Clark-Hall. Trials were carried out with a one-pounder semi-automatic gun mounted in one of Britain's latest aircraft, a Vickers EFB (Experimental Fighting Biplane) 1. The weapon was found to be unsuitable, but as a result of the trials it was decided to investigate the possibilities of fitting machine-guns to aircraft. Experiments were also made with a variety of bombs and rifle grenades to determine their suitability for use against airships.

By mid-May 1914 the Naval Wing's strength had increased to 111 officers and 540 men. There were now ninety-five aircraft of all types on the inventory, and a further fifty were on order. On the 23rd of the following month, the Naval Wing ceased to be part of the Royal Flying Corps; from now on it was to be a separate entity, to be known as the Royal Naval Air Service. To distinguish them from other branches of the Royal Navy, RNAS officers were to be given new ranks as follows: Wing Captain (instead of Captain); Wing Commander (Commander); Squadron Commander (Lieutenant Commander); Flight Lieutenant (Lieutenant); Flight Sub-Lieutenant (Sub-Lieutenant); and Warrant Officer, Grades 1 and 2. And on the left sleeve of a hundred officers' uniforms, above the rank braid, appeared the new insignia of the RNAS – an eagle, its wings outstretched and head inclined to the right.

In the afternoon of 18 July, nineteen aircraft of the RNAS drawn from six air stations – Eastchurch, Calshot, Yarmouth, Felixstowe, Dundee and the Isle of Grain – flew over the great armada of warships assembled off Spithead on the occasion of the Royal Review. The aircraft that took part were three Short Folders, four Short S-41s, four Farman MF-11s, a Sopwith Tractor Biplane, one of the new Sopwith Bat Boats, two BE 2s, a Sopwith Tabloid, a Bristol Scout, a fifty hp Avro Biplane and a fifty hp Short. Everything went off smoothly during the event, although three of the aircraft had to make emergency landings later because of engine failure. One came down on the Maplin Sands and was completely lost, although the crew was picked up safely.

On 28 July, Squadron Commander A. M. Longmore – flying

a Short Folder – made the first air launching of a torpedo in Britain. That same day, the Fleet was ordered to war stations. It was exactly one month since the assassination of Archduke Franz Ferdinand of Austria in Sarajevo, and war with Germany now seemed inevitable. On 1 August the RNAS deployed its available aircraft among the air stations around the east and south coasts, and No. 4 Squadron, RFC, arrived at Eastchurch to reinforce the naval aircraft already there. Three days later, at five minutes past eleven in the evening of 4 August 1914, Great Britain declared war on Germany.

To the RNAS personnel who manned the air stations along the coast, the fact that Britain and Germany were now at war was not immediately apparent. A few of the more imaginative had got up on the morning of the 5th half expecting to see a long line of Zeppelins bearing down on the coast; instead, the sky was empty. As a matter of fact, there was very little operational flying during the first week of the war by RNAS aircraft; it was not until 9 August that serious patrols were started along the east coast of England and Scotland. A seaplane patrol was also begun between Westgate and Ostend, across the Channel, and a temporary base was set up there on 13 August under the command of Flight Lieutenant E. T. R. Chambers. The main task of the small nucleus of aircraft based on Ostend in the early days of the war, together with the RNAS's handful of airships, was to provide air cover for the transports carrying the British Expeditionary Force to France.

On 11 August the Admiralty requisitioned three cross-Channel packets – the *Empress,* the *Engadine* and the *Riviera* – for conversion as seaplane tenders. As well as the *Hermes,* a second tender had just entered service; she was the *Ark Royal,* a steamer bought by the Admiralty in 1913. Initially, aircraft operating from these vessels were given the task of patrolling shipping lanes in the North Sea.

On 22 September, aircraft of the RNAS had the distinction of mounting the first air raid over enemy territory when five BE 2s of No. 2 Squadron, led by Flight Lieutenant C. H. Collet, took off from a temporary base near the German border to attack enemy airship sheds at Dusseldorf and Cologne. Collet and one other pilot bombed the target at Dusseldorf, causing a small amount of damage, but the three aircraft detailed to attack Cologne failed to locate their target because of fog. All the BEs returned safely. Dusseldorf and Cologne were attacked again, with greater success, on 8 October by Squadron Commander Grey and Lieutenant Marix, flying Sopwith Tabloids. The two aircraft, each carrying a small load of twenty-pound bombs, took off from Antwerp; a third aircraft also started, but had to turn back because of engine trouble. Visibility began to deteriorate rapidly as the two aircraft approached the Rhine. Lieutenant Marix came down to one hundred feet to get his bearings and found himself skimming over a wood, with the Rhine dead ahead. Slipping over the river, he climbed to one thousand feet and just managed to make out the target in the murk. Machine-guns opened up as he started his dive, but he held the Tabloid steady and released his bombs at two hundred feet. As he climbed away towards the river, he looked back and saw flames and smoke pouring from the airship shed.

Grey, meanwhile, had followed the Rhine southwards to Cologne, but in the thickening fog he had been unable to identify his target. After cruising around over the city for several minutes, he dropped his bombs on the central railway station, then dived flat out for the Rhine and safety. Grey's flight back to base was uneventful, but Marix had a few nasty moments when his fuel ran out and he had to make a forced landing in a Belgian field a few miles beyond the river. As he climbed out of the cockpit he saw some soldiers running towards him and raised his hands, thinking they were Germans. But it turned out to be a Belgian patrol, and within a couple of hours Marix was on his way back to Antwerp by car.

Early in November, a raid was planned on the heart of German airship production – the Zeppelin works at Friedrich-shafen, on the shores of Lake Constance. On 13 November three Avro 504 biplanes from Ostend arrived at Belfort, thirty miles from the Franco-German border, and waited for a break in the weather. The pilots were Squadron Commander E. F. Briggs,

Flight Lieutenant J. T. Babington and Lieutenant S. V. Sippe – the airman who should have taken part in the Cologne raid with Grey and Marix. The raid on Friedrichshafen involved a round trip of something like two hundred and fifty miles over mountainous, forested terrain; a considerable distance for the Avros, with their load of four twenty-pound bombs each.

The weather cleared a little on the 21st and Briggs decided not to delay the raid any longer. This time, all three aircraft took off without incident and crossed the frontier, flying low over the haze-shrouded Black Forest. The mist thickened as they crossed the northern tip of Switzerland, and over Schaffhausen Briggs lost contact with the other two Avros. Thirty minutes later, still inside Swiss territory, he droned over Kreuzlingen and saw the vast expanse of Lake Constance creep out of the mist ahead. Friedrichshafen was on the other side, due east of his present position.

Briggs located the Zeppelin factory without difficulty and dived down to five hundred feet, releasing two of his bombs through a storm of rifle and machine-gun fire. One of the bombs exploded between the two Zeppelin hangars, causing light damage. The other two Avros arrived on the scene and let go their bombs in turn: one exploded a few feet away from a hangar and blew out some windows. If the bomb had landed fifty feet to the left it would have gone right through the hangar roof and destroyed Zeppelin L.7, which in the event escaped unharmed. More bombs set a gas tank on fire, sending flames shooting up into the mist. As he circled over the target, Briggs was caught in a cone of machine-gun fire that riddled his aircraft and ruptured his fuel tank. By some miracle, the Avro failed to catch fire and Briggs managed to land near the hangars, in spite of blood pouring into his eyes from a head wound. He was taken prisoner and treated well by his captors, who seemed to have nothing but admiration for the way the raid had been executed. Briggs later managed to escape and make his way back to England; Sippe and Babington got away with only minor damage to their aircraft.

For the RNAS, the raid had been a form of revenge. Three

weeks earlier, the old *Hermes* – the Service's first seaplane-carrier – had been torpedoed off Calais by an enemy submarine while returning from Dunkirk. Fortunately, loss of life had been small; she had stayed afloat long enough to allow most of her crew to be rescued.

So far, no German airships had raided Britain – but on the night of 24 December a lone German aircraft dropped two bombs near Dover Castle, and this was followed up on Christmas night by another raider who penetrated as far as Erith, on the Thames, and dropped a single bomb. Neither raid caused any damage or casualties.

On the night of 24 December, a German U-Boat sighted a force of two British light cruisers and eight destroyers off Heligoland. It was the Harwich Force, and with it were the seaplane-carriers *Empress, Engadine* and *Riviera,* carrying a total of nine Short seaplanes. The force hove-to at 07.00 hours on the 25th and the carriers hoisted out their aircraft. By 08.00 seven were airborne; two others failed to get off the water.

At two thousand feet the seven British seaplanes – piloted by Flight Lieutenants Oliver, Hewlett, Ross, Kilner, Miley, Edmonds and Gaskell-Blackburn – headed for the German coast. Their target was the airship sheds at Nordholz, eight miles south of Cuxhaven. It was the second time that the Harwich Force had set out to attack this objective; the first attempt had been made on 25 October, but fog and rain had prevented the seaplanes from being launched.

At 09.12 hours the German airship L.5 – which was heading to attack the British warships – sighted three of the seaplanes over the River Weser and alerted Nordholz. The airship base was shrouded in dense fog, but at 09.25 one of the British aircraft was spotted through a gap and fired on by machine-guns. The aircraft came down to one thousand feet and released two bombs at a big gasometer, but they missed and exploded harmlessly in a nearby wood. No more British aircraft appeared over the base.

Meanwhile, the Harwich Force had come under attack by another Zeppelin, the L.6, commanded by Oberleutnant zur See Horst Baron von Buttlar. He released one 110-pound bomb at the *Empress,* missing the target by a good hundred feet, then sheered off into the clouds as anti-aircraft fire began to come up thick and fast. When he landed at Nordholz, having lost contact with the enemy, he found ten bullet holes in the airship's gas cells.

By this time, most of the British seaplanes were in serious trouble. Only one had found the target; the others, lost in the fog, had been forced to drop their bombs more or less at random. Among the latter was Vincent Gaskell-Blackburn, who had cruised around at six hundred feet, just under the cloud base, for what seemed an eternity. Finally, with his fuel running dangerously low, he had dropped his four twenty-pounders on what looked like a railway station.

As he turned away he flew straight into an anti-aircraft barrage. To escape it, he dodged into the clouds and flew blind for a while; then, when he judged that he was over the coast, he brought the seaplane down into clear sky once more. Seconds later, he flew smack into the middle of another withering barrage; he had broken cloud right above what looked like half the German battle fleet.

To the utter dismay of his observer, Chief Petty Officer James Bell, Gaskell-Blackburn calmly stooged around above the warships, counting and identifying the enemy vessels and making a mental note of their position. Suddenly, there was a roar like an express train and the seaplane lurched violently. Bell saw that one of the struts supporting the seaplane's port float had been shot clean away.

Gaskell-Blackburn nursed the damaged seaplane towards the open sea, heading for the rendezvous with the *Empress*. But there was no sign of the *Empress*. The needle of the fuel gauge was hovering on empty; they had only enough fuel for another five minutes' flying at the most.

Suddenly, they spotted a submarine travelling on the surface a few hundred yards away. The airmen had no way of telling whether it was British or German, but there were no other vessels in sight and they had no choice but to land as close to it as possible and pray that it would stop to pick them up.

As soon as the seaplane touched the water, the damaged float folded up and the aircraft nosed over sharply. Gaskell-Blackburn and Bell, both unhurt, scrambled out of their cockpit and climbed on to the starboard float, watching anxiously as the submarine nosed slowly towards them. As luck would have it, she was British: the *E*.11, Lieutenant-Commander Dunbar-Nasmyth. The crew of the *E*.11 threw the airmen a line and managed to pull them aboard after a struggle. Seconds later, two more seaplanes – Oliver's and Miley's – also landed close by, and their crews were picked up as well. Not a moment too soon – for at that instant the long silver shape of a Zeppelin appeared overhead.

It was the L.5, and she dropped two bombs as the *E*.11 began to submerge. Fortunately they missed, and after shooting up the three abandoned seaplanes with his machine-guns the L.5's commander, Oberleutnant zur See Hirsch, continued his patrol westwards.

Of the seven seaplanes that had taken off on the raid, only two returned safely – although all the crews were picked up by friendly vessels. Later, the abortive raid was hailed as a 'valuable reconnaissance' by the Admiralty. But there was no escaping the fact that because of the adverse weather conditions the RNAS crews had failed to achieve their primary objective: the destruction of one of the German Navy's most vital airship bases.

There was, however, one immediate result of the raid; the Germans mounted 88- and 37-mm anti-aircraft guns on their airship bases, camouflaged the conspicuous hangars and deployed flights of naval fighter aircraft to provide round-the-clock air defence.

It was going to be a long war.

2   The Giant-killers

On the morning of 19 January 1915, three German airships –
and L.3, L.4 and L.6 – took off from Fuhlsbüttel and set course
over the North Sea. L.3 and L.4 were to attack targets on the
River Humber; each carried a load of eight 110-pound explosive
bombs and ten 25-pound incendiaries. L.6, with orders to attack
the Thames, carried ten 110-pounders and twelve incendiaries.

In the event, L.6 was forced to turn back because of engine
trouble. The other two, however, crossed the English coast at
20.50 and 21.30 hours respectively, although they had been
blown too far south and made landfall over Norfolk. Following
the coast, L.3 dropped her bombs on Great Yarmouth, causing
some damage and killing two people; L.4 released her load on
King's Lynn, killing a woman and a small boy.

Three RNAS aircraft were on readiness at Yarmouth Air
Station at the time, but they never took off. Even had they done
so, they could not have been of much use. Their crews were
armed only with rifles, and the ceiling of their machines was far
below that of the airships. L.3 and L.4, the first enemy airships
to raid English soil, returned to base completely unscathed.

If the RNAS was ill-equipped to deal with the Zeppelin threat,
it was nevertheless capable of mounting successful offensive operations. Three days later, on 22 January, Squadron Commander
Davies and Flight Lieutenant Pierse flew to Zeebrugge, which
the enemy had been using as a submarine base since its capture,
and bombed it in reprisal for a German air raid on their own
base at Dunkirk. They reported one submarine severely damaged
and a number of gun batteries on the Mole destroyed. On 12
February, the Air Service mounted its biggest air raid to date
when a force of thirty-four aircraft and seaplanes of all types, led

by Wing Commander Samson, attacked several targets along the Belgian coast. This was followed by another raid on the 16th, when forty RNAS aircraft attacked enemy gun positions, the locks of the canal between Bruges and the sea, and craft in Zeebrugge harbour. The second raid was made in conjunction with a diversionary attack by French airmen on the German airfield at Ghistelles. No British aircraft were lost through enemy action during these two raids, although a small number came down in the Channel on the way home. All the crews were picked up safely. Smaller raids were carried out on 7 March and 1 April, when the U-Boat repair base at Ostend and the submarine yards at Hoboken, near Antwerp, were bombed.

In April, the Germans stepped up their Zeppelin attacks on Britain. On 14 April the L.9 dropped several bombs on Blyth – which the airship commander mistook for Tynemouth – and injured two people. The following night, three more airships set out for England. The L.5 attacked Lowestoft, the L.6 bombed Maldon in Essex, and the L.7 returned to base without reaching the target – although she had actually flown over the Norfolk coast without her crew knowing it. Flight Lieutenant de Courcy Ireland took off from Yarmouth at 01.00 hours to try and locate the enemy, but returned an hour later having made no contact. Another patrol was flown by Flight Sub-Lieutenant Nicholl three hours later, but he too was unsuccessful.

A third raid was made on the night of 29 April, this time by a German Army airship which dropped bombs on Ipswich and Bury St Edmunds. Four Sopwiths took off from Yarmouth in an attempt to catch her, but she escaped in thickening fog. The Zeppelins came again on 10, 17 and 27 May, and each time they managed to elude the defences. On the night of 31 May, the airship LZ.38, commanded by Hauptmann Erich Linnarz, dropped three thousand pounds of bombs on north-east London, killing seven people. It was the first time that the British capital had come under air attack.

It was the LZ.38's sister ship, the LZ.37, that became the first victim of the RNAS in air combat six days later – and it happened more or less by accident. At one in the morning of 6 June,

Flight Sub-Lieutenant R. A. J. Warneford, flying a Morane Parasol, was on his way from Dunkirk to bomb enemy airship sheds at Berchem Ste Agathe when he sighted the LZ.37 over Ostend. The airship was one of a combined force of naval and military craft that had set out to raid England, and she had turned back because of bad weather. Warneford managed to climb above the airship and release his bombs on her. The result was spectacular; she burst into flames and fell like a stone, exploding in the grounds of a convent near Ghent, killing all but one of her crew. Warneford's aircraft was hurled brutally around the sky by the turbulence of the burning airship, and a fractured fuel pipe forced him to land in enemy territory. However, he succeeded in making temporary repairs and took off again before enemy forces arrived on the scene. For his exploit, Warneford was awarded the Victoria Cross; tragically, he was killed in a flying accident ten days later.

A few hours after Warneford's kill, two other RNAS pilots from Dunkirk bombed the airship shed at Evere, near Brussels. Inside was the LZ.38, which – like the ill-fated LZ.37 – had turned back before reaching England. She was reduced to blazing wreckage.

Meanwhile, the RNAS's carrier force had received a new addition – the newly-converted steamer *Ben-my-Chree*. She was equipped with the new Sopwith 'Schneider' seaplane fighters; with a one hundred hp rotary engine, an upward-firing Lewis gun and the ability to climb to ten thousand feet in a little over thirty minutes, these aircraft presented the first serious threat to marauding Zeppelins. On 3 May the Harwich Force had attempted to attack the German radio station at Norddeich, but a heavy swell had prevented the aircraft from being launched. A second attempt was made on 11 May, but that too had to be called off because of an approaching storm.

The Harwich Force's next appearance in German waters was on 3 July, off Heligoland. Its mission was to launch fighter seaplanes to attack patrolling Zeppelins, and also to reconnoitre the estuary of the River Ems. The carriers involved were the *Engadine* and the *Riviera*, escorted by three light cruisers and sixteen destroyers. Shortly after 03.00 hours, four Short seaplanes took off and headed for the estuary, but two returned soon afterwards with engine trouble. One of the other two carried out its reconnaissance successfully, but the other got lost in cloud and came down near a Dutch trawler, which picked up the crew.

About 07.30 hours, four enemy airships appeared over the Force, and the *Engadine* immediately swung out her three Sopwith Schneiders. The attempt ended in a fiasco; the seaplanes' plywood floats broke up in the swell and two of the aircraft sank.

The seaplane-carriers *Ark Royal* and *Ben-my-Chree*, meanwhile, had arrived in different waters. The former had sailed from Harwich on 1 February 1915 for the Dardanelles, arriving at Tenedos on 17 February; while the *Ben-my-Chree* had sailed on 21 May, arriving at Mitylene on 12 June. The *Ben-my-Chree* carried two Short seaplanes, recently converted to launch torpedoes – and it was not long before they had a chance to prove their worth. On 12 August Flight Commander C. H. K. Edmonds took off from the Gulf of Xeros and flew over the Bulair Peninsula into the Straits, where he spotted an enemy transport off Gallipoli. Coming down to within twenty feet of the water, he launched his torpedo from three hundred yards and scored a direct hit. Five days later, he torpedoed another transport off Ak Bashi Liman and left her in flames. On that same day, Flight Commander G. B. Dacre, flying the other Short, had just landed on the water with a misfiring engine when he saw an enemy tug a few hundred yards away. He launched his torpedo while taxiing and had the satisfaction of seeing the vessel blow up and sink. Freed of its load, the Short managed to stagger into the air again and Dacre nursed it back to the carrier.

The success of the Short seaplane as a torpedo-carrier, however, was short-lived; in the hot climate of the Aegean, the aircraft had endless trouble with burnt-out exhaust valves and boiling radiators, and full-throttle sorties with torpedoes soon became impossible. After that, the normal load consisted of a pair of 112-pound bombs, which meant that as well as being able to carry a two-man crew the aircraft enjoyed a greatly extended combat radius. On 8 November 1915, carrying this type of load,

Edmonds and Dacre flew a hundred miles over enemy territory and bombed the Maritza railway bridge, a vital link in the enemy's main supply route from Germany via Bulgaria. Chiefly, however, the Shorts were employed as spotters for the guns of naval monitors, and the accuracy of the latter in blasting the Straits clear of enemy shipping was due in no small part to their airborne 'eyes'.

Although the Short seaplanes bore the brunt of the RNAS's work during 1915, and were in fact produced in larger numbers than any other type of British seaplane, new and exciting aircraft were beginning to reach the naval air units in increasing numbers by the autumn of that year. There was the Bristol Scout, a fighter biplane with an eighty hp Gnome, a speed of ninety-four mph and a ceiling of over fifteen thousand feet; it eventually formed part of the equipment of ten RNAS home defence units and carried either a non-synchronized overwing Lewis gun or a load of Ranken Darts, explosive cylinders for use against airships. Another new type was the Nieuport 'Baby' fighter, twelve of which served with Nos. 1 and 3 Wings of the RNAS from the autumn of 1915. There was the Morane Type L Parasol, which served with No. 1 Wing in France and with No. 2 Wing in the Aegean; and the Curtiss H-4 flying boat, the first batch of which was based on Gibraltar for patrol duties. The RNAS had fought its way through the first year of the war with a hotch-potch of nondescript aircraft, most of which were unsuitable for the tasks they had been called upon to perform; now, at last, as the new year approached, it was with the promise of new and improved equipment that would enable the naval pilots to establish at least a margin of air superiority.

At the beginning of 1916, as in 1915, the main concern of the RNAS was to find an effective means of defence against the Zeppelins – particularly as it was known that the enemy was about to start a series of intensive air raids on Britain. Six raids were in fact made between 31 January and 2 May – two of them by aircraft – but in spite of the fact that the British air defences had recently been strengthened by an increase of anti-aircraft batteries and the formation of a number of RFC squadrons whose sole task was night defence, the British airmen still failed to get to grips with the enemy.

On 2 May, five Zeppelins raided targets on the east coast. It was to be the last raid for nearly three months, because the majority of the airships had been earmarked for a more pressing duty: providing air cover for units of the German High Seas Fleet, which had put out from the Jade Estuary on the morning of 24 April. At five in the morning of the 25th, the *Lützow*, the *Derfflinger*, the *Moltke* and the *Von der Tann* appeared off Lowestoft and shelled the town for six minutes. The warships were attacked by six RNAS aircraft (three Short seaplanes and three BE.2cs) from Great Yarmouth, but no damage was inflicted. The pilot of one of the Shorts, Flight Sub-Lieutenant H. G. Hall, was badly wounded during the attack and just managed to reach base before collapsing from loss of blood.

On the morning of 3 May, the seaplane-carriers *Engadine* and *Vindex* – the latter a converted Isle of Man packet – sailed with an escort of cruisers and destroyers to attack the airship base at Tondern. The force hove-to off Sylt at four the following morning and eleven brand-new Sopwith Baby seaplanes were swung out from the carriers. The raid was a failure from the start; eight of the seaplanes failed to get off the water, a ninth hit the mast of a destroyer and crashed, killing its pilot, a tenth turned back minutes after take-off with engine trouble, and the eleventh and last missed the target and dropped one bomb on Danish soil. The only bright spot of the whole mission came when the light cruisers *Galatea* and *Phaeton*, covering the carriers, shot down the Zeppelin L.7 in flames.

The stage was now set for the greatest naval battle of the First World War. On 30 May, a force of German cruisers and destroyers led by Admiral Franz von Hipper's flagship, the 26,000-ton *Lützow*, steamed out past the Frisian Islands and Heligoland into the North Sea. The advance guard of the High Seas Fleet, the warships steamed northwards off the Danish coast, 'trailing their coats' in the hope that Admiral Beatty's battle-cruiser fleet would race out from Rosyth to meet them – and be cut to pieces by the main German force, lying forty miles to the south, under

Admiral Scheer. The movements of the British vessels were to be reported by U-Boats lying in wait off Cromarty, Rosyth and Scapa Flow.

But the submarines failed in their task; by midnight the whole of the Grand Fleet was at sea and steaming eastwards virtually undetected. Standing patrols of Zeppelins were also to have kept a lookout for the British warships, but they were prevented from taking off by bad weather. They did not get off the ground until the following afternoon, by which time battle had already been joined.

The opposing forces sighted each other at 14.20 hours on 31 May, and thirty minutes later the Battle of Jutland opened with a ranging shot from the light cruiser *Elbing* at HMS *Galatea*. A few minutes later the *Engadine* – accompanying Beatty's cruiser force – launched a Short seaplane to reconnoitre the enemy fleet. The pilot was Flight Lieutenant F. J. Rutland; flying low to keep under cloud, he followed a north-easterly heading until at 15.20 he sighted the armada of enemy warships and closed to within half a mile of them, flying at one thousand feet through a heavy anti-aircraft barrage. His observer, Assistant Paymaster G. S. Trewin, tapped out the course and disposition of the German ships over the W/T. Satisfied, Rutland turned away and the enemy was soon lost in the fog. Shortly afterwards, the seaplane had to make an emergency landing because of a fractured fuel line, but Rutland repaired it with the aid of a piece of rubber torn from his lifejacket and later rendezvoused with the carrier. It was the first time in history that an aircraft had taken part in a fleet action.

After the Battle of Jutland, new types of Zeppelin – with increased range and war-load – began to reach the German naval air units. By the end of July, everything was ready for a new wave of offensive operations against British targets.

At 05.15 on 31 July, Flight Sub-Lieutenant J. C. Northrop took off from Covehithe in a BE.2c and chased a Zeppelin thirty miles out to sea off Southwold, where he finally caught up with it. Closing in below, he fired two drums of explosive and tracer bullets into the airship, but with no result. Then a drum of ammunition he was changing slipped out of his hands and hit him on the forehead, stunning him, and his aircraft spiralled down out of control. By the time he recovered, the Zeppelin had disappeared in cloud. Two more interceptions were made on the night of 2 August by Flight Lieutenants Pulling and Galpin, but once again the Zeppelins escaped. It was not until 2 September that the first Zeppelin – or more correctly the Schütte-Lanz airship SL.11 – fell to the guns of a fighter over Britain, and the honour went to a RFC pilot, Lieutenant Leefe-Robinson, of No. 39 Squadron. Three more Zeppelins were brought down by RFC pilots during the following weeks; L.32 on 23 September, L.31 on 1 October, and L.34 on 27 November. And on that night a RNAS pilot scored a success at last, when L.21 was destroyed after concentrated attacks by Flight Lieutenant Cadbury and Flight Sub-Lieutenants Fane and Pulling, all flying BE.2cs.

While the Zeppelin menace was being countered with increasing success in British skies, the summer and autumn of 1916 saw the expansion and re-equipping of the RNAS squadrons in France. By the end of the year, in addition to the seaplane base at Dunkirk, there were eight RNAS squadrons on the continent, all based in the Dunkirk area. New aircraft that reached the RNAS in France during 1916 included the Sopwith Pup, Sopwith 1½ Strutter, Sopwith Triplane, Nieuport 17C-1, Caudron G-4, Handley-Page 0/100 and the Short Bomber. The last-named aircraft first went into action on the night of 15 November with No. 7 Wing based on Coudekerque, when four of them bombed submarine pens at Zeebrugge. Fifteen more equipped the 3rd Wing at Luxeuil and bombed targets in the Saar Valley. It was this unit which, in 1918, was to form the Independent Force, RAF – the ancestor of Bomber Command.

The summer of 1916 also saw a reversal in the fortunes of the air war over France. During the early months of the year, the German Fokkers – with synchronized machine-guns firing forwards through the propeller arc – had enjoyed undisputed air superiority over the Allied air arms. Then, in April 1916, the Sopwith 1½-Strutter entered service with No. 5 Wing RNAS in

France – and the Fokkers no longer had it all their own way. The 1½-Strutter was the first British aircraft to use synchronizing gear; it was armed with a Vickers machine-gun firing through the propeller and a Lewis gun in the rear cockpit, operated by the observer. It was first used to escort French bombers, but later in the year it was employed as a bomber itself with No. 3 Wing RNAS, carrying a load of four 65-pounders. Altogether, nearly fifteen hundred Strutters were built and used by the British and Allied air arms; fifty-eight of the RNAS Strutters were converted for carrier duties and served principally aboard HMS *Argus, Furious* and *Vindex*.

It was while flying a 1½-Strutter that Raymond Collishaw, the pilot who was to become the top-scoring ace of the RNAS, notched up his first victory. It happened on 12 October 1916, when he destroyed a Fokker over Oberndorf. A fortnight later, he shot down two enemy aircraft in a single sortie near Luneville while escorting a flight of French bombers, and was awarded the Croix de Guerre. When No. 10 RNAS Squadron was formed in February the following year, Collishaw got permission to form a special 'fighter flight' of five Sopwith Triplanes, all flown by Canadian pilots. The five Triplanes, which were painted all black, were named 'Black Maria' (Collishaw's own aircraft), 'Black Sheep', 'Black Prince', 'Black Death' and 'Black Roger'. Collishaw destroyed three more enemy aircraft by 15 May, when the squadron was attached to No. 11 Wing RFC, near Ypres. A fortnight later, his score had risen to nine – and when he was sent back to Canada on leave at the end of July, a total of thirty-seven enemy machines had gone down before his guns.

Another RNAS fighter pilot was carving out a name for himself. He was an Australian, Roderic Dallas, and he had been in France since November 1915, flying with No. 1 RNAS Squadron. He scored his first kill on 12 May 1916 when – flying a Nieuport Baby – he sent an Aviatik spinning down to crash with its pilot dead at the controls. Eight days later he shot down two out of a formation of five Friedrichshafen two-seaters on their way home after bombing Dover and Dunkirk, and from then on his score began to mount steadily. Like Collishaw's 'Naval Ten',

No. 1 Squadron was also attached to the RFC from the beginning of 1917. During those early months of 1917 the exploits of Collishaw, Dallas and their fellow RNAS fighter pilots provided a brief and solitary flash of glamour in the monotonous routine of normal RNAS operations: escorting bombers, maintaining day and night defensive patrols, reconnaissance, bombing targets on land and (infrequently) at sea, protecting the shipping lanes, and so on. The flying-boat and seaplane crews had the worst job of all, droning over the open sea for four or five hours at a time, often without seeing anything, and knowing that if engine-failure compelled them to alight their chances of being picked up were very slim. One flying-boat crew from Great Yarmouth, however, did have some excitement on 14 May. The machine was a Curtiss H-12, piloted by Flight Sub-Lieutenant Leckie, and was carrying out a routine patrol eighty miles out over the North Sea when the crew sighted a Zeppelin ahead and about three thousand feet lower. They crept in astern and dived on the airship – the L.22 – at ninety knots, opening up with their two Lewis guns from a range of fifty yards. Within seconds, the Zeppelin began to burn and plunged vertically into the sea.

In March 1917, work was started to equip the light cruiser *Furious* with a flight-deck on her forecastle. She was completed in July and entered service with a complement of five Sopwith Pups. One vessel in each light cruiser squadron was also to be fitted with a small platform over her forward gun-turret to enable a Pup to be launched. The first, HMS *Yarmouth,* was already in service suitably modified.

At 03.50 hours on 21 August the airship L.23 took off from Tondern to make a routine patrol. Two hours later, her commander reported sighting four light cruisers and fifteen destroyers thirty miles west of Bovbjerg. Among them was HMS *Yarmouth,* with her Sopwith Pup. The first trial from the *Yarmouth*'s wooden platform had been made by Flight Commander Rutland on 28 June, and the result had been satisfactory. Now, as the Zeppelin shadowed the warships at a respectful distance Flight Sub-Lieutenant B. A. Smart was ordered to take off in the Pup and attack her. Before doing so, Smart obliterated the

Pup's red, white and blue roundels with battleship grey paint in the hope that the airship's crew would not recognize the Pup as a British aircraft until it was too late.

Smart succeeded in getting above and astern of the Zeppelin before he was sighted, dived on her at 130 knots and ripped off a burst along one flank. He went on firing until he was only twenty yards away, then broke away and turned to make another attack – but, as he said later, 'the Zepp was one mass of flame and strumming like a huge piano'. The airship plunged seawards, rapidly disintegrating. Smart reported that one of the crew had baled out, but the man was never found. Smart himself landed on the sea close to the destroyer *Prince* and was picked up safely, but the Pup was lost as there was no means of retrieving it. The history-making pilot was later awarded the DSO.

Smart's success led to the equipment of battle cruisers as well as light cruisers with aircraft platforms. By the beginning of 1918, all British battle cruisers were equipped to launch their own aircraft.

If the role of the RNAS on the Western Front had little of the glamour or publicity that was attached to the operations of the Royal Flying Corps, the RNAS units in other parts of the world enjoyed even less of both. These were the forgotten men; men who had been fighting not only the enemy, but also hostile climatic conditions that ruined engines and rotted the wood and fabric of their machines. Apart from the Dardanelles campaign, RNAS aircraft had served in the humidity of Africa; in July 1915, three Short 827 seaplanes had arrived in Mombasa aboard the armed liner *Laconia* to assist the British monitors *Severn* and *Mersey* in their efforts to winkle the *Königsberg* out of her refuge seven miles up the steaming Rufiji River in Tanganyika. One of the seaplanes, flown by Flight Lieutenant J. T. Cull, spotted for the monitors' guns during the final action. The aircraft was hit and crashed in the river, but Cull and his observer were picked up safely by the *Mersey*.

The two surviving seaplanes, together with a third replacement aircraft, were sent to Mesopotamia in August and two were used as bombers against the Turkish advance on Kut-al-Amara the following December. Four more Shorts were sent out to Zanzibar on the *Laconia* in March 1916 and, operating alternately from Chukwani Bay and the *Laconia,* the *Himalaya* and the *Manica,* they spotted for the guns of the *Severn* at Lindi and reconnoitred enemy positions in preparation for the British landings. A few weeks later they were handed over to the Belgians, who took them overland to Lake Tongwe and used them to bomb the German lake cruiser *Graf von Goetzen* in Kigoma Harbour. Other Short seaplanes served in the Mediterranean, at Otranto and with the carrier *Ben-my-Chree,* which – as part of an RNAS force under Commander Samson – operated in the Eastern Mediterranean, the Red Sea and the Indian Ocean during the latter part of 1916 and early 1917, until she was sunk off Castellorizo in January of that year. She was replaced by the carrier *Raven II,* whose aircraft patrolled the Laccadive Islands in an unsuccessful search for the German commerce raider *Wolf* during the spring of 1917.

January 1918 saw the substantial reorganization of the RNAS units in France. More squadrons were formed, bringing the total of fighter and bomber units on the Western Front to fifteen. Nos. 1, 3, 8, 9, 10 and 13 Squadrons were now equipped with the magnificent little Sopwith Camel, No. 4 with the Pup, Nos. 2, 5, 6 and 17 with DH.4 and later DH.9 high-speed day bombers – and lastly there was the 'heavy brigade', Nos. 7, 14, 15 and 16 Squadrons with Handley-Page o/100s and o/400s. No. 11 Squadron had been disbanded in August 1917 and would not be reformed until the following April; No. 12 was based at Great Yarmouth where it operated Bristol Fighters, DH.4s, DH.9s and Camels. On the continent, the RNAS stations at Oudezeele and Cherbourg operated a variety of aircraft, the former DH.9s and SE.5s and the latter Short 260s and Wight seaplanes.

Naval air stations overseas included Imbros, Stavros, Thasos, Lemnos, Otranto and Taranto, all operating DH.9s and Camels. Units were also based on Gibraltar and Port Said. In Britain there were twenty-five major operational RNAS stations, their units engaged in a wide variety of tasks ranging from air defence to long-range anti-submarine patrols. During the winter of 1917–18, prospects for the Allies in general were far from bright. The worst single factor was the collapse of Russia, torn by the internal strife of revolution, and her withdrawal from the war with Germany – which meant the release of vast numbers of German troops and thousands of guns for service on the Western Front.

In the early morning of 21 March 1918, Germany's last all-out attempt to win the war began with a concentrated barrage on the British Third and Fifth Armies by 6,500 guns and 3,500 mortars. In misty weather that prevented Allied aircraft from making successful sorties, the German spearheads smashed through the British defences in the first phase of their planned thrust to the coast, aimed at cutting the British and French armies in two. Then, on 23 March, the weather cleared a little, allowing the RFC and its attached RNAS squadrons to begin operations in earnest. Under sustained air attack, the enemy advance began to lose its momentum, and its lines of supply and communication were thrown into chaos by the incessant strafing. It was the first time in history that a massive ground assault had been disrupted by a concentrated assault from the air. By the end of March, the advance was almost at a standstill.

On 1 April 1918 the Royal Flying Corps and the Royal Naval Air Service were amalgamated to become a single service – the Royal Air Force. For the men in the front-line squadrons, the new name had little significance. Most of them hardly noticed the change; they were too busy fighting. But the RFC and the RNAS had passed into history.

The great German offensive was smashed – but it had been a close thing. In four weeks of fighting, the British air services had lost close on a thousand first-line aircraft. The Royal Air Force had received a terrible baptism of fire; not for another two decades would it be called upon to face such odds again.

The closing months of the First World War were of tremendous significance for the development of British naval air power. On 17 July the aircraft carrier *Furious* sailed from Rosyth, accompanied by the First Light Cruiser Squadron, and headed out into the North Sea. The *Furious* was the Royal Navy's first true aircraft carrier, with a continuous flight deck broken only by her funnel and superstructure. She had accommodation initially for fourteen Sopwith $1\frac{1}{2}$-Strutters and two Pups, although by early 1918 she had been re-equipped with Camels. She was also fitted with workshops, lifts from her hangars to the flight deck and a primitive form of arrester gear, which usually failed at the crucial moment. A similarly-equipped sister ship, the *Cavendish,* was nearing completion; she was eventually commissioned in October 1918 and renamed *Vindictive,* but her operational career was limited to a brief foray in support of the Allied Intervention Force in North Russia during 1919. The most important development, however, was centred on three new carriers, all fitted with unbroken flight decks; the 10,850-ton *Hermes,* the *Argus,* and the *Eagle.* The latter – which had started life as a battleship laid down for the Chilean Navy – had a flight deck 640 feet long by 100 wide and was launched in June 1918. The *Argus* joined the fleet three months later.

On 19 July, however, as she reached her station off the Schleswig coast, it was the *Furious* that was about to make history by launching the first-ever naval air strike. Two flights of Camel 2F1s – six aircraft in all – roared off from her flight deck and set course for the German airship base at Tondern. Each aircraft carried two fifty-pound bombs. They took the Germans completely by surprise, destroying a huge hangar and the two airships inside, the L.54 and L.60. However, only two pilots – Captains W. F. Dickson and B. A. Smart – regained the carrier; three of the others ran into bad weather and had to land in Denmark, and the fourth crashed in the sea and was drowned.

It was the first and last air strike of its kind to be launched during the First World War. Plans were laid for the *Argus's* aircraft to hit selected enemy targets at a later date, but the carrier entered service too late. On 11 November 1918 the guns on the Western Front were silent after more than four years of bitter fighting.

One war was over: another was about to begin. It was a war of words and paper that was to last for nearly twenty years; a war on whose outcome the future of British naval aviation depended.

3 Years of Frustration

On 1 April 1918, with the formation of the Royal Air Force, the Admiralty lost all control of its own aircraft. It was to be twenty years before that control was fully regained.

RNAS aircrews had been given the choice of remaining with the Royal Navy or joining the Royal Air Force; the majority had chosen the latter course because they knew that if they stayed with the Navy their flying careers would be at an end as soon as the war was over. Others didn't really care; they were still flying and fighting, and one uniform was much the same as another. In all, 2,500 aircraft and 55,000 officers and men were transferred to the new Service.

For those who realized the importance of maintaining some form of independent naval air arm, the consequences of the large-scale transfer were serious. It meant that the Navy had lost all the officers and men who were experienced in aviation techniques; there was no nucleus left on which to build at a later date. Even seaborne aircraft were flown by RAF pilots and serviced by RAF crews, although the vessels from which they operated were still under Naval command. Known as Air Force Contingents, these seaborne RAF units were poorly trained, inexperienced in carrier operations, and flew aircraft that were either obsolescent or totally unsuitable for carrier work.

Late in 1918 the Admiralty wrote to the Air Ministry and proposed that all personnel connected with naval air operations afloat should be naval officers and ratings – although the RAF would still be responsible for their training. The proposal produced immediate and open hostility from senior officers in the Air Ministry, who regarded it as a sort of underhand first step to the formation of a separate naval air arm. The battle was on.

While the first verbal shots in the naval aviation 'war' were being fired, some of the seaborne air units were already committed to a real conflict – as part of the Allied Intervention Force fighting on the side of the White Russians against the increasingly victorious Red Army. First on the scene was the seaplane-carrier *Pegasus,* which arrived off Murmansk with her Short floatplanes in the spring of 1919 in support of the North Russian Expeditionary Force. Then, in July 1919, the new aircraft-carrier *Vindictive* joined the naval force under Admiral Cowan that was operating in the Baltic off Kronstadt; she carried a mixed bunch of Sopwith Camels, Fairey Campanias and $1\frac{1}{2}$-Strutters, twelve aircraft in all, which she disembarked for land-based operations from improvized airstrips on the Gulf of Finland before returning to Copenhagen for replacement machines, which had been brought out from England aboard HMS *Argus.*

On 30 July, the *Vindictive*'s aircraft carried out two raids on the Bolshevik-held naval base at Kronstadt, dropping their bombs through a barrage of well-directed anti-aircraft fire. They started two large fires, one near some oil tanks and one in the dry dock, but the overall result was not very encouraging. A second air raid took place on 17 August, this time by night and with the object of diverting attention of Bolshevik shore-batteries from a raiding force of British coastal motor-boats. Some of the aircraft returned a few hours later to assess the damage, and reported that the CMBs had sunk three Bolshevik warships.

Altogether, the shore-based aircraft – supplied with spares, fuel and ammunition by the *Vindictive* – made some sixty raids on Kronstadt. They also acted as spotters for the warships' guns during shelling of Bolshevik positions.

The *Vindictive,* however, was not a happy ship, and she was not alone in that respect. The soldiers and sailors of the Expeditionary Force were sullen, disgruntled, and utterly fed up. They had survived one war merely to be flung headlong into another – and, moreover, one which seemed to be no concern of theirs. Morale was at a low ebb during that summer and autumn of 1919.

In November, the unrest flared into open mutiny on the

Vindictive as she replenished her supplies at Copenhagen. Sixteen men were subsequently tried and punished. A few days later, the *Vindictive* returned to the Gulf of Finland, re-embarked her aircraft and sailed for England with the rest of the Baltic Force at the end of December.

At home, the continued bickering over the future of British naval aviation had not deterred the Admiralty from going ahead with the formation of a 'flying squadron' consisting of the carriers *Furious, Argus, Nairana, Pegasus, Vindex* and *Vindictive*. By March 1920, however, only the *Argus* remained in home waters; the *Pegasus*, together with her sister seaplane-carrier *Ark Royal*, had been sent to the Mediterranean because of the Turkish crisis; *Furious* was in the process of being fitted with a continuous flight deck; and the others had fallen victim to the post-war economy axe. The two new carriers, *Hermes* and *Eagle*, were not yet complete, although three squadrons – Nos. 185, 186 and 210, equipped with Sopwith Cuckoo torpedo-bombers – had been earmarked for service aboard the latter vessel. Initially, the Cuckoo was to be the mainstay of the carrier-borne Air Force Contingents during the immediate post-war years; the first British aircraft designed as torpedo-carriers from the outset, one hundred and fifty were built altogether. The great majority, however, operated from land bases.

In December 1919 the Admiralty laid down their requirements for the future development of naval aircraft. First priority was given to the development of a gunnery spotting aircraft, second priority to what would nowadays be called a multi-role aircraft for operation from carriers, third priority to a torpedo-carrier, and fourth to both long- and short-range flying boats and seaplanes for reconnaissance duties. There was also a requirement for the development of heavy armour-piercing bombs for use against warships. But the question of who was to control these new aircraft and the carriers from which they were to operate still remained unresolved; the Air Ministry showed no inclination to accept the Admiralty's insistence that the control of all naval air operations should be the Royal Navy's responsibility.

The state of deadlock persisted for nearly two years. Then, in July 1921, the Admiralty informed the Air Ministry that it intended to form a branch of specialist naval observers for aircraft duties. There was very little the Air Ministry could do to counter this move except fail to reply for several months; when the reply finally did come, it merely insisted that the observers should be trained at establishments within the Coastal Area of the Royal Air Force. Coastal Area, the forerunner of RAF Coastal Command, was responsible for maritime air operations around the British Isles. The formation of the Navy's own branch of air observers seemed a small victory at the time – but it was to have far-reaching importance in providing a sound basis for the formation of other naval aircrew branches in the years to come.

While the Air Ministry was pondering the Admiralty's latest move prior to replying to it, Sir Hugh Trenchard, the Chief of Air Staff, laid a proposal before the Committee for Imperial Defence in March 1921 in which he recommended that in addition to providing the main defence against a possible invasion of Britain, the RAF should also exercise control over naval and military weapons in the same way as it already controlled air units attached to the Army and Navy. This sparked off two months of heated discussions between the three Services. Finally, on 26 July, Mr Balfour – Chairman of the Defence Sub-Committee – circulated a report in which he outlined the Committee's conclusions. These were, firstly, that the RAF must play the leading part in defence against air attack; secondly, when acting in support of military or naval operations, the RAF units involved should come under the control of the senior Army or Naval officer in command; and thirdly, that in offensive operations against enemy territory, co-operation between the three Services should be the keyword rather than subordination.

This report was followed up almost immediately by a letter to the Admiralty from the C-in-C Mediterranean, who stressed that a Navy without its own aircraft would labour under a severe handicap in time of war. He also pointed out that in peace or war, the RAF was never likely to be in a position to meet the Navy's air requirements even halfway. The truth of that statement was to be made brutally apparent time and again. In August 1921 the Cabinet appointed a 'Committee on National Expenditure' under Sir Eric Geddes to study ways and means of effecting cuts in government expenditure. Not unnaturally, the armed forces were the Committee's primary target; after a detailed examination of the estimates for 1922–3, the Committee recommended drastic cuts in the budgets of all three Services. The Navy and Army Estimates were to be reduced by about £20 million each, while the RAF was to suffer a reduction of £5½ million, bringing its estimate down to £13 million. For the RAF particularly, with by far the smallest estimate of the three Services, it was a serious blow.

The Geddes Committee's recommendations were, of course, violently opposed by every Service department; and a new committee, under Winston Churchill, who was then Secretary of State for the Colonies, was at once set up to analyze them. The Churchill Committee's recommendations led indirectly to a victory for the RAF, for after studying them closely the Imperial Defence Committee set up a sub-committee to review the air defence of Great Britain. In April 1922 this sub-committee recommended that the strength of the RAF should be greatly increased, and the Cabinet gave its approval to the formation of twenty new squadrons – a total of some five hundred aircraft – for home defence. The following October yet another committee, under Lord Salisbury, began a further study of the situation; this led in 1923, to a recommendation for the creation of a home defence force with six hundred aircraft. However, the concrete decision to form a new RAF Command, the Air Defence of Great Britain, with a strength of fifty-two squadrons, was not actually taken until 1925.

Trenchard had fought to save the RAF and to turn the embryo Service into the beginning of a formidable striking force, and it seemed that he was well on the way to achieving his aim. Nevertheless, he still showed no inclination to relinquish control of the seven squadrons that were attached to the Navy, and it was not until early in 1924 that the stalemate was partially broken.

In April 1924, at the instigation of the new Labour Government, Trenchard and the Deputy Chief of Naval Staff, Admiral of the Fleet Sir Roger Keyes, got together to thrash out a plan for the future of the Fleet Air Arm, as the RAF's shipborne component was known by this time. The choice of Keyes as the Admiralty's negotiator was an appropriate one; he knew Trenchard well, being related to him by marriage.

A draft concordat was forwarded to the Lord Chancellor by the negotiators on 4 July 1924. It was a compromise, but at least it was a step in the right direction. Among other things, the agreement allowed the Admiralty to have the final say on the required performance and the numbers of aircraft it needed, although the Air Ministry would still be responsible for preparing specifications; the RAF would still be responsible for training naval pilots, although the Navy would state the type of training that was required; the majority of airmen serving aboard aircraft-carriers were to be replaced by naval ratings; seventy per cent of the Fleet Air Arm's officers would be drawn from the Royal Navy and Royal Marines, and they would be granted RAF rank during attachment to the Royal Air Force for training and other duties; and finally, all air observation duties on behalf of the Navy would be carried out by naval officers, who would remain completely independent of the RAF.

With the Trenchard-Keyes agreement approved and in the bag, the Admiralty now went ahead and called for volunteers to train as aircrew in the Fleet Air Arm. The need for a nucleus of trained naval aircrew was pressing, with the conversion of the carrier *Furious* approaching completion and work on the conversion of the former light cruisers *Courageous* and *Glorious* progressing well, in addition to the three carriers already in service: the *Argus*, *Hermes* and *Eagle*.

In 1925 Britain had more aircraft-carriers in service than any other nation. She was destined to hold this numerical superiority until 1942, when the US Navy turned to the aircraft-carrier as the basic unit in its task force policy following the Japanese attack on Pearl Harbour. Japan, too, had been quick to realize the potentialities of the aircraft-carrier. In fact, Japan had been the

46

first country to bring into service a carrier designed as such from the start – the *Hosho,* which entered service in the autumn of 1922. Her displacement was a mere 7,470 tons, but her flight deck was five hundred feet in length and she could steam at twenty-five knots; she was still in service twenty years later, when Japan entered the Second World War. The Japanese had two more carriers nearing completion in 1925: the *Akagi* (36,500 tons) and the *Kaga* (38,200 tons).

The US Navy had one makeshift carrier – the *Langley* – in commission; she was a converted collier and never looked like anything else, in spite of her flush flight deck. Far more promising were the two new carriers that were nearing completion, the *Lexington* and the *Saratoga,* each displacing 36,000 tons. Both these and the latest Japanese carriers exceeded the limit of 33,000 tons laid down by the Washington Treaty. The French had one carrier, the 22,146-ton *Béarn,* similar to the Royal Navy's *Eagle.*

Although the Royal Navy held a commanding lead in aircraft-carrier development, the Fleet Air Arm's aircraft of the mid-1920s were lagging behind their American counterparts in terms of performance. The standard torpedo-carrier was the Black-burn Dart; it was replaced by the Blackburn Ripon in 1926, beginning an unbroken association between Blackburn Aircraft and the Fleet Air Arm. There had been two main contenders for the job of Fleet fighter; the Fairey Flycatcher and the Parnall Plover. The Plover was in many ways the better aircraft, with much cleaner lines and a higher top speed; nevertheless, it was the Flycatcher that was accepted, eventually serving with Nos. 402 to 408 Fleet Fighter Flights. Only six Plovers entered service, operating with Nos. 403 and 404 Flights until they were replaced by Flycatchers at the end of 1924. The spotter-reconnaissance role was filled by the Fairey IIID, a three-seat fabric-covered aircraft of wooden construction that had first flown in 1920; it trundled along at a top speed of 106 mph, and was replaced by the Fairey IIIF in 1928. A total of 207 IIIDs served with the Fleet Air Arm.

Contemporary with the Fairey IIID was the Avro Bison, a spotter-reconnaissance aircraft that served in HMS *Furious* at home and HMS *Eagle* in the Mediterranean until it was replaced by the Fairey IIIF in 1929. The Bison's performance was inferior even to that of the IIID, aerodynamic efficiency being sacrificed to provide accommodation for a three-man crew in the bulky fuselage. Altogether, forty-one were ordered.

The Bison and the Fairey IIID replaced another aircraft that in many ways symbolized the economy-conscious mood of the early 1920s. It was the Westland Walrus (no relation to the later Walrus of air-sea rescue fame), and it was built largely of spare parts from DH.9A bombers. A three-seat deck landing aircraft, the Walrus served with the Fleet Air Arm's Nos. 420 and 421 Flights at Gosport, and with No. 3 Squadron of the RAF at Leuchars, until 1925.

By the standards of 1920–1, the majority of these aircraft were admittedly adequate enough for the tasks they had to perform. But many of the types were still in service in 1928 and 1929, some even later, and by that time they were obsolete. More serious still, the design of naval aircraft had been at a virtual standstill during the late 1920s. And as the Fleet Air Arm moved towards a new decade, the standards of ten years earlier still applied; there were no new, modern, high-performance British carrier aircraft on the horizon.

4 Rebirth

During the nineteen-twenties, the Royal Navy held a series of exercises during which the effectiveness of carrier-based aircraft was ably demonstrated. The first was carried out in 1925 by the Mediterranean Fleet, under Admiral Sir Roger Keyes.

The planners of the exercise, which was held in the Aegean, had assumed that the Japanese had occupied bases in the Dutch East Indies and were threatening Singapore (represented in this case by one of the many Aegean islands). The object of the exercise was to discover whether the British Fleet would be exposed to serious risks during its passage through the southern part of the Malacca Strait while sailing to the relief of Singapore.

Only one aircraft-carrier took part in the exercise – the *Eagle* – and she was allocated to the 'Japanese' fleet. Her aircraft made several torpedo attacks on the 'British' fleet and scored three hits. The conclusions drawn after the exercise were that operations by the Royal Navy in the Malacca Strait, faced with strong air-supported enemy naval forces, would be extremely risky. Another and even larger exercise was held in 1928, with Gibraltar representing Hong Kong, and the island of Alboran, off the Algerian coast, representing Singapore. The exercise lasted two months and over eighty ships were involved. Once again, the Japanese were the simulated enemy; the British Fleet's task was to defeat the 'Japanese' fleet before it could attack 'Hong Kong' and 'Singapore'. This time, each side had one aircraft-carrier – and with both sides more or less equally matched in air power, the result was a draw.

Shades of 1942!

In 1929 the aircraft-carriers *Furious, Courageous* and *Eagle* operated together in the Mediterranean for the first time. Their aircraft took part in several simulated strikes against other warships, but the results achieved – together with the results of other smaller air-sea exercises of the period – were unfortunately destroyed when the RN Staff College at Greenwich was bombed during the Second World War. It is on record, however, that in October 1931 a force of fourteen torpedo-bombers, operating from HMS *Glorious,* scored nine hits on warship targets in the Mediterranean; and that in the spring of 1933, aircraft from three carriers taking part in a combined fleet exercise scored twenty-one hits out of a possible thirty-two.

By the beginning of the nineteen-thirties, in spite of Britain's lead in the number of carriers in service, the number of aircraft deployed among them was less than the number deployed by both the Americans and the Japanese. The *Eagle,* for example, carried only eighteen aircraft; the *Furious* carried thirty; and the *Courageous* and the *Glorious* carried thirty-six each, although they had been intended to operate fifty-two. By way of comparison, the American *Lexington* and *Saratoga* operated seventy-two aircraft each, and the Japanese *Kaga* and *Akagi* sixty. The British carriers were, however, generally smaller than their American and Japanese counterparts, and their greater numbers enabled the Royal Navy to deploy them among each of its fleets stationed throughout the world, from the Atlantic to China. The Americans and Japanese, on the other hand, preferred to concentrate their carrier forces. Apart from their numerical superiority in carrier aircraft, the Americans had also taken the lead in catapult-launching techniques.

In 1928 the British Government announced that plans to lay down a new aircraft-carrier were to go ahead. Shortly afterwards, Admiral Dudley Pound, submitted an estimate of the aircraft strength that would be required by the Fleet Air Arm up to 1938. After comparing the FAA's strength with that of other naval air arms, he indicated his belief that a first-line strength of 251 aircraft by 1937 would be adequate to meet the Navy's requirements. In retrospect, it is difficult to understand how Admiral Pound arrived at his assessment; five years later, the Fleet Air Arm possessed only 159 aircraft in comparison with the

US Navy's 1000 and the Japanese Navy's 411, and the trend towards this disparity in numbers was already apparent in 1928.

Towards the close of the nineteen-twenties, relations between the Royal Navy and the RAF on the question of naval air power began to show a steady improvement. Trenchard resigned his post as CAS on 31 December 1929, and his place was taken by Air Chief Marshal Sir John Salmond, who viewed the situation from a more flexible standpoint than Trenchard had done. By this time, however, all three Services were fighting for survival in the midst of the worst economic crisis in Britain's history and the politicians's fool's paradise of disarmament.

By 1930, because of the country's fluctuating political fortunes, nothing at all had been done to authorize even the modest expansion of the Fleet Air Arm that the Admiralty had requested. The FAA now had a total of ninety-two naval officer aircrew, but the RAF was still responsible for their training and for the provision of new types of aircraft. In 1931, however, the Admiralty made an important decision when it decided to create the new post of Flag Officer (Air) and selected Rear-Admiral R. G. H. Henderson to fill it. Henderson was a firm believer in the vital importance of naval air power, and under his direction a completely new set of tactics governing aircraft-carrier operations was devised. These involved massed air attacks by aircraft operating from three or more carriers grouped into a single squadron, and as we have already mentioned the method revealed itself to be highly successful during combined air-sea exercises in the Mediterranean later that year. But Henderson's 'massed formations' were severely handicapped by the critical shortage of aircraft; the maximum number that could be used in a single large formation at any one time never exceeded fifty.

Moreover, the unserviceability rate among the FAA's Fly-catchers, Blackburns and Fairey IIIFs was steadily becoming higher with the passage of time. In 1932, as a replacement for the Flycatcher, the Fleet Air Arm received the first batch of Hawker Nimrod fighters – the naval version of the RAF's Fury. The first FAA Fighter Flight to be equipped with the Nimrod was No. 408 under Lt Cdr M. C. Abel-Smith, operating from the *Glorious* in the Mediterranean. A few weeks later, however, the Flight was disembarked at Hal Far, Malta, and the *Glorious* sailed back to Britain to undergo a refit. The following September a new Nimrod Flight, No. 409, formed at Netheravon and embarked on the *Glorious* when she sailed to rejoin the Mediterranean Fleet. By that time, No. 402 Flight was also operating Nimrods, and No. 404 Flight Nimrods and Hawker Ospreys. The latter aircraft, the naval version of the Hawker Hart, had been accepted by the Fleet Air Arm for the spotter-reconnaissance role soon after the Osprey's entry into service. Normally, each Flight had six aircraft.

On 3 April 1933 the Fleet Air Arm's Fighter Flights were amalgamated to form four squadrons. Nos. 402 and 404 Flights became No. 800 Squadron, operating nine Nimrods and three Ospreys; the same number of aircraft served with No. 802 Squadron, resulting from the amalgamation of Nos. 408 and 409 Flights; No. 801 Squadron, formerly No. 401 Flight, was smaller, with an establishment of six Nimrods and three Ospreys; and No. 803 Squadron was an Osprey unit, with only one Nimrod attached. No. 800 Squadron operated from the *Courageous,* No. 801 from the *Furious* and No. 802 from the *Glorious.* That same year, the Fleet Air Arm's new squadron structure was extended by the amalgamation of torpedo-bomber and reconnaissance flights.

In 1935 the Navy's long-awaited new carrier – the *Ark Royal* – was finally laid down. In July the following year, the first examples of a new aircraft for the torpedo-spotter-reconnaissance role – the Fairey Swordfish – were delivered to No. 825 Squadron, the first of thirteen Fleet Air Arm units to be equipped with the type over the next three years. Known affectionately as 'Stringbag' throughout her Service career, the Swordfish was already obsolescent in design compared with the latest American and Japanese types; nevertheless, she was loved by the men who flew her, and over the years she was to carve out an unforgettable place for herself in the annals of the Royal Navy.

In the spring of 1936 the total strength of the Fleet Air Arm was still only 178 aircraft. In the Defence White Paper published in March 1936, however, it was stated that the Fleet Air Arm would be expanded considerably to bring it closer to the level of the American and Japanese naval air arms. But the planned expansion came too late; when war broke out in 1939 the Fleet Air Arm still had a total of only 340 aircraft, 115 of which were spotter types carried in battleships and cruisers.

In July 1936 the Admiralty placed an order for 190 Blackburn Skua dive-bombers – the first British combat aircraft designed as a dive-bomber from the outset, and the first monoplane type to be ordered for the Fleet Air Arm. The first FAA squadron to receive the Skua, in November 1938, was No. 800 aboard the newly-commissioned *Ark Royal*. Nos. 801 and 803 Squadrons had also replaced their Nimrods and Ospreys with Skuas by September 1939. During the same period, No. 802 and a new FAA fighter squadron, No. 804, received Gloster Sea Gladiators – the naval variant of the RAF's last biplane fighter.

Meanwhile, in July 1937, the Admiralty had at last won its battle to gain operational and administrative control over the Fleet Air Arm – but it was not until May 1939 that all the paperwork was finally sorted out and full Naval control of the Air Arm became a complete reality. Once the decisions had been made, however, the Admiralty went ahead with a crash programme to expand the Fleet Air Arm literally at the eleventh hour. Orders were immediately placed for four new fleet carriers, to be followed by two more within two years.

At the end of 1938, the state of the Fleet Air Arm was as follows. The *Ark Royal* was completing her trials; the *Courageous* and the *Furious* were with the Home Fleet, the former operating No. 800 Squadron, which was shortly to embark on the *Ark Royal* with its new Skuas, and Nos. 810, 820 and 821 Spotter Reconnaissance Squadrons with Swordfish, and the latter with Nos. 801, 811 and 822 Squadrons; the *Hermes* was in reserve at Devonport; the *Glorious* was in the Mediterranean with No. 802 Squadron (Sea Gladiator) and Nos. 812, 823 and 825 Squadrons (Swordfish); the *Eagle* was on the China Station with Nos. 813 and 824 Squadrons (Swordfish); and the old *Argus* was in use as a training carrier at Portsmouth. There were also eleven Catapult Flights scattered among Royal Navy units throughout the world, equipped principally with the Fairey Seafox floatplane.

Five new fleet carriers of 23,000 tons were under construction; these were the *Illustrious, Victorious, Formidable, Indomitable* and *Implacable,* with the building of a sixth – the *Indefatigable* – scheduled to begin in 1939. Unlike former British carriers, these new vessels followed American lines in that they incorporated both hangars and flight deck in the main hull structure. They differed from their American counterparts, however, in the construction of the flight deck itself, which – like their hulls – was heavily armoured. Later, in the Pacific, the British carriers' armour was to save them time and again when they absorbed terrible blows that often proved fatal to American carriers, with their wooden flight decks. The use of heavy armour-plating reduced the number of aircraft that the British carriers could accommodate, but as events were to show the sacrifice was well worth while.

Meanwhile, in the Far East, the Japanese Navy's aircrews had been gaining something that the Fleet Air Arm lacked so far – combat experience. Since its beginnings in 1920, Japanese naval aviation had developed at an incredible rate. Japan's naval architects had learned a lot from early British experience with carriers; their first aircraft had in fact been British types, including Sopwith Pups and Cuckoos, Gloster Sparrowhawks and Parnall Panthers, and the design of the carriers *Kaga* and *Akagi* had incorporated a good deal of British know-how. Even as late as 1939, many western observers unjustifiably labelled Japanese naval aircraft as more or less straightforward copies of British and American types, although by this time Japanese designers were producing naval aircraft that were in advance of any others. In 1937 the Japanese Navy had introduced the world's first monoplane carrier-based attack aircraft, the Nakajima 97, later known to the Allies by its code name of 'Kate'. And in 1939 the Mitsubishi factories were building the prototype of a carrier fighter known as the Navy Type O – the famous 'Zero' that was to come as a nasty surprise to the Allies in 1942.

Japanese naval airmen first saw action in 1932, during the early phase of the conflict with China. Early operations showed the need for a long-range fighter to provide cover for attack aircraft, and it was the Zero that eventually filled this requirement. Just as the Spanish Civil War provided a testing-ground for the Luftwaffe's new aircraft and a baptism of fire for its crews, the Sino-Japanese conflict enabled the Japanese Navy to formulate new carrier tactics and to lay down clear requirements for new aircraft. By the end of 1939 the Japanese Naval Air Arm was probably the most efficient, highly-skilled striking force in the world. Five carriers were in service, the *Kaga, Akagi, Ryujo, Soryu* and *Hiryu,* and two more – the *Shokaku* and *Zuikaku* – were building.

If the Fleet Air Arm had been pitted against the Japanese instead of against the Germans in the early months of the war, the consequences for the Royal Navy would have been disastrous. Fortunately, neither the Germans nor the Italians had shown any interest in carrier development; both had a very small naval air arm, but it was restricted to shore-based aircraft and a handful of floatplanes such as the Arado 196 and the Heinkel 114, in the case of the Germans, for spotter duties aboard battleships and cruisers.

Nevertheless, when war finally did come the Fleet Air Arm was still badly under-equipped and unprepared. The lack of modern aircraft, and particularly of fighters, was to make itself felt during the coming months, when the hammer-blows of the Luftwaffe mercilessly battered the Royal Navy's warships in the seas off northern Europe.

c

5 Against All Odds

On 3 September 1939 the German submarine *U-30* launched a salvo of torpedoes at a large British passenger vessel sailing without lights outside the normal shipping lanes off Ireland. The ship was the liner *Athenia,* and she sank with the loss of 128 lives. On the very day that war broke out between Great Britain and Germany, the conflict at sea had claimed its first victims.

The Royal Navy immediately sent out two U-Boat hunting groups, each with its own aircraft-carrier. The first, with the *Ark Royal,* took station to the west of the Hebrides; the second, with the *Courageous,* patrolled the Western Approaches. On 14 September the *Ark Royal* had a narrow escape when she was sighted by the *U-39;* the submarine fired a salvo of torpedoes at her, but they were a new type fitted with magnetic pistols and exploded short of the carrier, causing only slight damage to the warship's paintwork. The *U-39* was immediately attacked by the *Ark Royal's* destroyer screen and sunk, her crew being taken prisoner.

Three days later, however, the U-Boats took their revenge and dealt a major blow to the Fleet Air Arm's carrier force. The *U-29,* commanded by Lt-Cdr Schuhardt, had been stalking what appeared to be a troopship when a dark smudge of smoke was sighted on the horizon to the west of the English Channel. It was the *Courageous,* and she was steaming towards the U-Boat. Two hours later she was within range, and Schuhardt had just worked out a plan of attack when the carrier suddenly altered course, her huge flank presenting the submarine's commander with a once-in-a-lifetime target. Schuhardt immediately fired three torpedoes and then crash-dived to evade the carrier's escorting destroyers. Soon afterwards, two tremendous explosions shook the U-Boat as the torpedoes struck home. The *Courageous* went down, taking her commander and over five hundred of her crew with her.

The U-Boats had struck the first crippling blow; now, suddenly, it was the Luftwaffe's turn. At 09.00 hours on 26 September the crew of a Dornier 18 flying boat were detailed to carry out a reconnaissance for the Navy's Northwest Command in the Fisher Bank area. It was known that units of the British Home Fleet were at sea in force, and the Luftwaffe was planning an air strike. It was not an ideal day for reconnaissance; a layer of almost unbroken cloud stretched over the sea. Nevertheless, the pilot kept a watchful eye on the sky; the day before, one of his colleagues in the Dornier squadron at Norderney had been shot down off the Norwegian coast by a flight of British carrier aircraft. (They were the Skuas of No. 803 Squadron from the *Ark Royal*, led by Lieutenant C. L. G. Evans, and they claimed the distinction of shooting down the first enemy aircraft of the war.)

Suddenly, an excited shout from his observer interrupted the pilot's thoughts. Looking down through a gap in the clouds, he saw a ship come slowly into view. It was followed by others: four battleships, an aircraft-carrier, and some cruisers.

At 11.00 hours the telephone rang in the ops room of the Luftwaffe base on the island of Sylt. 'Enemy naval surface units concentrated in square 4022. Recce aircraft maintaining contact. Load up with thousand-pounders and attack immediately.' At 12.50, nine Heinkel 111s of No. 1 Squadron, Kampfgeschwader 26, took off from Westerland. They were followed ten minutes later by four Junkers 88s of KG. 30. The two formations headed out for their rendezvous with the British warships.

The British force in fact consisted of the *Ark Royal*, the battleships *Nelson* and *Rodney*, the battle-cruisers *Hood* and *Renown* and three light cruisers. Some distance away was the Second Cruiser Squadron, with four more cruisers and six destroyers.

The main target assigned to the Junkers 88s, led by Lieutenant Storp, was the *Ark Royal*. Unlike the Heinkels, the 88s were dive-bombers and as such they would stand a greater chance of success. KG.30 had just begun to re-equip with the new bombers;

this was their first operational mission.

One of the pilots in Storp's flight was a Sergeant named Carl Francke. He had helped to test the Ju. 88 before the war, and knew the aircraft inside out. Now, as he droned towards the target, Francke had no idea that within twenty-four hours his name would be splashed over the front page of every newspaper in Germany.

Exactly one hundred minutes after take-off, the pilots in Storp's formation sighted the warships and split up to make individual attacks from different directions, to confuse the anti-aircraft gunners. From ten thousand feet, Francke started his dive, plummeting down through a maze of anti-aircraft bursts and keeping the *Ark Royal* firmly centred in his sights. The 88 leaped buoyantly as the bombs curved away from under its wings and the pilot pulled up in a steep climbing turn, craning his neck to see the result of his attack. A great fountain of water erupted close to the carrier's side, cascading on the flight deck. Something else caught his eye, too – a bright flash near the carrier's bow. Was it a hit – or the flash of an A/A gun? He had dropped two bombs, but only one had exploded in the sea.

With the defensive fire growing thicker every second, Francke felt indisposed to hang around – and anyway, he had no bombs left. Shoving down the 88's nose he raced for home, low over the waves. Back at base, a barrage of questions awaited him. Francke could only report one near miss – and what he thought might have been a hit. At 15.00 hours the speculation reached fever-pitch when reconnaissance aircraft reported that the British force was heading westwards at high speed – with no sign of the carrier.

Both Goering and his Luftwaffe chiefs, Milch and Jeschonnek, thought that it would be prudent to wait for a British announcement before making the sinking public. But Goebbels' propaganda machine was already in full swing, and the next morning the German papers were full of the news. Even Goering was going along with the fable now; he had Francke promoted immediately to Lieutenant and awarded the embarrassed pilot the Iron Cross, First and Second Class.

It was the *Ark Royal* herself that gave the lie to the German claim. At the beginning of October, she slipped out into the South Atlantic to take part in the search for the German pocket battleship *Admiral Graf Spee*.

Apart from reconnaissance and gunnery spotting missions flown by HMS *Ajax*'s Fairey Seafox floatplane, the Fleet Air Arm played no direct part in the naval action that has gone down in history as the Battle of the River Plate. Three carriers took part in the hunt for the German warship, but when she was finally brought to battle off the coast of Uruguay by the cruisers *Exeter, Ajax* and *Achilles* on the morning of 13 December, they were all several thousand miles away. The *Eagle,* as part of Force 'I', was at Durban, over four thousand miles distant; Force 'K', with the *Ark Royal* was two thousand miles to the north, off Pernambuco; and Force X, with the *Hermes,* was further north still, off St Paul Rocks. However, British Intelligence put out false radio signals that led the Germans to believe that the carriers were very much closer – and on 17 December, convinced that a strong British naval force including the *Ark Royal* was in position off Montevideo, Captain Langsdorff scuttled his ship in the estuary of the River Plate.

During the weeks that followed. Fleet Air Arm aircraft were involved in the search for the *Graf Spee*'s companion, the supply ship *Altmark,* whose holds were crammed with British seamen; later, it was learned that she had been spotted but not identified by *Ark Royal*'s Swordfish. Eventually, however, she was sighted off the coast of Norway on 15 February 1940 by Hudsons of RAF Coastal Command, and later was boarded by sailors from the destroyer *Cossack* in Josing Fjord. Apart from that, the long winter of 1939–40 was an endless routine of anti-submarine patrols, reconnaissance and convoy protection for the naval airmen, with a sprinkling of mine-laying operations in conjunction with Coastal Command.

Then, on 9 April 1940, the period of the 'phoney war' came to an abrupt end when German forces invaded Norway. Early that afternoon, units of the Home Fleet were attacked almost without pause for three hours off Bergen by forty-one Heinkels of

KG. 26 and forty-seven Junkers 88s of KG. 30. The battleship *Rodney* received a direct hit from a 1,000-pound bomb, but was saved from serious damage by her armour; the cruisers *Devonshire*, *Southampton* and *Glasgow* were also hit and damaged, and the destroyer *Gurkha* was sunk west of Stavanger. During this first encounter, the Royal Navy had learned to its cost what it meant to operate within range of large formations of shore-based bombers without fighter cover; the aircraft-carrier *Furious* had in fact been ordered out from the Clyde to join the Fleet, but she had left in such a hurry that there had been no time to embark her aircraft. Realizing that she could contribute nothing to the safety of his ships, the C-in-C, Admiral Forbes, ordered her to stay out of range. In the late afternoon of the 9th, he took his main force westwards to meet the carrier and the battleship *Warspite* to the north of the Shetlands.

In the early hours of the following morning scattered cloud hung over the Orkneys, drifting slowly before a chilly north-east wind. Over the airfield at Hatston, a few miles north of Kirkwall, the night air throbbed with sound as sixteen Skuas – seven from 800 Squadron and nine from 803 – taxied round the narrow perimeter track. The Skuas had disembarked from the *Ark Royal* early in the new year; on 9 April they had been ordered north to the Orkneys to bring them within striking distance of targets in Norway.

Each aircraft was laden with a 500-pound bomb, and under the unaccustomed weight take-off was a tricky business. Some cleared the end of the short runway by a matter of feet, but at last all sixteen were safely airborne. Forming up overhead, they set course north-eastwards. Three hundred miles away in the darkness lay their target: the German cruiser *Königsberg*, anchored in Bergen harbour.

For nearly two hours they droned on. Ahead of them now, the pink and green flush of dawn began to spread across the sky. At seven o'clock, a dark, broken line rose out of the horizon; the black cliffs of the Norwegian coast. The sun burst out over the mountains beyond and suddenly the pilots made out the entrance to Bergen Fjord, dead ahead. After flying three hundred miles through the night, they had made landfall in exactly the right place and within seconds of their ETA.

Throttles wide open, the sixteen Skuas went up to eight thousand feet and swept up the fjord. Bergen loomed up out of the thin morning haze and there was the *Königsberg,* moored hard up against Skoltegrund Mole. The first wave, led by Lieutenant W. P. Lucy, went into line astern and the nine aircraft seemed to falter as their big flaps went down. Then their wings flashed in the sunlight as they peeled off into a sixty-degree dive towards the target.

As a dive-bomber, the Skua was unsurpassed. It could dive almost vertically at near-constant speed, held back by its huge flap area, and the pilot's visibility was excellent. Lucy held his aircraft rock-steady, watching the long shape of the cruiser loom up in his sights. At four thousand feet the first scattered burst of flak started to come up, the blotchy bursts whipping past Lucy's Skua as he held her in the dive. At two thousand feet Lucy pressed the release and the bomb fell away, curving down to explode near the warship's stern in a geyser of foam. As Lucy pulled up out of his dive, he saw the *Königsberg*'s decks erupt in smoke and flame as the other Skuas of his formation bombed her in turn, followed almost immediately by the second wave led by Captain R. T. Partridge, Royal Marines.

The cruiser sustained three direct hits, one amidships between her funnels, one on the port quarter and one on 'A' turret. Two more exploded between the ship and the Mole, tearing gaping holes in her side; five pulverized the Mole itself, and the rest were all near misses. An enormous column of flame burst from the stricken warship and she began to list heavily. Five minutes later, a thin plume of brown smoke speared into the air as her magazines went up and she broke in half, sinking in a cloud of steam.

Skimming the water, the Skuas sped through a smoky spider's web of tracer from the shore. Two of them trailed thin streamers of smoke; a third staggered drunkenly and disappeared up the fjord, weaving from side to side. Neither it nor its crew, Lieutenant Smeeton and Midshipman Watkinson, were seen again.

The surviving Skuas formed up over Lyso Island and set

course for home. They landed at Hatston at 09.45, after a flight that had lasted four and a half hours. The engines of three aircraft spluttered and died as they turned clear of the runway; their tanks were empty.

Fifteen minutes after the attack, a flight of Messerschmitt 110s of Zerstörer-Geschwader 76, based on Stavanger, arrived over the fjord. They were too late. By that time, the Skuas were well on their way home. The Fleet Air Arm had achieved complete surprise. Eleven days later, this time operating from the *Ark Royal* in support of the Narvik operations, No. 800 Squadron's Skuas returned to Bergen and sank the supply ship *Bahrenfels*.

A few hours before the Skuas made their attack, the Second Destroyer Flotilla under Captain Warburton-Lee had forced its way into the German-held harbour of Narvik, sinking three enemy destroyers and damaging three more. But five enemy ships had escaped unharmed, and on the 13th the Admiralty sent up the *Warspite* and nine destroyers to finish them off. Swordfish from the *Furious* and the *Warspite*'s own Swordfish floatplane acted as spotters for the battleship's 15-inch guns, as well as searching the fjords for lurking destroyers. The Swordfish's crew pinpointed one enemy destroyer, which was promptly blown out of the water by torpedoes and gunfire from the *Warspite*; a few miles further on the aircraft located a U-Boat in Herjangsfjord, which it bombed and sank.

Throughout these operations, air cover was provided by the Skuas of 800 and 803 Squadrons and by Sea Gladiators from the *Glorious,* recently recalled from the Mediterranean. In the space of three days, Lieutenant Lucy – now operating from the *Ark Royal* with 800 Squadron – claimed the destruction of five enemy aircraft. But on 14 April, during a scrap with a Heinkel 111, a lucky burst from the bomber's rear-gunner tore into the Skua's fuel-tank and the aircraft exploded, killing Lucy and his observer.

Between 14 and 19 April, an allied expeditionary force of British, French and Polish troops went ashore at Namsos and Aandalsnes. On the 22nd, in support of the landings, eighteen Gloster Gladiators of No. 263 Squadron RAF sailed for Norway aboard the *Glorious*. They arrived on the 24th and, operating from a frozen lake, they destroyed six enemy aircraft during the next three days. But by the afternoon of the 27th only three Gladiators were left, there was no more fuel, and the surface of the lake was pitted with bomb craters. The RAF pilots were ordered to destroy the surviving aircraft and embark on the cargo vessel *Delius*.

On 14 May No. 263 Squadron sailed on the *Glorious* once more, this time equipped with more modern Gladiator IIs and bound for Bardufoss, near Narvik, to support the Allies' second Norwegian expedition. On 21 May, two flights of Gladiators – each led by a Fleet Air Arm Swordfish – took off from the flight deck of the *Glorious* in a blinding gale-driven storm of sleet. The pilots soon realized that they had no hope of finding Bardufoss and turned back; one section regained the carrier all right, but the other was not so lucky. The leading Swordfish, hopelessly lost, flew straight into the side of a fog-shrouded mountain at Soreisa, followed by the two Gladiators. The wreckage of the three aircraft blazed on the barren mountainside, three forlorn beacons glowing redly through the murk.

An advance force of eight Gladiators finally reached Bardufoss the following day and was immediately flung into action. For sixteen days, assisted later by the Hurricanes of 46 Squadron at Skaanland, they fought against hopeless odds. Then, on 7 June, the Norwegian campaign drew to a close and the fighters flew their last patrol before setting course over the sea, heading for the *Glorious*. Together with the surviving Hurricanes of 46 Squadron they all landed safely as dusk was falling, even though most of the pilots had never before attempted a deck landing. For the last time, the *Glorious* pointed her bow away from Norway, towards Scapa Flow and home.

She never reached Scapa. On the afternoon of 8 June, she was caught in the open sea by the German battle-cruisers *Scharnhorst* and *Gneisenau*. In a running fight lasting less than two hours, the cruisers pumped salvo after salvo into the carrier. At last, tiredly, she turned over and slid beneath the waves, leaving nothing but a few pitiful islands of wreckage bobbing on the icy sea. Only thirty-eight survivors were picked up, and the Gladiator pilots were not among them.

The *Glorious*'s two escorting destroyers, *Acasta* and *Ardent*, were also sunk – but before she went down the little *Acasta* made a suicidal attack on the *Scharnhorst* and severely damaged her with torpedoes. The cruiser limped into Trondheim, and on 13 June the *Ark Royal* flew off a strike of sixteen Skuas from 800 and 803 Squadrons against her. The aircraft attacked through rain and fog, the murk lit up by pearly streams of tracer and the red flashes of explosions. None of the bombs hit the target, and eight of the Skuas failed to return. Among them was Captain Partridge, who had taken part in the sinking of the *Königsberg;* he crash-landed his burning aircraft and was picked up, badly burned, to face the prospect of five years in a POW camp.

A few days later, on the 21st, a reconnaissance Sunderland reported that the *Scharnhorst* had left Trondheim and was steaming slowly south. This time, she was attacked by Beauforts and Hudsons of Coastal Command, assisted by a handful of Fleet Air Arm Swordfish. The British aircraft suffered heavy losses; the *Scharnhorst* escaped unhurt. The Norwegian tragedy was finally over.

For the Fleet Air Arm, the balance sheet at the end of the Norwegian campaign was depressing. Apart from the *Königsberg,* the Skuas and Swordfish had sunk one large transport and had sunk or damaged several smaller craft, but the attack missions flown by the Swordfish had been generally ineffective for the simple reason that in the shallow waters of the fjords, their torpedoes had often exploded short of their targets. The Skuas had destroyed fourteen enemy aircraft and the Sea Gladiators three, but there was no escaping the fact that two entire Sea Gladiator squadrons – Nos. 802 and 804 – had been lost with the *Glorious,* or that the Skua squadrons had been decimated during their operations as fighters, a role for which they were totally unsuited. Later in the campaign, the Fleet Air Arm's task had not been made any easier by the fact that the Luftwaffe possessed undisputed control of the skies over and around Norway, making it impossible for carriers to operate safely in the area. The

Skua squadrons had been forced to withdraw to the Orkneys, which meant a round trip of 600 miles or more, reducing the time spent on actual patrol and leaving little margin of fuel for combat flying. Several aircraft were lost in the sea on the return flight because of battle damage or lack of fuel.

There was to be no respite. Late in June, shortly before the *Ark Royal* sailed to join the Mediterranean Fleet, three Skua squadrons – Nos. 801, 803 and the recently-formed 806 – moved to bases in southern England to help cover the evacuation of the British Expeditionary Force from Dunkirk. In addition to its Skuas, No. 806 also had a few Blackburn Rocs, the fighter version of the Skua, fitted with a four-gun Boulton Paul turret. During the Dunkirk operations, No. 806 claimed the destruction of a pair of Junkers 88s, and two Messerschmitt 109s were also claimed by the pilots of 801 Squadron. Only one Skua was lost, but a number of others staggered back to base so badly shot up that they had to be written off. One aircraft landed at Detling literally shot to shreds, with the pilot dying at the controls.

After Dunkirk, a number of Fleet Air Arm pilots were attached to RAF Fighter Command and fought with distinction during the Battle of Britain.

But the Battle of Britain was the RAF's victory. For the Fleet Air Arm, the scene of combat now shifted to the Mediterranean – and it was there, while the RAF and the Luftwaffe tussled in the skies of southern England, that the naval aircrews helped to fight one of the war's grimmest and most tragic actions.

6 Mediterranean Theatre, 1940

Towards the end of June 1940 a powerful Royal Navy squadron assembled at Gibraltar under the command of Vice-Admiral Sir James Somerville. Known as Force H, it consisted of the aircraft-carrier *Ark Royal,* newly arrived from Britain, the battleships *Valiant* and *Resolution,* two cruisers and eleven destroyers, together with the battle-cruiser *Hood.*

Force H was only a week old when it was called upon to carry out one of the most tragic and melancholy operations in the history of the Royal Navy: the attempted destruction of the French Fleet at Oran and Mers-el-Kebir. Admiral Somerville was ordered to sail with his squadron to Oran and to offer an unpleasant ultimatum to the French commander, Admiral Gensoul. If the latter refused to join forces with the British, to sail to the French West Indies with reduced crews or to scuttle his ships, then Somerville had orders to destroy them. On 3 July Captain C. S. Holland, in command of the *Ark Royal,* was sent to Oran to parley with Gensoul – but the French Admiral refused even to consider any of the alternatives.

Shortly before 18.00 hours the *Valiant,* the *Resolution* and the *Hood* opened fire, their guns directed by spotter Swordfish from the *Ark Royal,* while another flight of Swordfish laid mines in the entrance of the nearby port of Mers-el-Kebir. The heavy shells tore into the magazine of the battleship *Bretagne* and she blew up; the *Dunkerque* and the *Provence* were badly damaged, and two destroyers were sunk.

As the sun went down, the battleship *Strasbourg* and five destroyers made a dash for safety. They were attacked by the *Ark Royal's* Swordfish, but in the face of heavy anti-aircraft fire and the gathering darkness the pilots' aim was poor and the French warships got away.

The following morning, the *Ark Royal* launched another strike of torpedo-carrying 820 Squadron Swordfish to finish off Gensoul's flagship, the *Dunkerque,* which was aground in Oran harbour. The Swordfish were escorted by Skuas of 803 Squadron, but this time the French were ready for them. When the British aircraft arrived over the harbour, they were hotly engaged by a mixed formation of Morane 406 and Curtiss Hawk 75A fighters from Groupe de Chasse 1/10. Two Skuas were shot down, while two 803 Squadron pilots claimed to have damaged a couple of French aircraft. It was fortunate that the French pilots lacked combat experience, otherwise they would certainly have taken a heavier toll of the outclassed Fleet Air Arm aircraft. As it was, the Skuas kept the French fighters occupied long enough to allow the Swordfish to make their runs; four of their torpedoes hit the *Dunkerque* and put her out of action.

Another French squadron – consisting of the Battleship *Lorraine,* four cruisers and a number of smaller warships – was at Alexandria, where it had been working under Admiral Cunningham, commander of the British Eastern Mediterranean Fleet, before France's collapse. Here, Cunningham managed to arrive at a peaceful settlement with his French opposite number, Admiral Godfroy, and the French warships were quietly demilitarized. That still left the new battleships *Jean Bart* and *Richelieu* in the West African ports of Casablanca and Dakar, and on 8 July a fast motor-boat from the carrier *Hermes* entered the harbour of Dakar and dropped depth charges under the *Richelieu*'s stern in an attempt to put her rudder and propellers out of action. But the depth charges failed to explode, and although the battleship was later attacked by Swordfish of 814 Squadron from the *Hermes* their torpedoes only inflicted light damage. She was attacked again two months later, this time by the *Ark Royal*'s aircraft, during the abortive British landing in Senegal; but once again the air strikes proved ineffective, and this time nine Swordfish and Skuas were shot down.

Meanwhile, having dealt with the question of the French

squadron in Alexandria, Admiral Cunningham had sailed from that port on 7 July with the twofold intention of providing protection for two convoys carrying badly-needed supplies from Malta to Alexandria, and also of throwing down a challenge to the Italian Navy by operating within sight of the southern coast of Italy. Cunningham's force was split into three; the leading unit consisted of five cruisers, the centre of the flagship *Warspite* and her destroyer screen, and bringing up the rear was the carrier *Eagle,* accompanied by ten destroyers and the two veteran battleships *Malaya* and *Royal Sovereign.* The British Fleet's air component consisted of just fifteen Swordfish, with three Sea Gladiators of 813 Squadron. Two days earlier, the Swordfish had scored a resounding success when, operating from an RAF airfield in Egypt, they had sunk the Italian destroyer *Zeffiro* and the 4,000-ton freighter *Manzoni,* as well as badly damaging the destroyer *Euro* and the 15,000-ton troopship *Liguria,* in a torpedo attack on Tobruk harbour.

Early on 8 July a patrolling submarine reported that a strong enemy force, including two battleships, was steaming southwards between Taranto and Benghazi. Reconnaissance Swordfish were launched, and they in turn reported that the enemy warships were following an easterly course, which led Cunningham to believe that they were covering a convoy en route to Benghazi. Hurriedly postponing the departure of the British convoy from Malta, he altered course in order to position himself between the enemy and their base at Taranto.

On the afternoon of that same day, the British Fleet was subjected to the first of a series of high-level attacks by the Italian Air Force, running in at over ten thousand feet. The *Eagle* was singled out as a special target, but in spite of several near misses she came through unscathed. Only one ship, the cruiser *Gloucester,* was hit and damaged; nevertheless, the Regia Aeronautica crews were very accurate in their bombing, and at the height they operated most of the British warships' anti-aircraft armament was ineffective.

The raids went on for five days, and several of them were intercepted by the *Eagle*'s Sea Gladiator flight. These three fighters were all in fact flown by Swordfish pilots of 813 Squadron: Commander C. L. Keighley-Peach and Lieutenants L. K. Keith and A. N. Young. Keighley-Peach, who had been the only pilot on 813 Squadron with fighter experience, had formed the flight earlier in the year and had personally trained the other two young pilots. Between 9 and 14 July, when they could be spared from their primary job of flying Swordfish, the trio shot down five Savoia S.M.79 bombers without loss to themselves.

At dawn on 9 July Cunningham was sixty miles off the south-west tip of Greece, with the enemy force – two battleships, sixteen cruisers and thirty-two destroyers – about one hundred and fifty miles ahead of him. By 11.45 hours only ninety miles separated the two forces, and the *Eagle* launched a striking force of nine Swordfish in an attempt to slow down the enemy. They failed to find the main force, which had altered course, but launched their torpedoes through a heavy barrage of fire at an Italian cruiser that was bringing up the rear, missed, and returned to the *Eagle* to refuel and rearm.

At 15.15 hours Cunningham's advance force of cruisers sighted the enemy, who immediately opened fire on them. Ten minutes later the *Warspite* arrived on the scene and pounded the Italian cruisers with her 15-inch guns until they were forced to withdraw under cover of a smoke-screen. At 15.45 a second Swordfish strike was flown off, and three minutes after the aircraft had gone the *Warspite* sighted the Italian flagship *Giulio Cesare* and opened fire on her at a range of 26,000 yards. At 16.00 hours, one of the *Warspite*'s 15-inch shells slammed home at the base of the *Cesare*'s funnel, causing considerable damage and reducing the warship's speed to eighteen knots. The Italian commander, Admiral Campioni, at once broke off the action and headed for the Italian coast, accompanied by the *Cesare*'s sister ship *Conte di Cavour*.

Half-an-hour later the nine Swordfish, led by Lt-Cdr Debenham, arrived on the scene and the pilots tried to make out their targets through the dense pall of smoke that drifted over the water. After a few minutes, Debenham spotted two large warships emerging from the smoke and led his aircraft in to the attack. In fact, the two ships were the 8-inch cruisers *Trento* and *Bolzano;* they immediately turned away into the smoke once more, throwing down a heavy barrage in the path of the attacking Swordfish as they did so. The torpedoes failed to find their mark, and all the aircraft returned safely to the carrier. They landed-on at 17.05 in the middle of yet another high-level attack by Italian bombers; fortunately none of the British warships sustained any direct hits, although both the *Eagle* and the *Warspite* were shaken by near-misses.

At 17.30, Cunningham abandoned the chase and set course for Malta. Without adequate fighter cover, it would have been suicidal to sail any closer to the Italian coast. Late the following day, however, the *Eagle*'s Swordfish flew off on one more strike – this time against a concentration of enemy cruisers and destroyers that had been reported in the Sicilian harbour of Augusta. The aircraft arrived over the harbour at dusk to find only one destroyer and an oil tanker still there; both were torpedoed successfully, the destroyer – the *Leone Pancaldo* – turning over and sinking within minutes.

Having refuelled and rearmed his force in Malta, Cunningham now turned to his main task: escorting the convoy to Alexandria. The ships were repeatedly attacked by the Regia Aeronautica during the next three days, but they reached Alexandria without loss on 14 July.

The 'Action off Calabria', as Cunningham's brush with the Italians later came to be known, was the first fleet action in which carrier aircraft took part. Presumably due to the lack of experience among the Swordfish crews, the Fleet Air Arm had made no material contribution other than to help convince the enemy, perhaps, that in the face of repeated if ineffective torpedo attacks withdrawal was the best policy. If the Italians had possessed an aircraft-carrier, even one as outdated as the *Eagle,* with a complement of fighter aircraft, the result might have been very different; there is little doubt that the Swordfish would have been very severely mauled.

As far as the Regia Aeronautica was concerned, the precision of their high-level bombing attacks had been little short of poetic – but totally ineffective against the elusive moving targets presented by the warships. It was not that the Italian aircrews lacked courage; far from it, as later events were to show. It was just that their tactics were based on precision bombing, as the Luftwaffe's were based on dive-bombing. The Regia Aeronautica's lack of success against Cunningham's force did, however, have one damaging effect. It bred a sense of complacency, a belief that bombing could not seriously interfere with the Royal Navy's freedom of movement in the Mediterranean. The complacency was to be rudely shattered before long, with the arrival of the first Stuka squadrons in Sicily and Italy.

Towards the end of August, the Royal Navy's striking force in the Mediterranean received a powerful new addition in the shape of the 23,000-ton armoured fleet carrier *Illustrious*. In addition to her two Swordfish squadrons, Nos. 815 and 819, she carried No. 806 Squadron – which, after the Dunkirk operations, had become the first FAA unit to exchange its Skuas and Rocs for the Fairey Fulmar, the Navy's new monoplane fighter. The Fulmar was fitted with eight Browning .303 machine-guns, and although its maximum speed of 270 mph made it a good deal slower than contemporary land-based fighters such as the Hurricane, it was a distinct improvement on the Sea Gladiator and Skua. Fourteen FAA squadrons were eventually equipped with the type.

For the first time, thanks to the Fulmars, Admiral Cunningham now had an effective means of countering the routine Italian high-level attacks and the reconnaissance aircraft that shadowed his warships at a respectful distance. The pilots of 806 Squadron soon began to chalk up an increasing score of kills against the lumbering Cant Z.501 flying boats and Z.506B floatplanes, as well as against the S.M.79 bombers. After some two months of operations, the Squadron tally stood at over twenty enemy aircraft. One of the most successful pilots was the CO, Lt-Cdr C. L. G. Evans, who had shared in the destruction of the first enemy aircraft of the war in September 1939; his score eventually rose to $16\frac{1}{2}$.

During September, the Swordfish of Nos. 813, 824, 815 and 819 Squadrons, operating from the *Illustrious* and the *Eagle,* made several dive-bombing attacks at night on Italian airfields in the Dodecanese. On one occasion, during a raid on Maritza airfield on the island of Rhodes, the Swordfish failed to get clear of enemy territory before sunrise and ran into a formation of Italian Fiat CR.42 fighters. Four of the thirteen Swordfish, all from the *Eagle,* were shot down. The Fleet Air Arm had its revenge on the night of 17 September, however, when fifteen Swordfish from the *Illustrious* sank two Italian destroyers and damaged several other vessels in Benghazi harbour.

The *Ark Royal*'s Swordfish were also in action during this period, carrying out a series of bombing raids on Italian airfields in Sicily to divert attention from the carriers *Furious* and *Argus,* which had just arrived from Britain with Hurricane fighters to reinforce the hard-pressed island of Malta. The island had been under attack by the Regia Aeronautica ever since Italy's entry into the war in June, and for nearly three weeks the sole air defence had been provided by three Sea Gladiators. They had originally been intended for service aboard HMS *Glorious,* but the ill-fated carrier had sailed for Norwegian waters without them and afterwards they had been shipped to Malta, in crates, prior to joining HMS *Eagle*. But they never reached the carrier; permission was granted for them to be assembled and used for the fighter defence of Malta. There were actually four aircraft, but the fourth was left in its crate to provide spare parts.

The three aircraft fought alone – hampered by the fact that they were slower than the bombers they were supposed to catch – until they were joined by the first flight of Hurricanes on 28 June. Later, the three Gladiators were immortalized by the names 'Faith', 'Hope' and 'Charity', but although official accounts state that they were referred to by these names during the actual period of air fighting, there is no evidence to support this.

As Malta prepared to weather the storm – the worst of which was yet to come – events in the Mediterranean were moving towards the action that was to form the very basis of the Fleet Air

Arm's fighting tradition in the years to come: the attack on the Italian Fleet at Taranto. The aggressive spirit of the Royal Navy, the courage and daring of the Fleet Air Arm's crews, are to this day symbolized by that one word: Taranto.

The plans for an attack on Taranto by carrier-borne aircraft had been laid long before 1940; as long ago as 1935, in fact, when Mussolini's forces invaded Abyssinia. There were actually two main Italian naval bases, one at Naples and the other at Taranto; and it was at the latter, in the autumn of 1940, that the Italians began to concentrate their heavy naval units to counter the threat from the British Eastern Mediterranean Fleet.

With only the old *Eagle* at Admiral Cunningham's disposal, an attack on the big Italian base had been regarded as impracticable – but the arrival of the *Illustrious* changed the picture completely. The old plans were dug out and revised, and it was decided to mount a big strike from the *Illustrious* and the *Eagle* on the night of 21 October – the anniversary of the Battle of Trafalgar. Before that date, however, a serious fire swept through the *Illustrious*'s hangar; some of her aircraft were totally destroyed and most of the others were put temporarily out of action, and the strike had to be postponed for a further three weeks. Perhaps it was just as well; it is now known that the Italians were expecting Cunningham to pull off something big on Trafalgar Day, and Taranto's defences were kept at a high state of alert throughout the 20th, 21st and 22nd.

Apart from that, early in November RAF Maryland reconnaissance aircraft of No. 431 Flight based on Luqa, Malta, reported that five out of the six battleships of the main Italian battle fleet were now at Taranto, as well as a large force of cruisers and destroyers. The battleships and some of the cruisers were moored in the outer harbour, the Mar Grande, a horseshoe-shaped expanse of fairly shallow water, while the other cruisers and destroyers lay in the inner harbour, the Mar Piccolo. The ships in the outer harbour were protected by torpedo nets and lines of barrage balloons. It was the balloons, perhaps even more than the anti-aircraft batteries, that would present the greatest hazard to the low-flying Swordfish.

73

The date of the attack – Operation Judgment – was fixed for the night of 11 November. Because of defects caused by the many near-misses she had suffered, the *Eagle* had to be withdrawn from the operation at the last moment; five of her aircraft were transferred to the other carrier.

The *Illustrious* and the fleet sailed from Alexandria on 6 November. Two days later, the warships rendezvoused with several military convoys in the Ionian Sea, on their way from Malta to Alexandria and Greece. The concentration of ships was located and bombed by the Regia Aeronautica during the next two days, but the attacks were broken up by 806 Squadron's Fulmars; the fighters shot down ten enemy aircraft without loss to themselves.

At 18.00 hours on the 11th, with the convoys safely on their way under escort, the *Illustrious* – together with a screen of four cruisers and four destroyers – detached herself from the main force and headed for her flying-off position 170 miles from Taranto. Twenty-one aircraft were available for the strike; twelve from 815 Squadron, led by Lt-Cdr Ken Williamson, and nine from 819 under Lt-Cdr J. W. Hale. Because of the restricted space available over the target, only six aircraft from each wave were to carry torpedoes; the others were to drop flares to the east of the Mar Grande, silhouetting the warships anchored there, or to dive-bomb the vessels in the Mar Piccolo.

At 20.40 hours the first wave took off and set course for the target, two-and-a-half hours' flying time away. The night was brilliantly clear, with the moon in its third quarter. Slowly, the Swordfish clawed their way up to eight thousand feet and droned along at a steady seventy-five knots indicated, the pilots jockeying to keep their heavily-laden aircraft in formation. It was bitterly cold in the open cockpits; the observers suffered most of all, for unlike the pilots they were mostly unoccupied. There was no third crew member; on this trip, the gunner's place was filled by an extra fuel tank.

At 22.20 hours, a wrinkled grey line showed up ahead in the moonlight: the enemy coast. The Swordfish formation now split in two, the torpedo-carriers turning away to make their approach from the west while the flare-droppers headed for the east of the

Mar Grande. As Williamson's six aircraft flew parallel with the coast, a series of twinkling flashes burst across the sky to starboard; the Italians had picked up the sound of the approaching aircraft and were putting up a haphazard anti-aircraft barrage over the harbour.

At 23.00 hours the aircraft were in position and turned in towards the target, diving in line astern with engines throttled well back. Seconds later the flares went down, hanging over the harbour in brilliant clusters. In the leading Swordfish, Williamson and his observer, Lieutenant N. J. Scarlett, swept over San Pietro Island through a storm of multi-coloured tracer, jinked their way between the cables of the southern line of balloons and levelled out at thirty feet, flashing over the stern of the battleship *Diga di Tarantola*. Williamson released his torpedo at the first warship that loomed up ahead, the destroyer *Fulmine;* it missed and ran on to explode against the side of a bigger target, the battleship *Cavour*. The Swordfish lurched drunkenly, shedding pieces as shells ripped through its wings and fuselage, and smacked into the sea. Williamson and Scarlett were taken prisoner.

The other Swordfish dropped their torpedoes and twisted desperately away from the pearly meshes of anti-aircraft fire. Two of their torpedoes slammed into the brand-new battleship *Littorio;* the aircraft all got clear of the target area and set course for the carrier. So did the other six Swordfish, whose bombs had damaged some oil tanks and started a big fire in the seaplane base beside the Mar Piccolo.

The second wave, which had taken off some fifty minutes after the first, had no difficulty in locating Taranto; the whole target area was lit up by searchlights and the glare of fires. There were only eight aircraft in this wave; the ninth had been forced to turn back to the carrier when it lost its extra fuel tank.

This time, the five torpedo-carriers came in from the north. The Italian warships were blazing away with everything they had except their main armament, but the Swordfish came through the murderous crossfire and released their torpedoes. Two hit the *Littorio* and another the *Caio Duilio;* a fourth narrowly missed the *Vittorio Veneto*. The fifth Swordfish, piloted by Lieutenant G. W. Bayley with Lieutenant H. J. Slaughter as his observer, ran into a concentrated cone of fire from a score of guns and exploded, scattering blazing fragments over the water. Both men were killed.

By 03.00 hours all the surviving Swordfish had regained the carrier safely. Incredibly, only two – Williamson's and Bayley's – had been lost, although several of the others had taken considerable punishment. One or two pilots had actually hit the water as they steep-turned away from the warships after dropping their torpedoes; if they had been flying a less robust aircraft, it would have been the end for them. Some of the crews who had bombed the vessels in the Mar Piccolo came back cursing; many of their bombs had failed to explode. One had hit the cruiser *Trento* amidships, only to bounce harmlessly off into the water.

The following day, RAF reconnaissance photos told the full story of the damage inflicted on the Italian Fleet by the Swordfish. The mighty *Littorio*, with great gaps torn in her sides by three torpedoes, was badly down by the bows and leaking huge quantities of oil; she would be out of action for four months. The *Cavour* and the *Duilio*, both badly hit, had been beached; the *Cavour* was back in service by May 1941, but the *Duilio* was out of action for the duration. Severe damage had also been inflicted on some of the cruisers and destroyers in the inner harbour; the bombs that had exploded had been dropped with beautiful accuracy.

It was the first time that a formidable battle fleet had been crippled by carrier aircraft, and the effect on the morale of the Italian Navy was shattering. After Taranto, the Italian Navy was permanently on the defensive – and the superiority of the Royal Navy in the Mediterranean was assured. The Italian warships were never again to present a serious threat to the safety of the British convoys that were passing through the Mediterranean in increasing numbers, en route to Malta, Port Said and Alexandria.

On the night of 24/25 November, three large British trans-

ports passed through the Straits of Gibraltar and headed eastwards, accompanied by the warships of Admiral Somerville's
Force H. Meanwhile, a detachment of the Eastern Mediterranean Fleet steamed westwards to meet the convoy south of
Sardinia and escort it on to Malta and Alexandria. On the morning of the 27th, however, when Force H and the merchantmen
were southwest of Sardinia, reconnaissance aircraft from the *Ark
Royal* sighted a large force of enemy battleships and cruisers to
the north. It included the *Vittorio Veneto* and the *Giuglio
Cesare,* the survivors of Admiral Campioni's once-proud battle
fleet, whose remnants had put out from Taranto two weeks
earlier to escape a possible second strike by the Fleet Air Arm.

Somerville immediately sent his five cruisers under Rear-
Admiral L. E. Holland after the enemy, backed up by the *Renown* and the *Ark Royal.* In the early afternoon, the British and
Italian cruisers sighted each other and exchanged fire; no hits
were registered and the enemy withdrew in the direction of the
Vittorio Veneto and the *Cesare.* At one o'clock, the latter opened
fire on Holland's cruisers and he turned away, but soon afterwards he saw the enemy battleships making off to the north-east
and continued the chase.

By refusing action, Admiral Campioni was obeying strict
orders from the Ministry of Marine, which forbade him to risk
his two remaining capital ships. Since both were faster than
Somerville's warships, the British Admiral's only hope lay in a
strike by the *Ark Royal*'s aircraft. Eleven torpedo-carrying
Swordfish were launched and they quickly overhauled the
Italian squadron. The two battleships were protected by a line
of seven destroyers, which threw a curtain of fire across the sky
ahead of the attacking aircraft; somehow, the Swordfish all came
through and dropped their torpedoes between the destroyer
screen and the capital ships, but the latter took violent evasive
action and no hits were scored. The only damage was to the
Vittorio Veneto's bridge, sprayed with bullets by the gunners of
three Swordfish that swept past it almost within touching
distance.

The enemy force was now in full retreat under a dense smoke-screen, and Admiral Somerville – realizing that the engagement had brought him within easy striking distance of enemy bomber bases – decided to break off the chase and return to the vital task of guarding the convoy. However, as the British cruisers turned southward, the *Ark Royal* launched a second strike against the fleeing Italian warships. Seven Skuas, carrying bombs, were to locate and attack an enemy cruiser that was reported to be damaged and stopped, while nine Swordfish were to have another go at the battleships themselves.

But the Swordfish were too late; the battleships were by this time close to the southern tip of Sardinia, and covered by an umbrella of fighters. The Swordfish leader accordingly decided to attack the Italian cruiser squadron that was bringing up the rear. They went in through a heavy barrage and dropped their torpedoes, but the cruisers took evasive action and there were no hits. All the Swordfish returned safely.

A few minutes later, the Skuas of 803 Squadron – who had been flying round in circles looking for a damaged enemy ship that apparently didn't exist – also sighted the cruiser squadron and bombed it. Half-a-dozen near-misses erupted in the water around the cruiser *Trento,* but she sailed on unharmed. Chased by streams of anti-aircraft fire, the Skuas dived away and headed back to the *Ark Royal.*

Not long after they had landed-on, the Regia Aeronautica appeared on the scene and subjected the *Ark Royal* to two hours of intensive high-level bombing. Skuas and Fulmars of 800 and 803 Squadrons took off to intercept the bombers and managed to shoot four of them down, but the great majority got through and unloaded their bombs on the *Ark Royal*. The carrier seemed to enjoy a charmed life; on several occasions, she vanished in the middle of a forest of massive geysers of water as explosions tore the sea around her – but she always emerged unscathed.

The attacks ceased at dusk, and a strange silence fell over the sea. The three merchantmen, escorted now by the battleship *Ramillies,* three cruisers and a screen of destroyers from the Eastern Mediterranean Fleet, went on their way safely; while Force H, its job done, set its face towards the west and Gibraltar.

7 Germany Strikes South

On 9 January 1941 a convoy of five big supply ships, escorted by the *Ark Royal* and other warships of Force H, entered the narrows between Sicily and Tunis on its way to Alexandria. The passage of the ships through the troubled waters of the central Mediterranean – known as Operation Excess – at first followed the well-worn pattern of earlier convoys. On the afternoon of the 9th the usual formation of Savoia SM.79s appeared, a cluster of brilliant dots sailing through a maze of black anti-aircraft bursts, and dropped their bombs on the twisting vessels far below without scoring any hits. Two of the Savoias were intercepted by the *Ark Royal*'s Fulmars and plummeted vertically towards the sea, trailing an arrow-straight pencil of smoke.

As darkness fell, the warships turned back towards Gibraltar, leaving three cruisers to shepherd the convoy through the Narrows under cover of night. At dawn on the 10th, the transports were met by the ships of the Eastern Mediterranean Fleet, including the carrier *Illustrious* and the battleships *Warspite* and *Valiant*, sixty miles west of Malta. Admiral Cunningham's ships had already suffered; shortly before first light, the destroyer *Gallant* had been badly damaged by a mine and had to be taken in tow by the *Mohawk*. Soon afterwards, the destroyers were attacked by a pair of torpedo-carrying Savoias, but the aircraft sheered off in the face of a heavy barrage put up by escorting cruisers and failed to achieve any results.

Two more Savoias also made a torpedo attack on the *Warspite* and the *Valiant*. They were brave pilots, these, and flew straight and level through a withering curtain of fire to release their torpedoes – but the big ships altered course and the tin-fish missed their target. The Savoias sped away to the west, low over the water, chased by two Fulmars from the *Illustrious*.

Ten minutes later, the carrier's radar picked up a large air formation coming in from the north. Four more Fulmars were flown off, while the warships' anti-aircraft crews huddled behind their weapons and peered anxiously into the northern sky, waiting for a fresh onslaught.

There they were – a host of black dots, sliding between scattered tufts of cloud. But these were no Italian bombers, cruising in impeccable formation; these were wicked-looking single-engined aircraft, with spatted undercarriages and gull wings. Sailors who had fought in the bitter waters off Norway and Dunkirk recognized them at once. Stukas! The Luftwaffe had arrived in the Mediterranean; from now on, it was going to be no picnic.

They were the Junkers 87s of Stuka-Geschwader 1 and 2, led by Major Enneccerus and Captain Werner Hozzel – part of the Luftwaffe's special anti-shipping group, Fliegerkorps X. They had arrived at Trapani in Sicily less than a week ago. Now, in three flights of twelve, the thirty-six Stukas roared over the fleet at twelve thousand feet and split up into groups of three, peeling off and plummeting down towards the warships with a banshee wail of sirens, hurtling through the middle of a thudding barrage of 4.5-inch and pompom shells.

They had singled out the *Illustrious* as their special target. The first bomb tore through S1 pompon on the carrier's port side, reducing the weapon to twisted wreckage and killing two of the crew before passing through the platform and exploding in the sea. Another bomb exploded on S2 pompom, which literally vanished together with its crew. A third slammed into the after-well lift, on its way to the flight deck with a Fulmar on it; debris and sheets of blazing fuel poured into the hangar below and it quickly became an inferno of blazing aircraft and exploding fuel tanks. Jagged splinters from the bomb ripped through the eight 4.5 gun-turrets aft, putting them all out of action. A fourth bomb crashed through the flight deck and ripped out of the ship's side, exploding in the water; splinters punched holes through the hull and the blast flung half-a-dozen aircraft into a heap of twisted wreckage in a corner of the hangar. Down there men fought the blaze amid a hell of exploding ammunition and spurting columns of white-hot flame.

Seconds later, a thousand-pounder tore through the flight-deck and the hangar-deck and exploded in the wardroom flat, killing everyone there and sending a storm of fire raging through the neighbouring passages. A sixth bomb hurtled down the after-lift well and exploded in the compartment below, putting the steering-gear out of action. Out of control, the carrier began to swing round in crazy circles. And still the Stukas came, the German pilots pressing home attack after attack through the smoke and the shell-bursts. One Stuka was hit halfway through its dive and disappeared in the explosion of its own bomb, a shower of blazing fragments falling from a spreading cloud of smoke. Above, a twisting dogfight developed as six Fulmars of 806 Squadron ripped into the enemy formation. A Stuka went into a spin, one wing torn off by a burst from a fighter's eight machine-guns. A Fulmar, caught in the cross-fire of two German machine-gunners, turned lazily over on its back and dived vertically into the sea. Another Stuka, with half its tail shot away, swept past the crippled carrier, struck the sea with its wingtip and cartwheeled in a cloud of spray and smoke. Another dropped through the maze of twisting aircraft like a falling leaf, turning over and over, and slammed into the sea. A parachute blossomed out, only to collapse again like a torn handkerchief.

Then, suddenly, the sky was empty. The Stukas droned away, leaving the wreckage of eight of their number behind. The guns of the Fulmars had accounted for five of them; one Fulmar had been lost. The surviving fighters circled the shattered *Illustrious* a couple of times, then, running short of fuel, they set course for Malta. On the way, they encountered a formation of Savoias and shot down two of them. The remaining Italian bombers made one run over the *Illustrious,* but their bombs fell wide.

The *Illustrious* was terribly hurt, but her heavy armour had saved her. Slowly, the crew regained a measure of control and she turned towards Malta, shrouded by a pall of smoke from the fires that still raged, steering on her main engines as the stokers worked in dense, choking smoke and a temperature of 140 degrees to maintain steam.

Two hours later the Stukas came again, but this fresh on-slaught had none of the fury of the earlier attack. Nevertheless one of their bombs found the target and added to the damage; the carrier was listing badly now. The Stukas had hardly droned away when another attack developed, but the fifteen dive-bombers again showed no inclination to brave the worst of the defensive fire and dropped their bombs from a fairly high alti-tude, scoring no hits.

As darkness fell, the *Illustrious* limped into Valetta's Grand Harbour and stopped alongside the dockyard wall. During the days that followed, she survived several more Luftwaffe attacks; it was as though fate had finished with her for the time being. But the Luftwaffe had done its job well; after being patched up to make her seaworthy, the battle-scarred carrier sailed for the United States, where she was to spend several months under-going extensive repairs. During February and March, the sur-viving Fulmars of 806 Squadron flew alongside the RAF's Hurri-canes in the defence of Malta.

With the *Illustrious* out of action, Admiral Cunningham was forced to restrict the operations of the Eastern Mediterranean Fleet for a period of several weeks because of the lack of air cover. Until March, with the arrival of the *Illustrious*'s sister carrier the *Formidable,* the full burden of Fleet Air Arm operations in the Mediterranean rested on the shoulders of Admiral Somerville and the *Ark Royal*. The carrier had recently taken on two new Fulmar Squadrons, Nos. 807 and 808, and with the air defence of Force H assured by these aircraft Somerville now made plans to use his Swordfish in a more offensive role, by striking at targets on the Italian mainland and in Sardinia.

On 2 February, eight Swordfish took off from the *Ark Royal* and set course for Sardinia. Their target was the dam on the River Tirso at the head of Lake Omodeo, the site of the island's only major hydro-electric plant. The mission was ill-starred from the start, however; the Swordfish pilots had a hard time of it flying down the twisting Tirso Valley, blinded by fog and lashed by drenching streams of rain – and when they reached the lake they were met by murderous fire from fully-alerted anti-aircraft defences. Only four Swordfish made a successful run-in and dropped their torpedoes, none of which reached the dam, and one aircraft was shot down. While this abortive attack was in progress, other Swordfish from the *Ark Royal* bombed an oil refinery at Leghorn.

On 9 March the carrier gap was filled when the *Formidable* joined the Mediterranean Fleet. She carried only four Swordfish; the rest of her aircraft complement was made up of ten Fairey Albacores – biplanes, like the Swordfish, but bigger and faster, with a longer range and an enclosed cockpit – of No. 826 Squadron, and the thirteen Fulmars of 803 Squadron, transferred from the *Ark Royal*. The fighter complement would be brought up to full strength the following month, when 806 Squadron joined the carrier from Malta. Before that, however, the *Formidable* and her aircraft were to play a decisive part in another large-scale action against the Italian Fleet.

At dawn on 28 March, while the Mediterranean Fleet was engaged in covering the passage of convoys of British troops and equipment to Greece to counter an imminent German invasion of that country, a reconnaissance Albacore from the *Formidable* reported a force of enemy cruisers and destroyers to the south of Crete. The force, consisting of the battleship *Vittorio Veneto*, six heavy cruisers, two light cruisers and a destroyer screen, was under the command of Admiral Iachino – who had put to sea in an attempt to intercept the British convoys only when the Luftwaffe promised him extensive fighter cover and reconnaissance facilities.

At 08.15 hours the Mediterranean Fleet's cruisers – which were about one hundred miles ahead of the main force – came under fire from the Italian warships and were in danger of being cut off by the enemy, who was steaming in a huge pincer movement. There was no hope of Admiral Cunningham's heavy brigade arriving in time to save the situation; only a torpedo strike by the *Formidable*'s aircraft could ease the pressure on the outgunned British cruisers. At 10.00 hours, six Albacores – the only ones available, as the other four were earmarked for reconnaissance duties – took off with an escort of two Fulmars and headed for the Italian squadrons. Their instructions were to attack the enemy cruisers; the first ship they sighted, however, was the mighty *Vittorio Veneto,* whose 15-inch guns were by this time pounding the British cruiser squadron. The Albacores went in at 11.25 hours, attacking in two waves, but the *Veneto* took violent evasive action and all the torpedoes missed. The two Fulmars, meanwhile, had tangled with a pair of Junkers 88s high above the warships; one crashed in flames and the other stuck his nose down and headed flat out for the horizon, slowly outstripping the two fighters that bayed at his heels.

Admiral Iachino, seeing his air cover melt away, now turned and headed westward at high speed, cutting down Cunningham's hopes of bringing him to action. The British commander ordered a second strike, this time with the object of slowing the *Veneto* down, and the *Formidable* accordingly flew off three Albacores and two Swordfish, escorted by another pair of Fulmars. They sighted the *Veneto* – which had meanwhile been attacked unsuccessfully by RAF Blenheim bombers from bases in Greece – an hour later. This time – primarily because they were anxiously watching out for more RAF aircraft – the Italian gunners failed to see the Fleet Air Arm aircraft until the latter had begun their run-in. The three Albacores swept in first, led by Lt-Cdr Dalyell-Stead. He was the last to release his torpedo; flying through a forest of massive water-spouts flung up by the battleship's main armament, he waited until the vast bulk of the *Veneto* filled his whole vision. Torn apart by a storm of shells, the Albacore blew up and plunged into the sea – but the torpedo ran on and blasted a gaping hole in the *Veneto*'s stern, jamming her steering gear and flooding the compartment with four thousand tons of water. The remaining aircraft scored no hits – but as they droned away, the *Veneto* slowed down and finally wallowed helplessly to a stop.

The Italian engineers worked frantically to remedy the damage, spurred on by the knowledge that Cunningham's battleships were now only three hours' steaming away. They succeeded in repairing the propeller shaft and gradually the battleship's

speed was worked up until she was able to forge ahead at between fifteen and eighteen knots, with the cruisers and destroyers forming a tight screen around her as insurance against
further attacks by torpedo aircraft.

The *Formidable*'s third and last attack was launched at dusk.
Led by Lt-Cdr W. H. G. Saunt, six Albacores and four Swordfish – two of the latter from Maleme airfield on Crete – caught
up with the crippled battleship and her escort and attacked
through a blinding glare of searchlights and multi-coloured
'flaming onions', their lurid, darting glow lighting up the thick
smoke-screen laid by the warships. The whole scene boiled like
some hellish cauldron and the Fleet Air Arm pilots flew straight
into it, furrowing the sea with the slipstream from their wingtips as they flung their aircraft away from the solid streams of
tracer the moment their torpedoes were released. One torpedo,
spearing straight for the *Veneto*, was blocked by the cruiser *Pola*
and burst against her side with a thunderous crash. The *Veneto*
herself escaped.

The *Pola* still managed to maintain some speed, but her progress was painfully slow. In the end, Iachino detached the
cruisers *Zara* and *Fiume* and four destroyers to escort her, while
the rest of the Italian force accompanied the *Veneto* to safety.

At 22.10 hours the *Valiant*'s radar picked up the three cruisers
and the destroyers. At 22.25 hours the guns of the *Valiant* and
the *Warspite* opened up, and within minutes both the *Zara* and
the *Fiume* were little more than blazing coffins, and two destroyers went in to finish them off with torpedoes. The crippled
Pola was also sunk before morning, as well as two of the Italian
destroyers. The enemy warships, which were not equipped with
radar, had no idea that they were steaming across the bows of
the British force until the *Warspite*'s first 15-inch salvo smashed
into them.

The Italians had lost five warships and nearly two thousand
five hundred officers and men; the British had lost just one Albacore. So ended the action that was to become known as the Battle
of Cape Matapan; an overwhelming victory for the British
Mediterranean Fleet, and one that had been made possible by

the Fleet Air Arm.

The jubilation, however, was destined to be short-lived. On 6 April German forces attacked Yugoslavia and Greece. Two days later the Yugoslav armies crumbled and the Wehrmacht smashed its way into Greek territory through the thinly-defended Aliakhmon Line, forcing an Allied withdrawal. The German Army, spearheaded by the inevitable Stukas, poured southwards through Greece and the Greek forces rapidly disintegrated before the onslaught, leaving the full burden of defence on the New Zealand Division, the 6th Australian Division and the 1st Armoured Brigade. By 2 May it was all over; battered ceaselessly from the air, overwhelmed by superior numbers, the Allies abandoned their hold on Greek soil. Forty-three thousand of them were evacuated; eleven thousand were withdrawn to the island of Crete, where they grimly prepared to meet the assault that was certain to come.

The island garrison's situation was perilous. With the enemy in possession of Greece and the Aegean islands, a seaborne invasion was likely – and it was the job of the Eastern Mediterranean Fleet to prevent it. Meanwhile, the island's air defences were strengthened by the arrival of the Fleet Air Arm's No. 805 Squadron under Lt-Cdr A. Black, DSC. The unit was equipped with a mixed collection of aircraft; mostly Fulmars, but also a handful of American-built Brewster Buffaloes (part of a batch originally ordered by Belgium before the war, twenty-eight of which subsequently found their way into Fleet Air Arm service) and a few Sea Gladiators. In the event, most of these aircraft were destroyed on the ground by strafing German fighters before they had a chance to fire their guns in anger; the surviving pilots promptly attached themselves to the RAF's two Hurricane squadrons on Crete, Nos. 33 and 80. On 16 May three Hurricanes flown by Fleet Air Arm pilots tackled a formation of thirty Junkers 88s escorted by fifteen Messerschmitt 109s; two of the British fighters were shot down almost immediately, but the surviving pilot – Lieutenant A. R. Ramsey – managed to destroy two of the enemy before he was forced to break off the fight.

On 20 May German airborne forces landed on Crete in the

wake of a massive air bombardment. The German plan to support the paratroops with a second wave of soldiers brought in by landing-craft failed, however, when the latter were intercepted by Admiral Cunningham's patrolling warships to the north of the island on the night of the 21st/22nd and were destroyed with heavy loss of life in a fight that lasted two and a half hours.

The following morning the Luftwaffe began a series of concentrated air attacks on the warships, and after twenty-four hours Cunningham was compelled to withdraw his forces to Alexandria, having lost the cruisers *Gloucester* and *Fiji* and the destroyers *Greyhound, Juno, Kelly* and *Kashmir*. Most of the the other warships in the area had also suffered varying degrees of damage. But the Royal Navy's task was far from over; on 27 May Cunningham's battered warships began to evacuate the first troops under intense air attack. It was like Dunkirk all over again – but this time there were no RAF or Fleet Air Arm fighters to patrol the beaches and fend off at least part of the onslaught. Nevertheless, the Navy managed to bring away some eighteen thousand men, but there was no disputing the fact that another twelve thousand had to be left behind – or that before the last soldiers were evacuated on 1 June, the cruiser *Calcutta* and the destroyers *Imperial* and *Hereward* had joined the others at the bottom of the Mediterranean. Yet again, the vulnerability of warships operating without an air umbrella in range of shore-based bombers had been tragically demonstrated.

While the struggle for Crete had been going on, HMS *Formidable* had been committed to convoy escort duties. The speedy passage of munitions and reinforcements to North Africa, where the British were now hard-pressed by Rommel's Afrika Korps, had been given the utmost priority. On the morning of 26 May, shortly after leaving Alexandria to meet an incoming convoy, the *Formidable* was heavily attacked by twelve Stukas. It was No. 2 Squadron of Stuka-Geschwader 2 again, led by Major Walter Enneccerus – one of the units that had dealt out such savage punishment to the *Illustrious* four and a half months earlier. They were now operating from Scarpanto, and they came across the carrier quite unexpectedly while searching for British

D

freighters en route to Alexandria. The *Formidable* immediately turned into the wind and flew off her Fulmars, but they were too late to break up the attack. The Stukas dived through thick anti-aircraft fire and planted three bombs on the carrier. One exploded on the flight deck and the other two ripped holes in her starboard side, but once again the carrier's armour saved her from serious damage and she limped back to Alexandria.

At the other end of the Mediterranean, the *Ark Royal* – as well as undertaking more or less routine convoy escort tasks – had also been heavily involved in flying desperately-needed fighter reinforcements to Malta. On 21 May she flew off two squadrons of Hurricanes from a position to the west of the island; and just three days later, in a classic example of the aircraft carrier's flexibility, she was in the Atlantic – her aircraft preparing to deliver the crippling blow that would at last bring to an end the long hunt for the battleship *Bismarck* ...

8 North Atlantic Crusade

High above the Norwegian fjord to the south of Bergen, a Spitfire described a graceful arc through the clear sky, its cameras whirring. In the cramped cockpit, Flying Officer Mike Suckling threw a quick glance behind, conscious that the white contrail streaming in the wake of his aircraft could be seen for miles. The sirens on Stavanger airfield must be going full blast. Any minute now, a shoal of Messerschmitts would be appearing over the horizon.

It was time to get out of it. His task completed, Suckling pushed down the Spitfire's nose to gain speed and streaked for home. Ninety minutes later, he was munching a hasty sandwich on an airfield in north-east Scotland while RAF photographic experts rushed to develop the precious film. Within minutes, Suckling was in his Spitfire once more – this time heading southwards in a mad dash to get the prints to the Air Ministry in London. A quick stop to refuel at Turnhouse and then he was on his way again, racing to beat the approaching darkness. Over the Midlands he ran into thick cloud and had to make a precautionary landing at a convenient airfield. He completed his journey in a fast car, speeding through the blackout at fifty miles an hour.

At one o'clock the following morning, Suckling – unshaven and still wearing his flying kit – handed over the package of photos to Sir Frederick Bowhill, Air Officer Commanding RAF Coastal Command. Bowhill studied the prints carefully – then reached for the telephone.

It was 21 May 1941, and at last the weeks of suspense were over. For there, pinpointed by Suckling's cameras in her Norwegian lair, was the object of the biggest combined search ever carried out by the RAF and the Royal Navy. The pride of Hitler's navy – the mighty 42,500-ton battleship *Bismarck*.

Less than two hours after Suckling had walked into Bowhill's office, a force of Whitley and Hudson bombers of Coastal Command was on its way to strike at the *Bismarck* and her companion, the heavy cruiser *Prinz Eugen*. But the weather was on the Germans' side; thick cloud had clamped down over the fjord. Only a couple of bombers were able to locate the target and drop their bombs, but no hits were registered. All that day the Coastal Command crews made sortie after sortie into the murk, but it was hopeless; the crews could see absolutely nothing.

Early the following morning, a Martin Maryland reconnaissance aircraft of No. 771 Naval Air Squadron took off from Hatston in the Orkneys and set course for Bergen. As it approached Norway, the pilot – Lieutenant N. E. Goddard, RNVR – peered anxiously through the rivulets of rain that streamed down the windscreen; too many Fleet Air Arm and Coastal Command pilots had smashed themselves and their aircraft to oblivion on the dark crags of the Norwegian coast.

Flying in the narrow three hundred-foot corridor between the grey murk and the sea, Goddard sped through the entrance to Bergen Fjord. The thunder of the Maryland's engines echoed and re-echoed from the grim walls on either side as the pilot kept down low, allowing his observer – Commander G. A. Rotherham – to get a good look at the few vessels anchored in the fjord. When he pulled up into the clouds, pursued by a few scattered tufts of flak, Goddard was no longer in any doubt: the *Bismarck* and the *Prinz Eugen* had gone.

Armed as she was with eight 15-inch and twelve 5.9-inch guns, with a top speed of 28 knots, the mighty *Bismarck* could outrun and outfight any British capital ship then in service. She was the biggest threat to Britain's lifelines that had so far materialized – and when it was learned that she was heading northwards at high speed for the icy waters of the Arctic Circle, the intentions of her commander, Admiral Lutjens, became crystal clear; he planned to break out into the North Atlantic through the Denmark Strait between Iceland and Greenland, to make a series of devastating attacks on Allied convoys.

Admiral Sir John Tovey, the C-in-C Home Fleet, immediately mustered every available warship to hunt her down and destroy her. Leaving Scapa Flow, the main body of the Fleet sailed westwards for Icelandic waters to reinforce the heavy cruisers *Norfolk* and *Suffolk* that were guarding the Denmark Strait. Three more cruisers were patrolling Lutjens's alternative breakout route, between Iceland and the Faeroes. First to arrive were the Home Fleet's two fastest ships, the battleship *Prince of Wales* and the battle-cruiser *Hood*. Behind them came the *King George V*, four cruisers, nine destroyers – and the new aircraft-carrier *Victorious*. She had been about to leave for the Middle East with a troop convoy, together with the cruiser *Repulse,* but Admiral Tovey had cancelled the departure of both vessels and committed them to the seach for the *Bismarck*. The *Victorious* was not yet fully worked-up; her complement of operational aircraft consisted of only nine Swordfish and six Fulmars.

On the evening of 23 May the *Bismarck* and the *Prinz Eugen* were sighted in the Denmark Strait by the cruiser *Norfolk*. Throughout the night she and the *Suffolk* shadowed the enemy ships by radar while the *Prince of Wales* and the *Hood* steamed up at full speed. The two opposing forces made contact at 05.35 hours on 24 May in improving visibility, and opened fire eighteen minutes later.

At 06.00 hours the third salvo of 15-inch shells from the *Bismarck* plummeted down through the *Hood*'s thinly-armoured deck and exploded in her magazine, and the battle-cruiser erupted in a gigantic explosion. She went down with horrifying speed, taking all but three of her crew of 1,419 officers and men with her. The *Prince of Wales,* badly hit, turned away under cover of a smoke screen; two of her 14-inch shells, however, had hit the *Bismarck* and damaged her fuel tanks. Although neither the warship's speed nor her fighting prowess was in any way impaired, Lutjens knew that with the loss of vital fuel his plans for a foray into the North Atlantic were now impracticable. Soon afterwards, he detached the *Prinz Eugen* and set course southeastwards for the French port of Brest.

As soon as they knew of Lutjens's intentions, the Admiralty called Admiral Somerville's Force H up from Gibraltar to cut off the German commander's escape route to the south. The battleships *Rodney* and *Ramillies* were also released from escort duties to take part in the chase. The main concern now was to reduce the *Bismarck*'s speed, giving the hunters a chance to close in for the kill – and that was where the *Victorious* and her aircraft came in. At 14.40 hours on the 24th, Admiral Tovey had sent her racing ahead of the main force to a position from which she could fly off her Swordfish against the *Bismarck*.

By 22.00 hours the distance between the *Victorious* and the enemy battleship had closed to about one hundred and twenty miles, and the nine Swordfish of 825 Squadron, led by Lieutenant-Commander Eugene 'Winkle' Esmonde, revved up their engines on the pitching flight deck. Take-off was a nightmare; the *Victorious* was steaming into the teeth of a gale that sent clouds of sleet driving before it through the darkness. One by one, the nine biplanes bounced down the deck and into the air, climbing away laboriously. Forming up overhead, they vanished into the darkness, helped along now by the strong tail-wind. Showers of sleet lashed into the open cockpits, blinding the crews and chilling them to the bone.

An hour later, through a clear patch, Esmonde sighted a group of warships and identified them as the *Prince of Wales,* the *Suffolk* and the *Norfolk*. Somewhere in the darkness beyond was the *Bismarck*.

They spotted her minutes later, a black streak trailing a long arrowhead of wake. The Swordfish split up and dived away to make their attacks from different directions, and almost immediately the *Bismarck* began to take violent evasive action. Vivid flashes illuminated her superstructure as her anti-aircraft gunners opened up, laying down a twinkling barrage in the path of Esmonde's squadron. In spite of the cold, sweat poured down the bodies of the Swordfish pilots as they concentrated on holding their aircraft steady in the face of the barrage, dropping their torpedoes at the last moment and turning steeply away from the glowing streams of tracer that rose lazily towards them. Eight of the torpedoes missed the battleship. The ninth exploded on her starboard side, but it struck one of her most heavily armoured points and she sailed on, her speed almost unchecked. The nine Swordfish battled their way back to the carrier through what was now a strong headwind, and all landed-on safely.

Meanwhile, the *Bismarck* had slipped quietly away into the murk and the hunters lost contact with her. However, there was no longer any doubt in Admiral Tovey's mind that Lutjens was making for Brest, and at 11.00 hours on 25 May the Admiralty instructed Somerville to place his Force H – the *Ark Royal*, the *Renown* and the cruiser *Sheffield* – across the *Bismark's* track between the warship's last known position and her refuge.

Twenty-four hours of suspense now followed; the Royal Navy's net grew tighter, but no one knew for certain that the elusive battleship was inside it. Then, at 10.30 hours on 26 May, she was located by a Catalina of No. 209 Squadron, RAF Coastal Command, piloted by Flying Officer Denis Briggs. Climbing to fifteen hundred feet, Briggs began to shadow the battleship, keeping under cover in low cloud. Then, abruptly, the cloud ended – and the Catalina was a sitting target, poised almost directly over the *Bismarck*. The aircraft rocked and lurched as anti-aircraft shells burst all around it. Shrapnel tore jagged holes in its wings and fuselage.

As his radio operator frantically tapped out the *Bismarck's* position, Briggs hauled his Catalina away from the murderous flak and plunged into the sheltering cloud once more. In spite of the battering the aircraft had taken, he continued to shadow the battleship. From time to time, shells blasted the air around the Catalina as the German gunners caught brief glimpses of the aircraft through rifts in the cloud. At last, early in the afternoon, Briggs was relieved by a second Catalina. Exhausted, he managed to nurse his shell-torn aircraft home to its base in Northern Ireland. A few days later, he received a well-earned DFC.

Coastal Command had done its work well; now, once again, it was the Fleet Air Arm's turn. Success or failure now rested with Force H, towards which the unsuspecting Lutjens was steaming, and with the *Ark Royal's* Swordfish.

By this time, two reconnaissance Swordfish from the carrier were assisting the Coastal Command aircraft to shadow the enemy battleship, while the cruiser *Sheffield* raced on ahead of Force H to make radar contact. At 14.50 hours the *Ark Royal* flew off a strike of fourteen Swordfish under frightful conditions of gale-force winds and driving rain, not to mention the extremely rough sea. For an hour the aircraft droned on through fog and low cloud, the pilots barely able to see the wingtips of the neighbouring aircraft in formation. Suddenly, the observer in the leading Swordfish caught a fleeting glimpse of a warship looming out of the murk. Certain that it was the *Bismarck,* the Swordfish pilots went down to the attack, running-in as usual from different directions.

The warship was, in fact, the cruiser *Sheffield,* and with admirable presence of mind her captain realized the mistake that had been made when the Swordfish dropped out of the cloud in a suspiciously aggressive manner. He spent the next fifteen minutes taking his ship through a series of hair-raising manoeuvres which, fortunately, caused all the torpedoes to miss.

For once, the *Ark Royal*'s pilots were heartily glad that their attack had been a failure. But precious minutes had been lost – and fourteen torpedoes wasted.

A second strike, consisting of the fifteen Swordfish of 818 Squadron, was flown off at 19.10 hours and set course for the target – which, fortunately, was still being shadowed – in the rapidly-gathering dusk. The aircraft, led by Lieutenant-Commander T. P. Coode, had some difficulty in locating the *Bismarck* in the dense fog that now swirled over the sea in waves. The formation became split up and the pilots made their way to the target in ones and twos, dropping down through the murk into a vicious flak barrage to make their attack. There was no longer any pretence of cohesion; it was every man for himself. The pilots, blinded by the glare of the tracer that homed on their aircraft and tore through wings and fuselages, flew in low through sheets of spray hurled up by shell-bursts and splinters and dropped their torpedoes as close as possible to the menacing giant before twisting away from the nightmare meshes of the flak. Two torpedoes hit the battleship; the first struck her armoured girdle and did little damage; the second, however, exploded against her stern, jamming her rudders and putting her steering-gear out of action.

She was crippled now, swerving erratically through the night with twisted propellers, still four hundred miles from Brest, with the battleships *Rodney* and *King George V* coming up relentlessly for the kill. At dawn on 27 May Admiral Tovey closed in from the north-west and his two battleships began firing at a range of 16,000 yards, pouring salvo after salvo into the dying *Bismarck*. By 10.20 she was little more than a blazing coffin. All her guns were silent, but still she refused to sink or strike her colours. Finally, at 10.36, shattered by torpedoes from the cruiser *Dorsetshire,* she rolled over and vanished under the tortured sea, her colours still flying. With her, she took all but 110 of her crew of over 2,000; they had fought their ship gallantly to the end,

Slowly, the British warships turned away from the patch of cold sea that was the *Bismarck*'s grave, marked only by a spreading oil slick, floating debris and a cryptic reference: 48° 10' North, 16° 12' West. Two Swordfish circled the scene once and then flew away to rejoin the *Ark Royal,* cruising on the horizon.

With the aircraft safely aboard, the carrier set her head southwards for Gibraltar and the warmer waters of the Mediterranean. Her crew could not know that before six months had gone by they would watch the waves close over their ship too, as they had closed over the proud *Bismarck* a short time ago.

9 The Gallant Sacrifice

12 February 1942. 12.30 hours.

Fifteen hundred feet above the grey, choppy waters of the English Channel, just off the coast of Kent, six Fairey Swordfish torpedo-bombers of No. 825 Squadron, Fleet Air Arm, turned in a tight circle. The crews anxiously scanned the fog-shrouded horizon, straining their eyes to catch the first glimpse of the escort of Spitfires that should be appearing at any moment.

Out there, under the overcast that hung low over the Channel, an armada of warships seamed at high speed through the narrow sea. For several months, the German battle-cruisers *Scharnhorst, Gneisenau* and *Prinz Eugen* had been holed up in the port of Brest under the watchful eyes of RAF reconnaissance aircraft, protected by the strongest anti-aircraft defences in occupied France. Bomber Command had been hammering the ships by day and night without inflicting serious damage; the last raid had been made on the night of 11 February by sixteen Wellingtons, which had unsuccessfully bombed the target in abominable weather. Soon after they droned away, the three warships had slipped their moorings and put to sea to join their escort of destroyers, minesweepers and E-Boats. Coastal Command Hudsons were patrolling the area, but the fleet escaped undetected in the murk.

In the early hours, the whole of the Luftwaffe's Fighter Command in the West was placed on the alert. The warships would have to pass through the Straits of Dover in broad daylight in their dash for the North Sea and sanctuary in the River Elbe, and the British could be expected to throw in everything they had in a bid to stop them. Admiral Ciliax, the German commander, had staked everything on two factors: the continuing bad weather and the Luftwaffe's ability to break up any air attacks.

By dawn on the 12th, the cruisers were well on their way up the Channel, still undetected. Their fighter umbrella, consisting of some three hundred Messerschmitt 109s and 110s, Focke-Wulf 190s and Junkers 88s operating in relays, flew low over the armada to avoid being picked up by the British radar, which was being jammed by German stations along the French and Belgian coasts under the direction of General Wolfgang Martini, head of the Luftwaffe Signals Command. The jamming was effective; although the British radar did detect some air and sea movements in the Channel, they were thought to involve an air-sea rescue operation.

Shortly after 10.00 hours two RAF pilots – Group Captain Victor Beamish, the station commander of RAF Kenley, and Wing Commander Boyd, leader of the Kenley Wing – took off and set course over the Channel through the fog and cloud, with the idea of finding a spot of 'trade' over France after several days of inactivity. Over the French coast they spotted two 109s and went after them. Suddenly, there were Messerschmitts everywhere – droves of them, scattering in all directions as the two Spits tore out of the fog and flew slap through the middle of them. And below, creaming through the sea, were the three huge battle-cruisers, surrounded by their escorts.

Beamish and Boyd sized up the situation with one hasty glance – then slammed their throttles wide open and headed for home flat out over the waves, pursued by a terrific concentration of flak. They managed to slip away in the low cloud and landed back at Kenley at 11.10 hours.

Their news sparked off a wave of feverish activity at RAF stations all over southern England and East Anglia as sweating armourers broke their backs to bomb-up 250 Whitleys, Hampdens, Wellingtons, Hudsons and Beauforts in the space of fifteen minutes. At Dover, the crews of the heavy coastal guns slammed shells into the breaches of their huge weapons and waited, while MTBs scurried out to sea like a pack of hounds.

At Manston, Lieutenant-Commander Eugene Esmonde

hastily assembled the six crews of 825 Squadron who had flown in from Lee-on-Solent a couple of days earlier and briefed them for a take-off at 12.15. The odds against the six Swordfish were high, but Esmonde had no intention of sending his men out on a suicide mission; 11 Group had promised to provide a fighter escort of five squadrons of Spitfires from Hornchurch and Biggin Hill, and with the RAF to keep the German fighters occupied the Swordfish would have at least a fighting chance. What Esmonde did not know was that both Biggin Hill and Hornchurch had been caught completely unawares. None of the squadrons were on readiness, because of the bad weather. At 12.15, just as the Swordfish were preparing to taxi out, Biggin Hill reported that both 124 and 401 Squadrons would be late. Esmonde decided not to wait; the German fleet was now ten miles off Ramsgate, ideally placed for the attack. Every minute was vital – and there were still three squadrons of Spitfires to provide top cover.

The six Swordfish took off at 12.20 and orbited the coast, waiting for their escort. A few minutes later, the crews breathed sighs of relief as they spotted the aggressive shapes of ten Spitfires skimming towards them under the cloud-base. They were the Spits of 72 Squadron led by Squadron Leader Brian Kingcome, who had broken all records in rounding up his pilots and getting them airborne from Gravesend. But no more Spitfires appeared, and the Swordfish crew were grim-faced now. Where the hell were the others?

There was no lack of courage in Esmonde's family background. The Esmondes came from Drominagh, set high on the wooded slopes of Lough Derg in Tipperary, and they were proud Irish nationalists to their fingertips. One of Eugene's ancestors, John Esmonde, had been hanged by the British during the rebellion of 1798 – but that had not prevented his son from joining the Royal Navy and working his way up to become captain of the frigate *Lion*. Another member of the family, Colonel Thomas Esmonde, had won the Victoria Cross in the Crimea; yet another had died in the Battle of Ypres. Every one of Eugene's five brothers had joined the British armed forces when war broke out; even his sister was in the WAAF. For centuries, the Esmondes had

98

been fighting against the English. Now, wholeheartedly, they were fighting for them.

It was courage, now, that led Esmonde to make his final decision. Fighter cover or not they had to strike now, to try and slow down the enemy warships with their torpedoes and give the Navy and the RAF a chance to finish the job before dark, or before the Germans slipped through the Straits. There was no other alternative. Resolutely, led by Esmonde, the six Swordfish pointed their noses out to sea. Above them, the Spitfires weaved from side to side.

Six antiquated biplanes and eighteen young men, heading for a rendezvous with the massed firepower of an enemy fleet and the cannon of three hundred fighters.

Meanwhile, at 12.25, the Spitfires of 124 and 401 Squadrons had at last got themselves airborne. Aware that they were late, their leader – Squadron Leader Douglas – decided to head out to sea and intercept the Swordfish on the way out. After a few minutes, however, it was obvious that the two formations had missed one another, so the Spitfires doubled back to Manston – to find that the Swordfish had already gone. There was nothing for it but to fly towards the battle area at full throttle, in the hope that they would arrive in time to take on the enemy before the torpedo-bombers started their attack.

Ahead, lost in the fog, the Swordfish flew low over the grey-green waves into weather that was growing steadily worse. Suddenly, a squadron of Messerschmitt 109s swept down out of the murk; guns blazing, they ripped through the Swordfish formation before the escorting Spitfires had time to react. Shells and machine-gun bullets tore long streamers of fabric from the biplanes' wings and fuselages. Then the Spitfire pilots recovered from their initial surprise and attacked the 109s ferociously, driving them away into the clouds. More enemy fighters came tumbling down out of the overcast, but the slow-flying Swordfish were able to escape the worst of the fire. Time and again, the fast Messerschmitts misjudged their speed and most of the cannon-shells went wide. The Swordfishes' wood-and-fabric structure saved them, too; shells tore right through it without exploding.

At 12.50 hours Esmonde and his pilots sighted the enemy fleet. It was a terrifying spectacle. The warships stretched away into the fog as far as the eye could see, their grey masses flecked with twinkling flashes from their medium-calibre guns. Overhead, like angry hornets, roved squadron upon squadron of Focke-Wulfs and Messerschmitts. The ten Spitfires of Esmonde's escort never hesitated; they dived into the middle of the mass of German fighters and soon the sky was covered with a maze of twisting dogfights. More air battles sprang up to the south; it was the Spitfires of the Biggin Hill Wing, better late than never; at least they were helping to divert some of the full fury of the Luftwaffe away from the torpedo-bombers.

Glowing strings of anti-aircraft shells enmeshed the Swordfish as they droned over the outer screen of German MTBs. They were flying straight into a nightmare. Ahead of them, the sea erupted in a great wall of lashing foam under a concentrated barrage from the destroyers and the heavy guns of the big battle-cruisers. With three thousand yards still to go, the Swordfish staggered on through the holocaust, tattered and holed like sieves. Behind them, German fighters queued up to blaze away with cannon and machine-guns.

Esmonde's aircraft was hit by tracer bullets and hungry flames began to lick along the fuselage. Esmonde's gunner, Leading Airman W. J. Clinton, climbed out of the cockpit and sat astride the fuselage, beating out the flames with his gloved hands; then, calmly he clambered back behind his gun.

Gigantic columns of water cascaded down on the Swordfish, threatening to smack them into the sea like flies. The giant water-spouts were lifted by the shells from the German cruisers' 11-inch guns. Behind Esmonde, in the second Swordfish, a bursting shell sent wicked splinters searing into the back of Sub-Lieutenant Brian Rose; he pulled out just in time, in agony, a few feet above the waves. Then they were through the inner screen of destroyers and heading straight for the great black bulks of the cruisers, wreathed in the flame-shot smoke of their guns.

Rose's observer, Sub-Lieutenant Edgar Lee, looked ahead at Esmonde's shot-riddled aircraft. At that precise moment, a shell ripped away its entire lower port wing; but incredibly, the Swordfish still flew. Half-a-dozen Focke-Wulf 190s came arcing down behind it, wheels and flaps down to reduce their speed. One by one, they pumped their cannon-shells into the bloodstained shambles of a cockpit. Esmonde's gunner and observer were already dead and the pilot himself was dying, his back torn by bullets. It must have been sheer courage alone that kept him hanging grimly on to life. He had just one more thing to do, and now he did it. The nose of his aircraft lifted slightly as he pressed the release; the torpedo fell into the water and began to run towards the great dark shape of the *Scharnhorst*. Then the Swordfish dived into the sea and vanished.

Rose, too, fired his torpedo – at the *Prinz Eugen*. Horribly slowly, the Swordfish lurched over the top of the big cruiser; looking down, Lee could see the white, upturned faces of the German sailors behind their spitting guns. Then, miraculously, the flak died away. Almost blind with pain, Rose brought the Swordfish clear of the destroyer screen and ditched her close to a British MTB. But they had ditched right in the middle of a pitched battle between the MTBs and German E-Boats – and it was two hours before they were picked up out of the freezing water. Rose's gunner, Leading Airman Johnson, had been killed earlier and went down with the shattered aircraft.

The third Swordfish in the leading flight, flown by Sub-Lieutenant Colin Kingsmill, also released its torpedo at the *Prinz Eugen*. Struggling to keep the crippled machine in the air, Kingsmill managed to get clear of the worst of the fire before ditching in the water. The three crew members, all severely wounded, clambered out of the wreck and were picked up by a torpedo-boat.

The other three Swordfish, led by Lieutenant Thompson, harried by the merciless fighters, torn to ribbons and with their crews dead or dying, vanished in the wall of water hurled up by the warships' guns. They were never seen again.

The sacrifice had been in vain; the torpedoes had missed their mark and the battle fleet, running the gauntlet of several attacks by RAF bombers and Royal Navy surface vessels later that afternoon reached the safety of the Elbe, although the *Scharn-horst* was damaged by two mines on the way. But for the three big battle-cruisers, time was fast running out. Only six months later, the proud *Scharnhorst* was battered into flaming wreckage by the Home Fleet in the icy waters off Norway's North Cape. The *Prinz Eugen,* damaged by a mine in the Elbe estuary, was being towed to a repair yard when a torpedo from a British submarine blew off her stern. After the war, the United States Navy seized her as booty; she was one of the 'phantom fleet' of surplus warships that was destroyed for test purposes by an atomic bomb at Bikini, in the Pacific, in 1946. As for the *Gneisenau,* she was so badly damaged by RAF bombers while she lay in dry dock that she never sailed again; the Germans turned her into a concrete-filled fortress ship, but she never again fired her guns in anger.

Every one of the men of 825 Squadron who took part in the gallant, suicidal attack on the warships was decorated, fifteen of them posthumously. For Esmonde, there was a Victoria Cross.

Over two months later, at the end of April, the body of a man was washed up on the shores of Kent. Around the sleeves of the uniform it wore were the gold rings of a Naval Lieutenant-Commander, surmounted by the wings of the Fleet Air Arm.

The cruel sea had given up its dead. And the body of Eugene Esmonde, VC would rest at peace in the warm earth of his native Tipperary.

10 The Battle of Malta's Lifelines

At 15.41 hours on 13 November 1941 a torpedo – one of three fired by the German submarine *U*-81 – struck the aircraft-carrier *Ark Royal* near her starboard boiler-room. A short while earlier, together with the old *Argus,* the *Ark* had flown off thirty-seven Hurricanes and seven Blenheims to Malta; she was homeward-bound for Gibraltar when the torpedo hit.

Almost at once, the carrier developed a heavy list to starboard and her Captain, L. E. H. Maund, ordered the evacuation of all surplus personnel. By 16.48, 1,487 officers and men had been transferred to the destroyer *Legion.* By 17.00 hours the list had steadied at about seventeen degrees and the destroyer *Laforey* was ordered alongside; after something of a struggle, leads were connected from her dynamos to provide at least some lighting and power for the crippled carrier.

Shortly after dark, the tug *Thames* arrived from Malta and the *Ark Royal* was taken in tow. At 22.30 Admiral Somerville arrived on the scene in person in a destroyer from Gibraltar to supervise the operation. For four hours the carrier and her escorts made their way painfully westwards. At 02.00 hours on 14 November, with Gibraltar only thirty miles away, the tug *St Day* appeared out of the night to assist with the towing operation. On the surface, things looked fairly bright – but in reality the *Ark* was slowly dying. Water was still pouring into her and, although the list had not increased, she was settling steadily.

Then, at about 03.30 hours, the list suddenly began to grow worse. There was nothing the crew could do to control it. The ship was going over rapidly now, helped on her way by aircraft and heavy equipment that broke loose and slid over to her starboard side. At 04.00 hours Captain Maund ordered the evacuation of the two hundred and fifty men who still remained on board.

At 04.30 the Captain himself left the dying ship and the destroyers and tugs moved clear. There was nothing they could do now but wait for the inevitable end. By 06.00 the flight deck was vertical, the waves lapping against the island. At 06.13, tiredly, she slid beneath the waves, leaving only a patch of oil and some floating debris. On the ships that stood by, like mourners round a tomb, there was silence for a time. Twenty minutes later, just before they turned away for Gibraltar, one of them picked up the last survivor: the ship's cat, clinging grimly to a piece of wood.

The loss of the *Ark Royal* was a savage blow. Without the protection of the carrier's aircraft, Force H was left virtually defenceless and unable to carry out its vital task of running convoys through to Malta. The carriers *Eagle* and *Argus* were attached to the force at intervals, but solely for the purpose of flying off fighter reinforcements to the island.

By the end of November 1941 things looked gloomy for the island garrison. On the 28th of that month Field-Marshal Kesselring, the Luftwaffe's newly-appointed 'Commander-in-Chief South', gave the order for the bomber squadrons based on Sicily to begin large-scale air attacks on the island. The first air offensive, by General Geisler's Fliegerkorps X in the spring of 1941, had been aimed at pinning down the British bomber squadrons on Malta while Rommel's Afrika Korps was being ferried across to Tripoli, and in this it had largely succeeded. Then, in April and May, the Luftwaffe had been heavily committed in the offensive against Greece and Crete, and the following month many of the units had been withdrawn from the Mediterranean Theatre to take part in Operation Barbarossa – the invasion of the Soviet Union. The result was that during the summer of 1941, Malta had enjoyed a welcome respite; the island's defences had been given a chance to regain some of their strength. By the end of October, three convoys totalling thirty-nine freighters – only one of which was lost – had reached the island, bringing badly-needed fuel, ammunition, weapons and food.

Meanwhile, the small RAF and Fleet Air Arm striking force based on Malta – consisting of some sixty-five Blenheims, Beauforts, Baltimores, Wellingtons, Swordfish and Albacores scattered along the six miles of runway at Luqa and Safi – continued to hit the Axis supply routes to Libya. Losses were appalling – up to thirty-per-cent a trip – and both aircraft and crews were constantly being replaced; nevertheless, in the seven months between May and December 1941, this determined bunch of pilots succeeded in sinking no less than fifty-six per-cent of the merchant tonnage at the disposal of the Germans and Italians in the Mediterranean. The enemy also suffered heavy losses at the hands of the Malta-based 10th Submarine Flotilla and the cruisers and destroyers of Force K, which was stationed on the island from the autumn of 1941. On 18 September the submarine *Upholder* torpedoed and sank the 20,000-ton Italian troopships *Neptunia* and *Oceania,* laden with equipment and five thousand men; and on 9 November Force K surprised an enemy convoy in brilliant moonlight and sank every ship – five freighters and two tankers, totalling 39,787 tons.

For the Afrika Korps, the consequences were catastrophic. Deprived of essential supplies, Rommel's forces were pushed back by the 8th Army's autumn offensive until they reached Marsa el Brega, the point from which they had started the previous spring. The alternatives were crystal clear: either Malta had to be subdued, or the Afrika Korps would be destroyed.

By the end of December, practically the whole of Fliegerkorps II – five Gruppen with Junkers 88A-4s, one Ju 87 and one Me 110 Gruppe, plus the Me 109Fs of the top-scoring JG 53 – had been assembled in Sicily: a total force of 325 aircraft. Only about 230 were serviceable at any given time, but that in itself was formidable enough. The objective of Fliegerkorps II was threefold; first, to knock out Malta's fighter defences by a series of surprise attacks on Takali airfield; second, to attack the bomber bases of Luqa, Hal Far and Calafrana; and third, to destroy the harbour installations at Valetta.

At first, the plan was held up by bad weather. The Luftwaffe was restricted to sending small formations of bombers over the island, and these suffered heavy losses. The first concentrated assault did not take place until 20 March 1942, when sixty Junkers 88s blasted Takali into a burning shambles. It was the start of Malta's ordeal; during the next five weeks, the German bombers made 5,807 sorties over the island; the tonnage of bombs dropped almost equalled that dropped on the United Kingdom during the whole of the Battle of Britain.

In April and May, the gap left by the loss of the *Ark Royal* was filled by the American carrier *Wasp*, which made three trips to fly off reinforcements of Spitfires, assisted by the *Eagle* and the *Argus*.

While the battle for Malta continued, Fleet Air Arm squadrons were active in the Western Desert, where their main task was to provide fighter cover for British convoys during the final stage of their journey to North African ports. In September 1941, Nos. 803 and 806 Squadrons had been transferred from the damaged *Formidable* to Egypt, where they joined up with No. 805 to form one big unit commanded by Lt-Cdr Alan Black. Nos. 803 and 806 exchanged their Fulmars for Hurricanes, while No. 805 – which had lost all its equipment in Crete – was now flying Grumman Martlets, the Fleet Air Arm versions of the US Navy's stocky little Wildcat fighter. The Navy pilots established close co-operation with the RAF, escorting Blenheims and Baltimores during raids on Rommel's supply-lines and flying offensive fighter sweeps. It was during one of these escort missions, on 28 September, that the unit scored its first kill when one of the Martlet pilots, Sub-Lt W. M. Walsh, shot down an Italian Fiat G.50 fighter.

On 20 November Lt-Cdr Black was leading 803 Squadron's Hurricanes at eight thousand feet, with an RAF Tomahawk Squadron above, when they ran into a formation of twelve 87s escorted by twice as many 109s. Within seconds, the sky was filled with a whirling mass of aircraft as the Hurricanes and Tomahawks tore into the Stukas and cut them to pieces. One 803

Squadron pilot, Sub-Lt P. N. Charlton, shot down three before a burst from a 109 forced him to take to his parachute. His was the only aircraft lost; not a bad day's work, in exchange for seven Ju 87s destroyed. As the British aircraft broke off the combat and returned to base, short of fuel, the last thing Lt-Cdr Black saw – as he said later – was 'two Messerschmitts knocking hell out of a third'.

As the British forces advanced beyond Tobruk, the Fleet Air Arm fighters returned to the task of convoy protection. On 28 December 1941 a Martlet of 805 Squadron piloted by Sub-Lt A. R. Griffin, RNVR, was detailed to fly a lone patrol over a supply convoy. He was orbiting over the ships when suddenly he spotted four torpedo-carrying S.M. 79s coming in to the attack and dived hell for leather to meet them. He shot one down in flames and forced two more to jettison their torpedoes and make off; the fourth Italian pilot was made of sterner stuff and closed on the convoy under a heavy barrage. The gunners ceased firing as Griffin dived on the lone bomber, which dropped its torpedo haphazardly and missed. At that moment, the Martlet dived into the sea at full throttle, killing its pilot.

At dawn on 5 May 1942 an Allied Expeditionary Force landed on the island of Madagascar, held by the Vichy French, with the object of siezing the naval base at Diego Suarez to prevent it being used by the Japanese as a submarine base in the Indian Ocean. The landings were covered by a naval force commanded by Vice-Admiral E. N. Syfret, flying his flag in the battleship *Ramillies*. Air cover was provided by two carriers; the recently-commissioned *Indomitable* and the *Illustrious,* back in action again after her enforced rest in the United States. The *Indomitable* was the flagship of Rear-Admiral D. W. Boyd, C-in-C Aircraft Carriers, Eastern Fleet.

At first light on the 5th, a striking force of Albacores from the *Indomitable* bombed the airfield near Diego Suarez, setting some installations on fire. A short while later, eighteen Swordfish from the *Illustrious* torpedoed the armed merchant-cruiser *Bougainville,* which blew up, sank the submarine *Bévezières* and bombed the sloop *D'Entrecasteaux*. The leader, Lieutenant R. N.

Everett, had to ditch in the sea near the beach after his aircraft was hit by anti-aircraft fire; he and his crew were taken prisoner, but were released shortly afterwards by the invading forces. Fighter cover throughout the operation was provided by the Martlets of 881 and 882 Squadrons, operating from the *Illustrious,* and the *Indomitable*'s Sea Hurricane squadron, No. 880. The Martlets shot down two Potez 63s and four Morane 406s, while three more Moranes were destroyed on the ground by the Sea Hurricanes. Throughout the operation, the Martlets were used for ground-strafing enemy positions which were holding up the advance. Only one Martlet was lost, shot down by a Morane 406. The pilot escaped unhurt. The Vichy French defenders capitulated on 8 May and the invading forces secured Diego Suarez and the neighbouring town of Antsirane. Nevertheless, it was to be a further six months before the whole of Madagascar was in Allied hands – and during the long and arduous campaign Fleet Air Arm aircraft where to play a considerable part, flying from bases on the African mainland and working in close co-operation with the South African Air Force.

To return to the Mediterranean: by the beginning of June 1942 the plight of Malta was desperate. Unless supply ships could battle their way through to the island, the defence would crumble through the critical shortage of supplies. Early in June two convoys were assembled; one at Alexandria, consisting of eleven transports escorted by the Mediterranean Fleet and strengthened by reinforcements from the Eastern Fleet, and the other – consisting of six freighters – at Gibraltar, where the warships of Force H, some of which had recently been in action off Madagascar, had been considerably strengthened by reinforcements from the Home Fleet. Air cover for the Gibraltar convoy was to be provided by the old carriers *Eagle* and *Argus,* the former operating the sixteen Sea Hurricanes of 801 Squadron and the latter half-a-dozen Fulmars.

The convoy from Haifa and Port Said, however, had no carrier and consequently no air cover. It sailed on 13 June, and Admiral Vian left Alexandria on the same day with seven cruisers and seventeen destroyers to accompany it. The following day, however, it was attacked in force by enemy aircraft; two freighters were sunk and two damaged. That same evening, Vian learned that the Italian Fleet, consisting of the battleships *Littorio* and *Vittorio Veneto*, four cruisers and twelve destroyers, had left Taranto and was steaming southwards. Knowing that he had little hope of defending the convoy in the face of such superior strength, particularly since the British ships were under constant and heavy air attack and were running short of ammunition, Vian at last decided to abandon the operation and withdrew to the east, towards Alexandria. The abortive operation had cost him a cruiser and three destroyers, not to mention the merchant losses.

The convoy from the west, code-named 'Harpoon', entered the Mediterranean on the night of 11 June. By the time it reached 'Bomb Alley' between Sicily and North Africa, only one transport had been lost. Things began to hot up on the 14th, however, when the convoy came under persistent air attack by high-level and dive-bombers, and torpedo aircraft escorted by droves of fighters. The Hurricanes and Fulmars put up a spirited defence, 801 Squadron claiming the destruction of six Italian aircraft during the course of the day. On the 15th, after the main escort had turned back, enemy surface forces joined the battle; although they were beaten off by the convoy's five escorting fleet destroyers, more heavy air attacks developed while the destroyers were otherwise occupied and three more merchantmen were lost. Only two of the freighters succeeded in reaching Malta, but their vital supplies brought the battered island a welcome breathing-space.

The respite, however, was short-lived. By the beginning of August, the situation on the island was once again extremely critical. On 10 August thirteen freighters and the tanker *Ohio* passed through the Straits of Gibraltar in a desperate, do-or-die attempt to relieve the island. To support the convoy, every available warship had been assembled; the escort included the carriers *Victorious, Indomitable* and *Eagle,* the battleships *Nelson* and *Rodney,* three anti-aircraft cruisers and twenty destroyers. A further three cruisers and fourteen destroyers were to meet the convoy and escort it through 'Bomb Alley' on the last twenty-four hours of its perilous journey. The convoy included the old carrier *Furious,* which would accompany the main body to a point one hundred and fifty miles west of Malta and fly off thirty-eight badly needed Spitfires.

The convoy was sailing into the teeth of formidable odds. On airfields in Sardinia and Italy the Germans and Italians had massed nearly eight hundred aircraft. Across the convoy's route, between Gibraltar and the Narrows, twenty enemy submarines were lying in wait. In the Sicilian Channel, a force of cruisers, destroyers and MTBs was lurking, ready to attack under cover of darkness after the main escort had turned away.

The first day passed fairly quietly. The fighter pilots stayed on readiness beneath the hot sun; the crews of the torpedo aircraft were helping to man the carriers' guns. Early the next morning, however, the first Junkers 88 reconnaissance aircraft appeared and circled the armada at a respectful distance. The *Indomitable* sent up two flights of Sea Hurricanes from Nos. 800 and 880 Squadrons to try and intercept them, but the Junkers simply poured on the coals and headed for the horizon at high speed, quickly outpacing the pursuers. One Hurricane pilot managed to get in a burst at extreme range and reported that he had hit one of the enemy, who left the scene trailing smoke.

Suddenly, at 13.16 hours, a series of heavy explosions reverberated through the convoy. The pilots of 880 Squadron, about to climb into their aircraft for another standing patrol, looked around anxiously to see what was happening. Then someone said, very quietly: 'Oh, Christ. Look at the *Eagle.*'

She was listing, shrouded in smoke, torn apart by four torpedoes from the submarine *U*-73. The other ships immediately increased speed and began to take evasive action, depth-charging at random. Just eight minutes later the *Eagle* had gone, sliding towards the bottom a thousand fathoms down, taking two hundred of her crew with her. It had all happened so quickly, too quickly for comprehension. Some of the *Eagle*'s aircraft, Sea Hurricanes of 801 Squadron and Fulmars of 804, were airborne; they landed on the *Victorious* and the *Indomitable,* the pilots dazed by the speed of the disaster, their faces white and down-cast. Their colleagues in the other squadrons looked on sympathetically; there were no words. Some said that losing a ship was like losing a good friend, but there was more to it than that. Sometimes, it was like losing part of one's own body.

Minutes after the *Eagle* had sunk, the white track of a torpedo crossed the bows of the *Victorious*. As the convoy continued to take evasive action, a submarine was sighted and the escorts raced away to unload their depth-charges on it, but without any visible result. Altogether, six U-Boat sightings were reported during the hours that followed.

Shortly before sunset, the *Furious* flew off her Spitfires and turned back towards Gibraltar, her mission completed. As dusk began to spread over the sea, a strange and deceptive silence fell over the ships. The pilots of the squadrons on readiness sat in the cockpits, munching a hasty sandwich; the crews stood at their positions, waiting for the call 'Fighters stand-to'.

It was not long in coming. A cluster of black dots away to the north heralded the first air attack of the day and the carriers vibrated with the roar of engines as the Fulmars and Hurricanes took off to meet it. The raid, by thirty-five Junkers 88s, was well timed; the enemy dropped their bombs and vanished in the dusk before the fighters had a chance to get to grips with them. Three of the 88s were hit by the anti-aircraft barrage and plummeted into the sea, lurid torches in the gathering darkness. None of the ships was hit, but one of the Hurricanes from the *Indomitable* caused something of a drama when, out of fuel, it tried to land on the *Victorious* while the carrier was still turning and out of the wind. The aircraft slammed into another, parked near the island, and burst into flames. The fire was put out and the wreckage cleared in six minutes flat, allowing more fighters to land-on. Six of the *Victorious*'s own aircraft were missing, but they turned up safe and sound on board the *Indomitable*.

First light on the 12th revealed a pair of S.M. 79s shadowing the convoy. The Italian pilots must have been novices; they failed to spot 809 Squadron's Fulmars until it was too late. Both of them went down into the sea. It was a good start to the day, but everyone knew that the real test was still to come. The convoy was now coming well within range of enemy airfields; the bombers that came that day would undoubtedly have fighter escorts. The first raid materialized at 09.00 hours, when a formation of twenty Junkers 88s appeared at eight thousand feet. They were intercepted by the *Indomitable*'s Hurricanes, who shot down two during the first pass and forced several others to jettison their bombs. More Hurricanes and Fulmars from the *Victorious* arrived a couple of minutes later and piled into the melée, destroying two more bombers; the remainder turned away and headed flat out for home.

After two more small and unsuccessful attacks that morning, a really big raid appeared at noon. More than a hundred aircraft – Junkers 87s and 88s, S.M. 79s and 84s, and Cant 1007s, with a strong fighter escort – were hotly engaged by every available Fleet Air Arm aircraft as they approached the convoy. Harried by the fighters, the enemy formations became dislocated while still some distance from the target. The only real damage was caused by a formation of eleven Junkers 87s that managed to break through the fighter screen and bomb a freighter. Badly damaged, the vessel began to lag behind the convoy and had to be left to fend for herself. She was later attacked and sunk just before dusk by two torpedo-bombers.

The *Victorious* had one narrow shave when a pair of Italian Reggiane Re. 2000 fighter-bombers came down in a very fast dive on the carrier's port quarter. Levelling out just above the sea they came streaking in and pulled up over the flight-deck, releasing two bombs. One was a dud; the other bounced off the armoured deck and exploded in the water. The anti-aircraft gunners had not opened fire; they had mistaken the Reggianes for Hurricanes.

During the attack, the enemy used a variety of weapons which had not been encountered before. The first was a new type of torpedo which was dropped under a parachute and followed a circular course through the water, designed to close in on the target ship in ever-decreasing spirals. It didn't work. Then there was a primitive type of pilotless aircraft, packed with explosive and launched from an S.M. 79 mother plane which was supposed to guide it to the target under radio control. That didn't work either; it droned harmlessly away over the horizon, presumably to explode somewhere in North Africa. Nevertheless, it was a taste of things to come.

That afternoon, the convoy ran into a submarine ambush laid by the Italian Navy. One submarine was brought to the surface by depth-charges and rammed by a destroyer; a second was reported damaged. None of the torpedoes launched by the submarines scored hits. The convoy was under continual air attack throughout the afternoon, but emerged relatively unharmed. By 17.00 hours, however, the ships were in range of Fliegerkorps II's dive-bombers in Sicily, and from now on the raids were pressed home with great determination. For two hours the bombers came over without pause, allowing the exhausted Fleet Air Arm fighter pilots no respite. A mixed formation of twenty Junkers 87s and 88s, harried by Fulmars and Martlets, broke through and dropped three bombs on the *Indomitable*. They failed to penetrate her flight-deck, but for the time being she could no longer operate her aircraft; those of her fighters that were still in the air had to land on the *Victorious*.

By 19.30 the last of the raiders had droned away; the convoy was still more or less intact and was now only one hundred and thirty miles from Malta. As dusk fell, two flights of RAF Beaufighters came whistling up from the island and circled the ships watchfully. Their job done, the *Indomitable* and the *Victorious* turned away towards the sunset. They had lost thirteen of their aircraft – not counting those that had gone down with the *Eagle* – but there was no denying that their pilots had enjoyed something of a field day. Their total claims amounted to thirty-nine enemy aircraft definitely destroyed during the three days of air fighting, plus a further nine probables. It had been a classic example of the value of carrier-borne fighters; the Navy pilots had amply demonstrated their ability to break up even the most determined enemy attacks. The fact that the convoy had got this far without suffering serious harm was due entirely to the air defence put up by the carriers.

But now the carriers had turned for home, leaving the convoy to steam on through the dusk with only the scant air cover that could be spared by the RAF on Malta. And the story of 13 August was to be tragically different from that of the three preceding days.

During the night, the convoy was repeatedly attacked by enemy MTBs and submarines, followed up by a savage air onslaught that began at dawn and lasted until the surviving ships reached Malta. Only five of the merchantmen – including the vital tanker *Ohio* – got through, and the escorting warships suffered heavy losses. Nevertheless, the supplies that did reach Malta enabled the island to keep going until November, when relief reached the defenders following the Allied landings in North Africa and the 8th Army's decisive victory over Rommel at El Alamein.

Operation Torch, the Allied invasion of North Africa, was the biggest circus that had so far faced the Fleet Air Arm. The plan involved three assaults; the first on Casablanca, by the ships and carriers of the wholly American Western Task Force; the second on Oran by the Central Naval Task Force under Commodore T. H. Troubridge, RN; and the third on Algiers by the Eastern Naval Task Force, commanded by Rear-Admiral Sir Harold Burrough. The American force sailed direct from the United States; the other two task forces left Britain and passed through the Straits of Gibraltar on 6 November, D minus two, shepherded by Hudsons and Sunderlands from the Rock.

The operation was supported by seven British carriers; the *Formidable, Victorious, Furious, Argus* and three escort carriers, *Biter, Avenger* and *Dasher*. Soon after the Task Forces entered the Mediterranean, a Vichy French Potez 63 reconnaissance aircraft flew overhead at about ten thousand feet. It was intercepted by a patrol of 888 Squadron Martlets from the *Formidable* and shot down in flames by Lt D. M. Jeram. Apart from that one incident, the day passed fairly quietly; the sky was brilliantly clear, with a light wind blowing off the African coast.

During the evening of the 7th the ships turned in towards the coast, the two task forces splitting up to make for their objectives.

The assault convoys were in position by 23.00 hours and ready for the attack, scheduled to begin at 01.00 on the 8th. The carriers *Furious, Biter* and *Dasher* moved closer inshore off Oran, ready to fly off their fighter squadrons. To the rear, with the warships of Force H, the *Formidable* and the *Victorious* also prepared to launch their aircraft at first light. Two of the *Furious* squadrons, Nos. 801 and 807, were equipped with Seafires – the naval variant of the famous Spitfire. Here, in North African skies, the Seafire was about to receive its baptism in combat. Further to the east the *Argus* and the *Avenger* also moved in to cover the landings at Algiers.

The first phase of the operation went off smoothly, the landings being met with little opposition. Everything had been done to foster the impression that American and not British forces were involved; even the Fleet Air Arm aircraft carried American markings. The planners of Torch had felt that the French would be less likely to resist an American invasion than a British one.

The first enemy aircraft appeared over the fleet at about 04.00 hours and dropped flares, but for some reason no attack materialized. At 06.00 the *Formidable* flew off five Albacores to carry out a reconnaissance of the beaches and also to keep a watch for enemy submarines and surface vessels. Fifteen minutes earlier, as soon as the sky began to lighten, four Martlets of 882 Squadron had left the carrier *Victorious* for the airfield at Blida, thirty miles to the south-west of Algiers, with orders to prevent any French aircraft from taking off. Two aircraft were in fact taxying out when they arrived, but the FAA pilots sprayed them with machine-gun fire and they were hastily abandoned by their crews. A second patrol was flown over the airfield a couple of hours later, and the leader – Lieutenant B. H. C. Nation – noticed people waving white handkerchiefs. After calling up the carrier and asking what to do, he received authorization to go ahead and land. This he did, while the other three Martlets circled watchfully overhead, and taxied over to the airfield buildings where he was met by the French station commander, who surrendered to him and informed him that the base was at the disposal of the Allies. Nation couldn't think of anything else to do but wait until Allied forces arrived, which they did a short while later – to find the Fleet Air Arm pilot drinking coffee and chatting amicably with the French officers.

As the morning progressed, however, enemy resistance stiffened in several quarters and the Albacore squadrons, engaged in bombing and strafing operations in support of the advance, began to suffer badly at the hands of enemy fighters. It was while escorting an Albacore squadron that the Seafires claimed their first victory, when Lt G. C. Baldwin shot down a Dewoitine D. 520 fighter. Five more D. 520s were also destroyed by the Sea Hurricanes of No. 800 Squadron, flying from HMS *Biter*.

At about 17.00, the *Furious*'s Seafires had just taken off for a patrol when a formation of fifteen Junkers 88s appeared out of the gathering dusk and dive-bombed the carrier, scoring one hit and several near misses. The damage was not serious, but the Seafires that were airborne were compelled to land at Maison Blanche and return to the carrier the following day. There were several more raids during the course of the operations, but they usually took the form of aircraft flying over the fleet in ones and twos at great heights, dropping their bombs ineffectively and escaping before the defending fighters could get to grips with them. One Heinkel 111 was, however, shot down by the Martlets of 882 Squadron on the 9th, followed by a Junkers 88 destroyed by 888 Squadron on the 10th.

At Oran, the main Fleet Air Arm operations were directed against the airfields of La Senia and Tafaraoui. At La Senia, the Albacores and Sea Hurricanes destroyed forty-seven aircraft on the ground. Four Albacores were shot down, but only one crew was killed.

On 11 November the carriers withdrew, leaving the RAF and USAAF to provide air cover over the landing zones. The Fleet Air Arm had played an enormous part in ensuring the success of the landings; it had effectively kept the French Air Force pinned down, bombed and strafed ahead of the advancing forces and carried out vital reconnaissance missions. Losses had been sustained, but most of these had been due to pilots overstretching the range of their aircraft and running out of fuel, writing-off their aircraft on landing, and to finger trouble in general, rather than to enemy action. As far as the Fleet Air Arm was concerned, the North African landings had been a classic example of co-operation.

11 Convoys to Russia

During the last week of July 1941 the aircraft carriers *Victorious* and *Furious* sailed from Seidisfjord in Iceland – where they had stopped to refuel on the way out from Scapa Flow – and set course north-eastwards, heading deeper inside the Arctic Circle with their escort of two cruisers and six destroyers. Five weeks earlier, on 22 June, the German armies had smashed their way into the Soviet Union, and now the Fleet Air Arm was on its way to strike the first blows in support of Britain's new ally by attacking vital enemy lines of communication at two points in northern Norway; Kirkenes and Petsamo. The operation had a second objective: to keep the enemy occupied while the mine-layer *Adventure* slipped through the dangerous waters off North Cape to Archangel, carrying a vital consignment of mines.

Initially, it had been hoped that the attacks would come as a complete surprise to the Germans; but the hope vanished when a lone Junkers 88 appeared in the vicinity shortly before the carriers reached their flying-off position at noon on 30 July. Nevertheless, the attack went ahead as planned. In the early afternoon the *Victorious* flew off her striking force of twenty Albacores from 827 and 828 Squadrons, escorted by the nine Fulmars of 809 Squadron, for the raid on Kirkenes; while nine Albacores of 817 Squadron, nine Swordfish of 812 and six Fulmars of 800 Squadron left the *Furious* and headed for Petsamo. The three remaining Fulmars of 800 Squadron, together with the four Sea Hurricanes of 880 Squadron 'A' Flight, stayed behind to provide air cover for the warships.

Flying low, the twenty Albacores of 827 and 828 Squadrons swept up Varanger Fjord and turned in towards Kirkenes harbour. The cliff walls echoed and re-echoed to the clatter of gun-

1. The first wings afloat: a Wright seaplane, looking like a huge moth on the water, makes a sharp contrast with the vessels in an unidentified American harbour in 1910

2. A view of the Short 310A-4, used by the RNAS as a long-range patrol aircraft in 1917-18. Aircraft was used against enemy submarines in the Adriatic, but without success

3. *Below:* One of the Short S.41 floatplanes that took part in the raid on the Zeppelin sheds at Cuxhaven in 1914

4. Sopwith 2F1 Camel taking off from an unidentified aircraft carrier in the Firth of Forth, early in 1918

5. Sopwith 1½-Strutter on gun turret platform of cruiser, 1917

6. Hawker Nimrod I with interchangeable wheel and float undercarriage. The FAA version of the Hawker Fury, the Nimrod equipped three squadrons

7. *Below:* Hawker Osprey I with wings folded. The Osprey was the standard fleet spotter during the 1930s

8. The Fairey Flycatcher, the standard fleet fighter during the late 1920s

9. Parnall Plover of No. 404 Fleet Fighter Flight: the fourth of six aircraft delivered to the FAA

10. Blackburn Ripon III, S1272, which was used for experimental flying and weapons trials

11. *Below:* The Blackburn Shark torpedo spotter, which was replaced by the Swordfish in FAA service

12. A flight of Blackburn Baffins, with the carrier HMS *Furious* in the background at top left

13. A Wildcat hits the barrier during a North Atlantic convoy, March 1944

14. Sea Hurricane ends up in the 'goofers' gallery on HMS *Ravager* after slewing off the deck

15. *Below:* Albacores

16. Swordfish of 756 Sqn from RNAS Katakurunda, Ceylon, on patrol over the Indian Ocean

17. Fairey Barracuda Mk II, one of a batch built by Blackburn Aircraft

18. *Below:* Fairey Firefly FR. First used operationally during the Tirpitz strikes of 1944, the Firefly saw combat over Korea nearly a decade later

19. Remarkable sequence of photos showing Swordfish 'T' of 834 Sqn, flown by Sub-Lt John McVittie, trying to overshoot after a missed landing, clipping a lump out of another Swordfish on the way, then ditching. The three-man crew was picked up safely

20. Sea Fury crossing the round-down of HMS *Illustrious*

21. The Armstrong Whitworth Sea Hawk, the first FAA jet to see combat (Suez, 1956)

22. *Below:* The Supermarine Attacker, the Navy's first jet. Intended as an interim aircraft, the type remained in FAA service until 1957

23. Fairey Gannet AEW 3 early warning aircraft

24. *Below:* Westland Wasp of 829 Squadron (XS463) about to land on the helicopter platform of the frigate HMS *Nubian*

25. Blackburn Firebrand V hooking the wire. The type equipped two
FAA squadrons

26. *Below:* Sea Fury leaving HMS *Glory* for a strike on Korean targets, 1952

27. Impressive study of a Buccaneer S.2 (XN980) of No 801 Squadron, piloted by Lt-Cdr J. de Winton, RN, flying over Nelson's Column in October 1965 to mark the 160th anniversary of the Battle of Trafalgar

fire as a murderous barrage of twenty-mm flak streamed out to meet the aircraft. A blinding light filled the sky as an Albacore exploded, scattering burning debris over the flak-ship that had destroyed it. Another plunged into the cliff face and blew up, sending an avalanche of boulders tumbling into the water below. The surviving Albacores pressed on through the holocaust and selected their targets. A 2,000-ton freighter blew up and began to sink, pulverized by three torpedoes, and a second caught fire and began to list heavily.

Suddenly there was a lull in the flak as an avalanche of Messerschmitt 109s and 110s came tumbling down on the fjord. The nine Fulmars turned to meet them and a vicious dogfight developed. Two of the Fleet Air Arm fighters were shot down almost immediately, but the rest accounted for a 109 and a 110. Meanwhile the other enemy fighters had got in among the Albacores. One after the other, the biplanes started to go down in flames. One Albacore pilot got in a lucky shot with his single front gun at a Junkers 87 which, surprisingly, appeared doing a steep turn in front of him; the Stuka went into a spin and crashed.

Somehow, shepherded by the seven Fulmars, the surviving Albacores fought their way clear and flew back to the carrier. There were nine of them. Nine out of twenty.

In terms of losses, the Petsamo force had fared a little better. Only one Albacore and two Fulmers were lost, but the damage to the enemy was limited to a small steamer and a few harbour installations. With the surviving aircraft safely on board, the two carriers left the danger area and set course for Scapa Flow. The following day, a Dornier 18 flying-boat was seen shadowing the force and two of 880 Squadron's Sea Hurricanes, piloted by Lt-Cdr Judd and Sub-Lt Howarth, were flown off to intercept it. After a short chase, they shot it down – the first kill to be scored by a Sea Hurricane.

During the last days of August, the first Russian Convoy sailed for Archangel. With it went the thirty-nine Hurricanes of the RAF's No. 151 Wing destined for operations at Murmansk; fifteen of them were crated in the holds of the merchant liner

Llanstephan Castle, and the remaining twenty-four were carried intact by the carrier *Argus.* The *Argus* also carried a pair of Martlet IIIs of No. 802 Squadron 'B' Flight for her own protection.

The trip was uneventful. On 7 September, when within flying distance of the Soviet mainland, the RAF pilots flew their twenty-four Hurricanes off the *Argus* and landed at Vaenga airfield, seventeen miles from Murmansk. Shortly afterwards, intense enemy activity flared up in the vicinity of the port, and the convoy had to be re-routed to Archangel, four hundred miles further east. It was met there by the *Victorious,* which took on the *Argus's* two Martlets before sailing for Bodo with units of the Home Fleet to strike at enemy shipping in the area. The carrier's Albacores sank two freighters and damaged a factory near Glomfjord for no loss to themselves. A second raid was made on 9 October, when several more enemy transports were damaged. Again, all the Albacores returned safely to the carrier, but two were written off in landing accidents.

No losses were sustained by the North Russian convoys during 1941. Towards the end of February 1942, however, the biggest threat since the *Bismarck* materialized in the shape of the new battleship *Tirpitz,* which had slipped out of the Baltic to a new refuge in Trondheim Fjord and to which Admiral Ciliax had transferred his flag from the damaged *Scharnhorst* after the 'Channel Dash' a couple of weeks earlier.

On 6 March the *Tirpitz* set out to intercept convoys PQ 12 and PQ 8 – the first bound for Murmansk, the second on its way home. The battleship's movements were, however, reported by a patrolling submarine, and units of the Home Fleet – including the *Victorious* – under Admiral Tovey placed themselves between the threat and the convoys, which passed one another off Bear Island at noon on 7 March. Ciliax detached some of his destroyers to search for the convoys and they sank one straggling Russian freighter, but apart from that no contact was made and the German Admiral turned southwards again.

Thanks to intercepted radio signals, Admiral Tovey knew of the Germans' intentions and headed towards the Lofoten Islands to try and cut them off. At daylight on the 9th, a reconnaissance Albacore from the *Victorious* spotted the *Tirpitz,* and twelve torpedo-carrying Albacores took off soon afterwards to attack the battleship. The attack, unfortunately, was carried out in line astern, which gave the *Tirpitz* ample room to avoid all the torpedoes – although one passed within thirty feet of her stern. Two Albacores were shot down.

The failure of the attack was a bitter pill for the Fleet Air Arm to swallow, but it did have one result; on Hitler's orders, the *Tirpitz* never put to sea again if carried-based aircraft were known to be in the vicinity.

The Germans, however, now had a formidable striking-force of aircraft, warships and submarines scattered among the fjords and airfields of northern Norway, and convoy losses inevitably began to mount. Between 27 and 31 March, PQ 13 became split up due to bad weather; two of its freighters were sunk by the Junkers 88s of K.G. 30, operating from Banak, and three more by U-Boats and destroyers. PQ 14 (8-21 April) found that the ice, not the Germans, was the main enemy; it ran into ice-floes in thick fog, and sixteen out of twenty-four vessels had to return damaged to Iceland. One more was sunk by a U-Boat. PQ 15 (26 April – 7 May) had three ships sunk by torpedo aircraft, and PQ 16 (25-30 May) was attacked by large formations of Ju 88s and Heinkels, losing seven freighters plus several more badly damaged.

Then came the disaster of PQ 17, which led to a complete revision of the convoy system.

The thirty-six freighters of PQ 17 sailed from Iceland on 27 June 1942 protected by a close-support force and a cover group of four cruisers and three destroyers. Additional long-range support was provided by a cover force of the Home Fleet, consisting of the battleships *Duke of York* and *Washington,* the carrier *Victorious,* two cruisers and fourteen destroyers.

As soon as they learned of PQ 17's departure, **the German** Navy's Battle Groups I and II – the *Tirpitz,* the heavy cruiser *Admiral Hipper,* the two pocket-battleships *Lützow* and *Admiral Scheer,* and twelve destroyers – slipped out of Trondheim and Narvik and headed northwards for Altenfjord. There they simply waited, the German Admirals unwilling to risk their ships until they had more information about the strength of the convoy's covering forces.

On 4 July, however, the Admiralty in London received a completely false report that a Russian submarine had sighted the German warships heading for the convoy. This, in addition to reports that the convoy was being continually shadowed by enemy aircraft, led to one of the most tragic decisions of the whole war: to withdraw the covering cruisers and destroyers and to scatter the convoy, the merchantmen making their way individually to the Russian ports.

It was the signal for droves of enemy aircraft and U-Boats to fall on the luckless transports and pick them off one by one. The slaughter began on 5 July and went on for five days, right up to the moment when the surviving ships entered the White Sea and Archangel. Twenty-four out of the thirty-six ships were sunk.

The next eastbound convoy was PQ 18, its departure delayed until September because all the available aircraft-carriers were engaged in running through the desperately-needed August convoy to Malta – and, after the PQ 17 fiasco, the departure of another convoy to Russia without a close carrier escort could not be considered. When PQ 18 finally sailed from Iceland on 9 September it was accompanied by the *Avenger* – an American-built 'utility' escort carrier. A converted merchantman, she was the second of her kind; a similar carrier, *Audacity*, had already proved her worth on the UK-Gibraltar route. A third, HMS *Archer*, was already in service and two more, the *Biter* and the *Dasher*, were scheduled to follow during the coming months. The *Avenger* carried Nos. 802 and 883 Squadrons, each with six Sea Hurricanes, together with the three Swordfish of a flight of 825 Squadron. Six more Hurricanes were carried in crates, as reserves.

The fighters were in action almost from the moment the convoy set out. On the 12th, when the ships were approaching North Cape, a three-engined Blohm und Voss 138 flying-boat appeared to the south, shadowing the convoy, and the Hurricanes were flown off to shoot it down. They failed, using up a lot of valuable ammunition – and while they were chasing the elusive and heavily-armoured BV 138, six Junkers 88s of KG 30 swept down on the convoy to make a dive-bombing attack. No ships were lost and the attackers were beaten off, but soon afterwards forty torpedo-carrying Heinkel 111s of KG 26 came boring in, low over the water. The formation leader, Major Werner Klümper, tried to locate the carrier but failed to find it. He even began to doubt whether it existed at all, especially as there was no sign of any fighters. In fact, the Hurricanes were still away over the horizon chasing the BV 138, and the *Avenger* had stationed herself some distance from the convoy to be in a better tactical position.

Through dense anti-aircraft fire, the forty Heinkels attacked the convoy's starboard column. In exactly eight minutes eight freighters were hit and sunk. All the German aircraft returned safely to base, but six of them were so badly shot up by the flak that they had to be written off.

The following day, Major Klümper was ordered to concentrate all his available aircraft against the carrier – the existence of which had been verified by the BV 138 crews. In the early afternoon Klümper led the twenty-two Heinkels of No. 1 Squadron, KG 26, in to the attack and this time spotted the *Avenger* steaming to the north of the convoy. He had just ordered his formation to split up when the Hurricanes of 802 and 883 Squadrons swept down on the bombers out of a clear sky. Klümper yelled a warning over the R/T, but it was too late. Hounded by the fighters, the Heinkels swept right over the convoy and straight into a murderous curtain of fire. One Hurricane pilot saw two of the bombers launch their torpedoes at the *Avenger* and miss; they then flew along the side of the carrier, level with the bridge, and were literally torn to shreds by a concentrated cone of fire.

In this attack, I/KG 26 lost five aircraft. Of the remaining seventeen, nine – although they reached base – were so badly damaged that they never flew again.

Subsequent attacks, later on the 13th and on the 14th, were

broken up by the *Avenger*'s Sea Hurricanes. In all, the fighters and the flak – mainly the latter, which because of the fighters' efforts was able to concentrate on individual aircraft – accounted for forty-one enemy bombers. Four Sea Hurricanes were lost, three of them being shot down by the convoy's own gunners.

After the failure of the Luftwaffe, the German Navy had a try. U-Boats attacked the convoy on the 15th and 16th and destroyed three freighters, but one of them – the *U*-589 – was located by 825 Squadron's Swordfish and sunk by escorting destroyers.

On the 18th, as the convoy entered the Kola Inlet, the Luftwaffe had a last fling and sent in two formations of torpedo-carrying Heinkel 115 floatplanes. Two more merchantmen were sunk, but two Heinkels were shot down by a Hurricane catapulted from the freighter *Empire Morn*. This was an RAF aircraft of the Merchant Service Fighter Unit, piloted by Flying Officer A. H. Burr. After the engagement, Burr flew to Key Ostrov airfield near Archangel and landed safely.

By this time, with PQ 18 in sight of safety, the *Avenger* had turned back to escort a homeward-bound convoy. It was not attacked en route; the Luftwaffe had learned its lesson.

The *Avenger*'s success in escorting PQ 18 was additional proof of how effective a small escort carrier could be in defence against aircraft and submarines. The value of such a vessel had already been demonstrated during the last three months of 1941, during the short life of HMS *Audacity*.

The *Audacity* was in fact a British conversion – a captured German merchant ship, the *Hannover,* fitted with a 460-foot flight deck. There was no hangar space; her fighters' six Martlets of 802 Squadron, were ranged on deck. The carrier began operations in September 1941 on the UK-Gibraltar route. She made two round trips, escorting four convoys; three of them came under air and U-Boat attack, and in the course of these operations 802 Squadron's Martlets shot down five Focke-Wulf 200C long-range patrol aircraft, damaged three more and drove off another. Nine U-Boats were also spotted by the aircraft, one of them – the *U*-131 – being sunk by escorting destroyers. Two

Martlets were lost, one being hit by machine-gun fire from a Focke-Wulf 200 and the other by flak from a U-Boat that elected to stay on the surface and shoot it out.

In the bitterest of these air-sea battles, while escorting a home-ward-bound convoy on 21 December 1941, the *Audacity* herself was hit by a torpedo. A fierce blaze raged through her fuel system and she blew up and sank. Her loss left a gap that was not filled until the American-built escort carriers began operations on the Atlantic trade routes in 1943.

The first of the escort carriers to be attached to the North Atlantic convoys was HMS *Biter*. Having received her baptism of fire during the 'Torch' landings in North Africa in November 1942, she sailed on her first convoy protection mission in April the following year. She carried the nine Swordfish of 811 Squadron, together with a fighter flight of three Wildcats – the well-proven Martlet, which had by this time reverted to its US Navy name. Her first success came quickly, when one of her Swordfish shared the destruction of the *U*-203 with the destroyer *Pathfinder* on 25 April. Soon afterwards, another 811 Swordfish shared the killing of the *U*-89 with the destroyers of the 5th Escort Group. These, however, were the only successes chalked up by the *Biter* during the sixteen convoys she escorted up to August 1944.

In May 1943 the *Biter* was joined by the escort carrier *Archer*, with the nine Swordfish of 819 Squadron and the three Wildcats of 892. On 23 May one of 819's Swordfish located the *U*-752 and sank her with rockets. However, the carrier made only one more convoy support run before serious mechanical defects forced her to be withdrawn from service the following October.

The destruction of the *U*-752 was the last claimed by aircraft from an escort carrier until February 1944, when 842 Squadron's Swordfish from HMS *Fencer* – which joined the convoy routes in October 1943 – sank the *U*-666. This was followed in March 1944 by the destruction of the *U*-653 by Swordfish of 825 Squadron operating from the newly-commissioned *Vindex* during an anti-submarine sweep, the kill being shared with the destroyers of the 2nd Escort Group. The success was repeated on 6 May, when the *Vindex*'s aircraft co-operated with surface forces in the sinking of the *U-765*.

Although a fighter flight was carried by every escort carrier, the complement of one carrier – the *Pursuer* – consisted entirely of fighters. These were the twenty Wildcats of 881 and 896 Squadrons, and on one occasion – while escorting a Gibraltar convoy in February 1944 – they broke up an attack by a formation of Heinkel 177s carrying glider-bombs, shooting down two of the enemy aircraft and driving off the rest. On the same run early in 1944, Sea Hurricanes of 835 Squadron, operating from the *Nairana,* surprised two lumbering Junkers 290 transports over the Bay of Biscay and shot them both down; another 290 and a He 177 were destroyed by Wildcats from the *Biter* and the *Fencer.*

By the end of May 1944, in addition to the escort carriers, nineteen Merchant Aircraft Carriers were in service on the North Atlantic routes. Known as MAC-Ships, they were all either grain ships or tankers, fitted with a simple flight deck. The first of them, the *Empire MacAlpine,* had sailed for Halifax with her first convoy on 29 May 1943. She was followed in July by the *Rapana* and the *Empire MacAndrew,* then by the *Amastra* and the *Empire MacRae* in September. During that month, two Swordfish from the *Empire MacAlpine* successfully attacked and drove off with rockets a U-Boat that threatened convoy ONS 18, bound for Halifax. A few weeks later, Swordfish from the *Rapana* made several attacks on a submarine and inflicted some damage.

During their wartime lives – after which most of them reverted to their more usual role – the MAC-Ships made 170 trips with the Atlantic convoys. Their Swordfish, drawn from Nos. 836, 840 and 860 Squadrons, based in Northern Ireland, flew 4,177 sorties. Although no U-Boat kills were directly credited to them, they co-operated with surface forces in the destruction of several – and of all the convoys accompanied by the MAC-ships, only one was successfully attacked by the enemy. It was from a MAC-ship, the *Empire MacKay,* that a Fleet Air Arm Swordfish made its last operational flight on 27 June 1945.

Meanwhile, as the mid-Atlantic tussle between the escorts and the U-Boat packs continued, the battle had flared up in Arctic waters once more. In September 1943 the *Scharnhorst* and the *Tirpitz* had made one sortie to bombard installations on the island of Spitzbergen before scurrying back to their Norwegian lair; and in December the *Scharnhorst* had put to sea once more in an attempt to intercept a Russian convoy. On 26 December she was cornered by the Home Fleet off North Cape and destroyed.

The *Tirpitz* herself had been damaged by X-Craft (midget submarines) during a gallant attack on 18 September 1943, but it could only be a matter of months before she was made seaworthy again, and her presence in Norwegian waters was a perpetual thorn in the Royal Navy's flesh.

In a bid to knock her out once and for all, the C-in-C Home Fleet planned a massive Fleet Air Arm strike against her. To simulate her anchorage in Altenfjord, a dummy range was built on Loch Eriboll, in Caithness, and during March 1944 this was the scene of intense activity as aircraft from the *Victorious* and the *Furious* rehearsed the attack. The strike was to be carried out by the 8th TBR (Torpedo Bomber Reconnaissance) and the 52nd TBR Wings, made up of Nos. 827, 829, 830 and 831 Squadrons operating Fairey Barracudas, a type that had first seen action with No. 810 Squadron during the Salerno landings eight months earlier. In addition to the TBRs, the *Victorious* and the *Furious* also carried Nos. 1834 and 1836 Squadrons, equipped with American-built Chance-Vought Corsair fighters, and Nos. 801 and 880 Squadrons with Seafires. More fighter cover was to be provided by the Hellcats of 800 and 804 Squadrons (HMS *Emperor*) and the Wildcat Vs of 891, 896, 882 and 898 Squadrons (HMS *Pursuer* and *Searcher*), while anti-submarine patrols were to be flown by the Swordfish of 842 Squadron on board HMS *Fencer*. The carrier group was to be escorted by the Second Battle Squadron of the Home Fleet, made up of the *Duke of York*, the cruisers *Anson*, *Sheffield*, *Jamaica* and *Royalist*, and a screen of destroyers.

The forces assembled on the afternoon of 2 April about 220 miles to the north-west of Altenfjord. From there they moved in to the flying-off position, 120 miles north-west of Kaafjord, reaching it during the early hours of the following morning.

At 04.30 hours the twenty-one Barracudas of No. 8 TBR Wing climbed away from the *Victorious* into a brilliant dawn sky and set course for the target, keeping low over the sea to avoid detection by the enemy radar. They were escorted by a mixed fighter umbrella of Corsairs, Hellcats and Wildcats, some forty fighters in all; the Seafires, which did not have sufficient range to accompany the bombers, flew patrols over the warships.

Fifty miles from the target, the Barracudas – labouring under the weight of their 1,600-pound armour-piercing or 500-pound SAP bombs – climbed up to eight thousand feet. Minutes later, the sirens began to wail around Altenfjord as the host of blips appeared on the German radar screens. Dense clouds of smoke started to spread out over the water from the generators that circled the warship.

It was too late. With a deafening snarl of engines, the first wave of Hellcats and Wildcats skimmed up the fjord, hammering the flak positions on the surrounding hilltops and the shore with highly-accurate machine-gun fire while the Corsairs circled watchfully overhead. Then the Barracudas arrived, diving in line astern and unloading their bombs on the naked battleship. One Barracuda was hit and plunged into the water, killing its crew; the rest escaped unscathed. All the fighters returned safely to the carriers.

An hour later, a second attack was made by nineteen Barracudas of No. 52 TBR Wing, escorted by thirty-nine fighters. The pattern of the earlier strike was repeated, the fighters keeping the flak batteries occupied while the bombers made their attack. By this time the smoke screen was fully developed, but it hindered the German anti-aircraft crews far more than it did the Barracuda pilots, who had little difficulty in locating their target. Once again, only one Barracuda was lost.

During the two attacks the *Tirpitz* sustained fourteen direct hits. Although the bombs failed to penetrate her heavy armour, they caused extensive damage to her superstructure and fire control systems, as well as killing or wounding 438 of her crew. Three other ships in the fjord were also damaged.

The strike, known as Operation Tungsten, put the mighty battleship out of action for three months. On 17 July 1944 she was attacked again, this time by the Barracudas of 820 and 826 Squadrons from HMS *Indefatigable* and 827 and 830 Squadrons from the *Formidable*. This attack marked the appearance in combat of a new Fleet Air Arm fighter: the Fairey Firefly. No. 1770 Squadron, the first to equip with the type, operated from the *Indefatigable*.

The enemy had plenty of warning on this occasion, and they succeeded in laying a dense smoke-screen around the *Tirpitz* with the result that no hits were scored. Four more attacks were mounted between 22 and 29 August, but these too failed for the same reason – although two hits were in fact scored on the battleship on 24 August, the Barracuda crews bombing blind through the smoke.

The Navy suffered one casualty: the Canadian-manned escort carrier *Nabob,* torpedoed by the *U*-354 off North Cape on 22 August. The carrier, although badly damaged, managed to limp back to Scapa Flow, but she was classified beyond repair and written off. Appropriately enough, the *U*-354 was herself sunk by the *Vindex*'s Swordfish three days later.

As for the *Tirpitz*, she was towed south to Tromsö for repairs. It was there, on 12 November 1944, that she was finally destroyed by 12,000-pound bombs from the Lancasters of Nos. 9 and 617 Squadrons, Royal Air Force.

12 Over the Beaches

On 13 May 1943, German resistance in North Africa finally came to an end after over two years of bitter fighting. Two months later, on 10 July, British and American forces landed on Sicily by sea and air. Operation Husky, the first step in the liberation of Europe, had begun.

The landings were covered by the two fleet carriers *Formidable* and *Indomitable*, the latter taking part in her first action since she was damaged by enemy bombs during the August Malta Convoy of 1942. To counter any possible action by the Italian fleet, which still possessed sixty-one warships – including six battleships and seven destroyers – the carriers were positioned 200 miles to the east of Malta. The Italians failed to take up the challenge, however, and the Fleet Air Arm's activities were restricted to patrols over the invasion area, flown by the Wildcats of 888 and 893 Squadrons, while the Seafires of 807, 880, 885 and 899 Squadrons maintained air cover over the warships. However, they were unable to prevent a dusk attack on the 11th by a lone Junkers 88, which took the British force completely by surprise and torpedoed the *Indomitable*, causing considerable damage that put her out of action for almost a year. The 88 sped away unharmed; not a single gun had opened up. The *Indomitable* was the last aircraft carrier to be hit by enemy air attack in the Mediterranean.

At the end of the second week in August, the Germans broke off contact with the Allies in Sicily and withdrew across the Straits of Messina to the Italian mainland. On 3 September British forces landed at Reggio in Calabria, and on the 9th – the day after the Italian surrender, resulting in the Germans siezing control of the country – a second landing was made at Salerno, with the object of capturing the port of Naples and cutting off the German forces retreating before the British advance from Reggio. But things went badly from the start; the Germans, under Field-Marshal Kesselring, counter-attacked ferociously and for a time it looked as though the British and American forces would be hurled back into the sea. This time, because of the distance of Salerno from the recently-captured airfields in Sicily – which meant that shore-based fighters could only patrol the invasion area for less than thirty minutes at a time, and then only in small numbers – it fell to the Fleet Air Arm to provide air cover over the beach-head.

Combat air patrols and close-support missions were flown by over a hundred Seafires operating from the escort carriers *Attacker, Battler, Hunter* and *Stalker,* which formed part of Force V under the command of Rear-Admiral Sir Philip Vian. As before, the Fleet carriers of Force H, the *Formidable* and the *Illustrious* – which had been called in to replace the damaged *Indomitable* – were positioned out to sea well clear of the beaches to deal with any intervention by enemy surface vessels that might materialize. Initially, it was thought that the Fleet Air Arm's commitment would be short; hopes were pinned on the rapid capture of Montecorvino airfield, which would enable air support operations to be taken over by shore-based fighters.

By the end of the first day, however, during which the Seafires flew 265 sorties, the airfield was still in enemy control, and for the hard-pressed Allies the situation showed no sign of improving. The Seafire pilots were forced to continue operating without respite for another two and a half days, until the Americans managed to level out a rough airstrip in their sector. By the end of that time, the escort carriers could muster only twenty-five airworthy fighters; because of the Seafire's fragile undercarriage, the accident rate during landing-on operations had been alarming, some forty aircraft having been written off. Ten more had been lost to enemy fighters and flak; on the credit side, only two enemy fighter-bombers had been shot down and another four damaged, largely because the Seafires were not fast enough to catch the Messerschmitt 109Fs used by the Luftwaffe.

The surviving Seafires were flown to the rough-and-ready American airfield at Paestum, from which they continued to operate until 15 September, while their carriers returned to Palermo. Five days later, Force V was disbanded. Soon afterwards, with the Allied Air Forces now firmly in control of the Mediterranean skies and the Italian Fleet immobilized, the task of Force H also came to an end. For over three years, it had borne the brunt of the enemy onslaught by sea and air; now it was disbanded and its warships dispersed to other theatres of war.

The stage was now being set for Operation Overlord, the Allied invasion of Normandy. In this case, since the beach-heads were well within range of fighter aircraft operating from bases in southern England, carrier-borne aircraft played no part. Four Seafire squadrons – Nos. 808, 885, 886 and 897 – No. 885 recently detached from HMS *Formidable* – did in fact cover the D-Day landings and the subsequent Allied advance, operating first from bases in the UK and later from advanced airstrips in France.

Operation Dragoon, the Allied landings in southern France which took place between St Raphael and Fréjus from 15 to 20 August – originally planned for June but delayed because of the greater priority in landing-craft allocated to Overlord – was a different story. Here, the distance of the invasion area from Allied airfields again meant that the task of providing air cover fell to carrier-based aircraft, and a mixed force of British and American carriers was mustered for the purpose. Known as Task Force 88 and under the joint command of Rear-Admiral Sir Thomas Troubridge and Rear-Admiral C. T. Durgin, USN, it consisted of the British carriers *Attacker, Emperor, Khedive, Pursuer, Searcher, Hunter* and *Stalker* and the American carriers *Tulagi* and *Kasaan Bay*. Only feeble resistance was encountered and the Allies swept rapidly inland, the carrier aircraft being employed mainly for strafing and reconnaissance. The only air combats took place on 19 August, when over a hundred Seafires and Hellcats surprised three Dornier 217s and two Junkers 88s over Toulouse and shot down the lot. Sixteen Allied aircraft were shot down during the five days of operations, a further twenty-seven – mainly Seafires – being lost through deck-landing accidents. With the arrival of USAAF units on the captured airfields around Marseille, the carriers were withdrawn on 24 August.

The following month, the seven Royal Navy carriers that had taken part in Dragoon sailed for the Aegean, where their aircraft flew in support of the Allied forces engaged in recapturing Crete and the other German-occupied islands. The fighters wrought massive destruction among the fleets of small craft, packed with the retreating enemy. The *Searcher* and the *Pursuer* rejoined the Home Fleet during September, but the other five remained in the area until the end of October, by which time all the major islands had been re-occupied. It was the last wartime offensive operation mounted by carriers in the Mediterranean theatre.

During the last year of the war in Europe, with the U-Boat packs decimated or immobilized by the capture of the Atlantic ports, the Fleet Air Arm switched a major part of its task from convoy protection to offensive operations against enemy shipping in Norwegian coastal waters. Between April and September 1944, No. 8 TBR Wing, operating from the *Furious,* destroyed over 25,000 tons of enemy shipping and damaged a further 21,000 tons. It was the old *Furious*'s last fling; twenty-eight years old, battle-weary and worn out, she was finally withdrawn from service that autumn. The fleet carriers *Victorious, Indefatigable* and *Implacable* played a major part in the series of strikes; the latter was the last carrier to enter service with the Home Fleet. Her first action took place in October 1944, and between then and the end of December her aircraft destroyed 40,000 tons of shipping, as well as damaging one submarine, the *U-1060,* which was driven aground and later destroyed by the RAF.

Most of the work in northern waters, however, was done by the escort carriers *Campania, Emperor, Fencer, Nairana, Premier, Pursuer, Puncher, Queen, Searcher, Striker* and *Trumpeter.* Between them, they carried out a total of forty-five offensive operations off the Norwegian coast between April 1944 and

May 1945. Only one of them, the *Puncher,* carried Barracudas; the rest had either re-equipped with Grumman Avengers or else they still soldiered on with the Swordfish. There were three exceptions; the *Emperor,* the *Pursuer* and the *Searcher* were fighter carriers, equipped with Wildcats, Hellcats or Fireflies. These fighters covered all minelaying and strike operations so successfully that none of the Barracudas or Avengers was lost to enemy aircraft during any mission, while some forty German planes were shot down or destroyed on the ground by the Fleet Air Arm. Because most of the enemy fighters were by this time committed to the Battle of Germany, there were few interceptions. The Luftwaffe made only one serious attempt to intervene, during a strike by Avengers on 26 March 1945, and the escorting Wildcats immediately pounced on the attacking Messerschmitt 109Gs and shot down five of them without loss to themselves.

By the beginning of 1945, the only carriers still operating Swordfish in the Norwegian operations were the *Campania* and the *Nairana.* Their aircraft were engaged mainly in reconnaissance and minelaying duties, but on one memorable occasion – on 28 January 1945 – the Swordfish of the *Campania's* 813 Squadron carried out a night strike against shipping at Vaagsö. In brilliant moonlight, they attacked with rockets and sank three armed trawlers.

Meanwhile, escort carriers were once again sailing with the Arctic convoys. The *Chaser,* the first carrier to accompany a Russian convoy all the way since PQ 18, scored a notable success in March 1944 when the Swordfish of 816 Squadron destroyed two U-Boats and shared the destruction of a third with the destroyer *Onslaught* on three successive days while escorting the homeward-bound convoy RA 57. During the next convoy, in April, Swordfish, Avengers and Wildcats of 819 and 846 Squadrons, operating from the *Activity* and the *Tracker,* destroyed two U-Boats, damaged three more and shot down six Junkers 88, Fw 200 and BV 138 shadowing aircraft in the space of two days. Successes continued to mount; in another two-day period early in May, seven U-Boats were sunk by the forces escorting convoy

JW/RA 59 – three of them by Swordfish from the *Fencer*'s 842 Squadron.

During the nine JW/RA convoys that made the round trip to Russia in 1944, only four merchantmen were sunk out of a total of 304. One more U-Boat was destroyed, by the Swordfish of the *Campania*'s 813 Squadron in December 1944, bringing the total of submarines sunk, damaged or shared with surface forces by carrier aircraft on the Arctic routes during 1944 to sixteen. A similar number of enemy aircraft were also destroyed during the same period. The last escort mission by a carrier – HMS *Queen* – in Arctic waters was carried out in May 1945, several days after the German surrender, in case of possible suicide attacks by fanatical Nazi U-Boat commanders.

On 4 May 1945 forty-four Avengers and Wildcats from the carriers *Trumpeter, Searcher* and *Queen* swept down on the Norwegian port of Kilbotn, near Harstad, and pulverized the 5,000-ton submarine depot ship *Black Watch,* together with the U-711 which was lying alongside. The flak was intense, but only two aircraft were lost.

It was the Fleet Air Arm's last strike in European waters. Four days later, the Germans surrendered. The enemy plans to transfer most of their forces from Northern Germany and Denmark to Norway for a desperate last-ditch stand that might have prolonged the war for several months had not materialized. The combined efforts of the Fleet Air Arm and RAF Coastal Command had tipped the scales against such a plan, which could not have succeeded without control of the air over Norway and the seas around it. The Norwegian fjords were littered with the sunken wrecks of ships, the Norwegian airfields littered with the charred remains of aircraft in mute testimony of the fury that had descended from the skies.

The fjords, which had echoed to the noise of gunfire for five long years, were silent now. Out in the Atlantic, ships could once more sail without fear of the white torpedo-track streaking towards them out of the darkness. Debris and oil from shattered ships would come floating in on the tides for a month or two, and then the sea would wipe away the last traces of the conflict as though it had never been.

But ten thousand miles away, on the other side of the world, another conflict still raged. It would be three bitter months yet before the red sun of Japan finally slid below the horizon.

13 Return to the Pacific

The morning of 24 January 1945 had dawned with the promise of heat. By eight o'clock the sun had already dispersed the thin layer of mist that hung over the network of Japanese fighter airfields around Palembang, in southern Sumatra.

The sun glittered on the wings of the forty Tojo fighters of the Imperial Japanese Army Air Force's 87th Squadron, drawn up in a long line beside the dusty runway of an airfield near Pladjoe. The early morning patrol of three fighters had just landed and taxied-in in a cloud of red dust; the pilots had nothing to report. The morning seemed peaceful enough as sunburned mechanics worked on the other aircraft, fuelling and arming them in readiness for the day's flying. In the mess tent, the pilots were just finishing their breakfast.

Suddenly, at exactly five minutes past eight, the strident tones of a siren brought the pilots tumbling out on to the airfield. Grabbing odds and ends of flying kit, they dashed for their aircraft as the smoky trails of two alarm rockets arced across the sky. One by one, started up by the mechanics, the big Nakajima radial engines burst into life and the pilots flung themselves into the cockpits.

The first flight, led by Captain Hideaki Inayama, had just turned on to the runway and opened up for take-off when half a dozen squat, gull-winged shapes blasted across the airfield like a whirlwind, their machine-guns churning up fountains of red earth among the Japanese aircraft. Corsairs!

Behind Inayama, a pair of Tojos – torn apart by the storm of bullets – slewed off the runway and blew up. Inayama hauled his fighter into the air and pulled up in a steep climbing turn, heading flat out for a thin layer of cloud. For a few moments, it

seemed as though he was the only Japanese fighter among a whirling mass of Corsairs and Hellcats. Then, as he burst through the
cloud layer, he saw a few other Tojos, widely scattered, climbing
hell-for-leather towards the column of black smoke that rose
vertically into the sky above the Pladjoe oil refinery.

A week earlier, on 16 January, a British task force consisting
of the fleet carriers *Illustrious, Indomitable, Indefatigable* and
Victorious, under the command of Rear-Admiral Sir Philip Vian,
had left its base at Trincomalee in Ceylon. The force's destina-
tion was Sydney, which was to be its main base for operations
against the Japanese in the Pacific.

On the way, Vian planned to carry out an operation which, as
well as dealing a severe blow to the Japanese war effort, would
also help to convince the Americans that the British Pacific Fleet
meant business: a strike by his carrier aircraft on the vital oil
refineries of Pladjoe and Soengi Gerong, which supplied a large
part of Japan's aviation fuel.

The strike was originally scheduled to take place on the 22nd,
but because of torrential rain in the launch area it had to be
postponed for forty-eight hours. At dawn on the 24th, however,
the morning silence that hung over the Indian Ocean two hundred miles off the coast of Sumatra was shattered by the thunder
of engines as a hundred and thirty aircraft revved up on the
flight decks of the four carriers. The strike was to be carried out
by forty-three Avengers drawn from Nos. 820, 849, 854 and 857
Squadrons, supported by the twelve rocket-firing Fireflies of the
Indefatigable's 1770 Squadron. Top cover and strafing attacks
on airfields in the area were to be the task of the Corsairs and
Hellcats, while – as usual, because of their limited range – the
Seafires of 887 and 894 Squadrons were to provide air defence
for the task force.

At ten minutes past eight, while the Corsairs and Hellcats
swept in to strafe the Japanese fighter airfields, the Avengers –
with ten miles still to go to the target – ran into the first heavy
anti-aircraft fire. A twin-engined Kawasaki 45 'Nick' was seen
circling some distance away, presumably engaged in directing the
A/A fire or fighters; it was chased and shot down by Lt P. S. Cole

of 1830 Squadron, flying a Corsair. A second Nick was destroyed a few minutes later by a Hellcat of 1839 Squadron.

At 08.15 hours the Avengers and Fireflies dived on their target through a thick barrage of anti-aircraft fire and balloons – the latter an unexpected complication that fortunately caused no losses. By 08.23 the refinery was blazing fiercely and the Avengers left for the rendezvous, escorted by the Fireflies; the main escort was still tangling with about twenty-five Tojos which, having escaped the strafing attacks had arrived on the scene somewhat belatedly. The Hellcat and Corsair pilots shot down eight of them; Sub-Lt A. French of 1836 Squadron accounted for two and so did Major R. C. Hay of the Royal Marines, the Air Co-ordinator on the *Victorious*. A total of fourteen enemy aircraft – Tojos, Oscars and twin-engined Nicks – were destroyed in air combat; a further thirty-four were destroyed on the ground. Seven Fleet Air Arm aircraft of all types were lost, the majority accidentally during landing-on after sustaining battle damage. The seven included two Avengers, both of which were shot down by Captain Inayama. Pulling up steeply after his first victory – which crashed into the jungle after a burst at point-blank range, burning fiercely – Inayama spotted a Hellcat pumping bullets into a twisting Oscar fighter. He turned and fired and the Hellcat flipped over on its wingtip, racing to meet him head-on. At the last moment, the British pilot broke away and shot beneath Inayama's fighter, missing it by a hair's breadth.

Inayama pulled round in a tight turn, looking for the Hellcat, but it had vanished. A minute later, however, he spotted an Avenger trailing smoke and quickly caught up with it, weaving to escape the tracers that snaked towards his fighter from the Avenger's gun-turret. A long burst from the Tojo's guns and it was all over; the Avenger dived into the ground in flames.

As he turned away, Inayama found himself flying alongside another Avenger. He could see the white face of the British pilot staring at him! The bomber itself was torn by anti-aircraft fire. Inayama climbed away, intending to come round on the bomber's tail and finish it off, but the Avenger escaped into some cloud. Wearily, his fuel and ammunition almost gone, the

Japanese pilot returned to his base.

During the attack, something like one hundred and fifty 500-pound bombs had gone down on the refinery, destroying sixty-per-cent of the installations. The storage tanks were completely burnt out and it was not until the end of April that the damage was repaired and the refinery's output regained the level it had attained before the strike.

Five days later, on the 29th, the Japanese had just started to clear up the mess when the Fleet Air Arm came back, this time with forty-six Avengers to hit the refinery at Soengi Gerong. On this occasion, the strike met with fiercer resistance from the Japanese fighters and sixteen FAA aircraft were shot down over the target area, but the escort accounted for twenty enemy aircraft in air combat and the strafing attacks destroyed a further thirty-eight on the ground, bringing the enemy losses sustained during the two strikes to over a hundred aircraft. In addition, the refinery had been well and truly plastered and production brought to a complete standstill for two months.

The two strikes had succeeded in cutting the flow of aviation fuel from Sumatra to the Japanese war theatres in Burma, the Philippines and China by a good sixty-five-per-cent. It was the severest blow ever dealt to the enemy by a British force in the Far East – and a far cry from the day, three years and six weeks earlier, when an avalanche of Japanese torpedo-bombers had swept down on the naked battleships *Prince of Wales* and *Repulse* and destroyed them within minutes, shattering the hopes of the Royal Navy in the Indian Ocean at one blow. . . .

During the early months of the war with Germany, between January 1940 and February 1941, the Royal Navy had not been able to spare an aircraft-carrier for trade protection duties in the Indian Ocean. The two carriers which had operated there for a time to counter any possible threat from the German battleship *Graf Spee* – the *Eagle* and the *Glorious* – had been withdrawn to European waters in January 1940, after the battleship's destruction in the River Plate.

The first British carrier to enter the Indian Ocean after that was the *Formidable*, on the way round the Cape to replace the damaged *Illustrious* with the Mediterranean Fleet. On 2 February 1941 the Albacores of her 826 and 829 Squadrons attacked the harbour of Mogadishu in Somaliland, towards which British forces were advancing. Further up the East African coast, the carrier's aircraft also bombed the Italian port of Massawa in Eritrea on 13 and 21 February and on 1 March.

A week after the attack on Mogadishu, the small fleet carrier *Hermes* arrived in the area and began a blockade of the port. Six enemy merchant ships were located by the Swordfish of 814 Squadron while attempting to break out; five were quickly captured by surface vessels, but the sixth refused to stop and was bombed by the Swordfish. Badly damaged, she was forced aground, where she later broke up.

Following these operations, the *Hermes* took up her primary duty of trade protection, her aircraft taking part in the search towards the end of February for the pocket-battleship *Admiral Scheer,* which was reported to be in the Indian Ocean. The *Scheer,* however, escaped from the net and slipped back into the Atlantic a few days later.

Late in April, after escorting a troop convoy from Bombay to Basra, the carrier took up station in the Persian Gulf as insurance against the insurrection that was looming in Iraq. When the fighting broke out at the beginning of May, six of her Swordfish immediately made a demonstration flight over Basra, and on the 7th two flights of 814 Squadron were disembarked and transferred to the airfield at Shaibah to extend their radius of action. Between 7 and 16 May these aircraft made ten bombing attacks on railway bridges, petrol and oil tanks, barracks and troop concentrations around the Shatt' 'al Arab. Several of the aircraft were hit by the very accurate fire of the Iraqui rebels; one of them was forced to land near the barracks at Samawa where it was at once surrounded by Iraqis, who fired on the crew as they advanced. Lieutenant J. H. Dundas, sizing up the situation, landed his Swordfish on the appallingly rough ground and took the stranded crew on board, taking off through a storm of automatic fire.

The rebels were finally overcome by the end of May, but aircraft from the *Hermes* continued to patrol the area for another two months. Then, after a further two months of ocean patrols, she sailed for Colombo and disembarked her Swordfish squadron – which stayed there from September 1941 until February 1942, while the carrier underwent a refit at Simonstown in South Africa.

Meanwhile, with war against Japan looming on the horizon, plans were being made to send six capital ships, a fleet carrier and a strong force of light cruisers and destroyers to Singapore. Losses and commitments in the Atlantic prevented the requirement from being met fully, however, and on 2 December the warships of the makeshift Force Z – centred on the *Prince of Wales* and the *Repulse* – assembled at Singapore without the essential air component. The latter was in fact to have been provided by the new carrier *Indomitable,* but she went aground off Jamaica while working up and there was a delay of nearly a fortnight before she finally sailed to join Force Z. She had only got as far as Capetown when, on 10 December, Japanese bombs and torpedoes tore the *Prince of Wales* and the *Repulse* apart and sent them to the bottom.

After this disaster, the *Indomitable* called in at Aden, where she exchanged her own squadrons for fifty RAF Hurricanes, which were flown off to Batavia in Java late in January 1942 in a desperate attempt to reinforce the decimated and outclassed RAF fighter squadrons, mostly equipped with Brewster Buffaloes, in the East Indies. In the event, most of the Hurricanes were destroyed on the ground before they had a chance to meet the Japanese in combat. After delivering another fifty Hurricanes to Ceylon, the carrier returned to Aden and picked up her Fleet Air Arm squadrons before sailing to join the Eastern Fleet at Addu Atoll, in the Maldive Islands. The *Hermes* and the *Formidable* were already with the Fleet, the latter carrier operational again after a break of ten months following the damage she had suffered off Crete in May 1941. Between them, the three carriers had a total of fifty-seven strike aircraft and forty fighters; in addition, the Fulmars of Nos. 803 and 806 Squadrons were based ashore at Ratmalana in Ceylon, where they had recently arrived after several months of operations with Hurricanes in Syria and the Western Desert.

Against this comparative handful of Fleet Air Arm aircraft the Japanese had some three hundred combat aircraft of all types, based on the carriers *Hiryu, Soryu, Akagi, Zuikaku* and *Shokaku* of the 1st Carrier Striking Force – the units which had carried out the devastating attack on Pearl Harbour. On 4 April, an RAF reconnaissance Catalina reported that the enemy fleet was approaching Ceylon, and Admiral Somerville took the Eastern Fleet out in an attempt to launch a night strike against the Japanese carriers. However, he failed to make contact and at dawn the following day – Easter Sunday – a strong force of Japanese aircraft attacked the harbour of Colombo in the hope of surprising the Eastern Fleet at anchor. The Aichi D3A 'Vals' were hotly engaged by the RAF's Hurricanes, but the latter were hopelessly outclassed by the Zeros of the Japanese fighter escort and thirteen of them went down in flames. The Zeros also pounced on a luckless formation of six 814 Squadron Swordfish, on its way from Trincomalee to Minneriya, and shot them all out of the sky. Only seven enemy aircraft were lost.

Later that same day, Japanese torpedo-bombers swept down on the cruisers *Dorsetshire* and *Cornwall* – on their way to rejoin the main body of the fleet after a detachment – and sank both of them. Albacores from the *Indomitable* made a night radar search for the enemy carrier force, but it had withdrawn to the south-east to refuel before heading to strike at Trincomalee naval base. Once again, the carrier force was sighted by a reconnaissance aircraft and all naval units in the base – including the *Hermes* – were able to get clear before the attack developed on 9 April. On the way back from the target, the Japanese pilots sighted the *Hermes* – and three hours later, when she was sixty-five miles from Trincomalee, they returned to attack her. She had no aircraft on board and radioed desperately for help, but the fighters at Trincomalee were still recovering from the devastating raid carried out by the Japanese earlier that day. The Fulmars of 803 Squadron were first to reach the scene, but by then it was too late; the pilots were just in time to see the old carrier go under, shattered by forty bombs in the space of ten minutes. The Fulmars tore in among the bombers in a gallant attempt to break up their concentrated attacks on the handful of ships that had accompanied the *Hermes,* but it was no use. Thirty minutes later, the Australian destroyer *Vampire,* the corvette *Hollyhock* and two Fleet Auxiliaries had joined the carrier at the bottom of the Indian Ocean.

Fortunately perhaps for the Eastern Fleet, Japanese carriers never again made an appearance in the Indian Ocean. After the attacks on Ceylon, Admiral Nagumo withdrew his task force to the Pacific in readiness for the next big Japanese venture: the occupation of Midway Island. In the event it proved to be a costly venture, for during the Battle of Midway on 4–5 June the carriers *Akagi, Kaga, Hiryu* and *Soryu* were sunk by air strikes from the USS *Enterprise, Hornet* and *Yorktown.*

Meanwhile, in May, the *Indomitable* had been detached from the Eastern Fleet to join the *Illustrious* in the attacks on the Vichy French-held island of Madagascar, leaving only the *Formidable* under Admiral Somerville's command. The following August, however, the *Formidable* also had to be redeployed to replace the *Indomitable* after the latter was badly damaged during the vital 'Pedestal' convoy to Malta. With the Fleet Air Arm's main carrier-borne elements now earmarked for the coming invasion of North Africa, that left the *Illustrious* as the only Allied carrier in the Indian Ocean; as well as providing air cover for the campaign in Madagascar, she made a few sweeps into the Indian Ocean from her base at Mombasa before she too rejoined the Home Fleet in January 1943.

Towards the end of 1942, in response to persistent American appeals for carrier reinforcements, the *Victorious* left the Home Fleet and sailed for the south-west Pacific, where – after her four squadrons had re-equipped with American aircraft – she formed part of Task Group 36.3, together with the USS *Saratoga, Indiana* and *Massachusetts* during the landings in the Solomon Islands between May and July 1943. Her stay in the Pacific, however, was short-lived; in August, she sailed for home waters by way of the United States.

In October 1943, after a break of nine months, another British carrier appeared in the Indian Ocean: HMS *Battler,* with the Swordfish and Seafires of No. 842 Squadron. She formed the nucleus of an anti-submarine group which, during the early months of 1944, began hunter-killer operations against the German and Japanese submarines which were preying on shipping in the area from their base at Penang. The first success came on 12 March 1944, when the *Battler's* Swordfish located an enemy submarine supply ship off the Seychelles and vectored destroyers on to her. The loss of this ship, together with another which had been destroyed a fortnight earlier, drastically reduced the time spent at sea by the enemy submarines, with a consequent reduction in the tonnage of Allied shipping sunk.

Later in the year, the *Battler* was joined by the escort carriers *Shah, Begum, Atheling* and *Ameer.* In August, one submarine – the *U*-198 – was destroyed by Avengers of 832 and 851 Squadrons, operating from the *Begum* and the *Shah,* during a hunter-killer sweep.

January 1944 saw the return of the *Illustrious,* which arrived at Colombo on the 27th accompanied by three capital ships. The first operation carried out by the strengthened Eastern Fleet was a sweep in search of three Japanese cruisers, which made a short foray into the Indian Ocean and sank two freighters off the Cocos Islands before withdrawing. Afterwards, the Fleet rendezvoused with the American carrier *Saratoga,* lent to the Royal Navy at Admiral Somerville's request to enable him to mount a big strike against Japanese targets in Sumatra.

On 16 April 1944 twenty-seven warships drawn from six Allied navies – including the two carriers – sailed from Trincomalee, arriving at their flying-off position one hundred miles south-west of Sabang Island shortly before dawn three days later. At first light on the 19th, eighty-three aircraft – seventeen Barracudas of 810 and 847 Squadrons covered by thirteen Corsairs of 1830 and 1833 Squadrons from the *Illustrious,* together with eighteen Dauntlesses, eleven Avengers and twenty-four Hellcats from the *Saratoga,* headed towards the target – Sabang harbour. While the Corsairs and Hellcats strafed the enemy airfields, knocking out twenty-five Japanese aircraft, the bombers made a series of beautiful precision attacks on the harbour installations, causing severe damage and sinking two small freighters. Only one aircraft, a Hellcat, was lost: the pilot was picked up safely by a British submarine. Later, a small formation of twin-engined Mitsubishi G4M 'Betty' bombers attempted to attack the Allied warships, but three out of the four attacking aircraft were destroyed by Hellcats.

The Eastern Fleet's next operation was a strike on the big Japanese aviation fuel dump at Surabajo in Java. Since the strike aircraft had to fly across the breadth of Java, 810 and 847 Squadrons temporarily exchanged their Barracudas for Avengers, the American aircraft having the greater range. Forty-five Avengers and Dauntlesses covered the 180-mile distance from the flying-off position to the target at daybreak on 17 May, one wave attacking the fuel dump and the nearby refinery while the second wave dived on the harbour. The results were disappointing; the refinery was only lightly damaged and only one small ship was sunk. Japanese fighters failed to challenge the forty Corsairs and Hellcats of the escort, and only one Allied aircraft – an Avenger – was lost. After the strike, the *Saratoga* – having been ordered to return to the United States for a refit – left the main force and sailed for Pearl Harbour. The *Illustrious* returned to Trincomalee with the remaining warships.

On 22 June aircraft from the *Illustrious* raided targets on the Andaman Islands in the Bay of Bengal. The weather was poor, and the damage was limited to a few coastal vessels sunk and damaged by the Barracudas and a dozen or so enemy aircraft destroyed on the ground at Port Blair airfield. It was the last operation before welcome reinforcements arrived in July, in the shape of the *Victorious* and the *Indomitable*. A few days later, the *Victorious* and the *Illustrious* struck at Sabang harbour once more, the Barracudas planting their bombs squarely on top of the fuel tanks that had been carefully repaired by the Japanese after the April raid, reducing them to burning wreckage again. While this was going on, some of the Corsairs acted as spotters for the guns of the British force's three battleships and seven cruisers, which pounded the shore installations to good effect. One or two of the warships suffered slight damage from bombs dropped by Japanese aircraft, but the attacks lacked any real cohesion and four of the enemy were 'splashed' by the fighters of the combat air patrol. This was the last operation directed by Admiral Somerville; on 21 August he was relieved by Admiral Sir Bruce Fraser, who until recently had been the C-in-C Home Fleet.

After the Sabang strike the *Illustrious* sailed to Simonstown for a refit. During the last week in August, Barracudas from the *Victorious* and the *Indomitable* struck at two more targets in Sumatra: the port of Emmahaven and the cement works at Indaroeng. The latter target was badly hit, but the harbour was only lightly damaged. However, no FAA aircraft were lost and the escorting Corsairs and Hellcats encountered no enemy fighter opposition. This was followed up by a third strike, on 18 September, on the vital railway junction at Sigli in northern Sumatra. Results could have been better; as in the earlier strikes, the Fleet Air Arm crews suffered from a lack of target intelligence, the result of the shortage of long-range reconnaissance aircraft based in India and Ceylon.

On 19 October a huge armada of American warships approached Leyte, in the Philippines, on the eve of what was to be one of the most decisive battles of the Pacific war – the Battle of Leyte Gulf, as what was left of the Japanese naval forces in the area made an abortive attempt to draw off the American fleet as a preliminary to smashing the invasion that was taking place. As part of their plan, the Americans had asked Rear Admiral Moody's British carrier squadron to mount a series of strikes on the Nicobar Islands in the hope that they would divert some of the Japanese forces from the main American objective.

The strikes began early on 17 October with waves of Barracudas from the *Victorious* and the *Indomitable* mounting a series of 'softening-up' attacks which, it was hoped, would convince the Japanese that an invasion of the Nicobars was imminent. The enemy, however, refused to rise to the bait – although for the first time since July Japanese fighters came up in strength to meet the attackers. On the 19th, Corsairs of 1834 Squadron from the *Victorious* shot down four Nakajima Ki 43 Oscar fighters in two engagements. During the three-day operation, only two FAA aircraft – a Hellcat and a Barracuda – were lost.

The Nicobar Islands strike was the Barracuda's last major operation. During the following weeks, they were replaced in Nos. 815, 817 and 831 Squadrons by Avengers. While the squadrons were working up with their new aircraft and undergoing a period of intensive training at Trincomalee, two significant events occurred: first, the *Illustrious* returned from her refit in South Africa – and second, the carrier force got a new commander in the person of Rear-Admiral Sir Philip Vian.

The first operation under this redoutable officer's command was a strike by twenty-seven Avengers, escorted by as many Corsairs and Hellcats, on the port of Belawan Deli in Sumatra on 20 December. This was actually a secondary target; the strike had originally been flown off against the refinery at Pangkalan Brandan, but low clouds and driving rain had prevented the attack on the primary. The raid on Belawan Deli caused only light damage, and no Fleet Air Arm aircraft were lost. The Corsairs and Hellcats strafed several airfields in the vicinity, destroying a number of enemy aircraft; two of 1839 Squadron's Hellcats from the *Indomitable* caught a Mitsubishi Ki 21 Sally twin-engined bomber slipping along just under the clouds and shot it down in flames.

Soon after the carrier force returned to Trincomalee it was joined by the *Indefatigable,* fresh out from the Home Fleet with her five squadrons of Hellcats, Seafires, Fireflies and Avengers. Vian stayed at Trincomalee just long enough to refuel and rearm before making another sortie against Pangkalan Brandan, this time with the *Indomitable,* the *Victorious* and the *Indefatigable* – the three carriers possessing some 170 combat aircraft between them. This time the weather was fine, and the strike – carried out on 4 January – was highly successful. While the Avengers inflicted severe damage on the refinery, the FAA fighters had something of a field day; the Corsairs of the *Victorious*'s 1836 Squadron shot down five Oscars, two of them being accounted for by

Sub-Lt D. J. Sheppard, while 1834 Squadron destroyed a Sally and a Mitsubishi Ki 46 Dinah. Total claims in air combat amounted to twelve, with twenty more enemy aircraft destroyed on the ground. Only one Avenger was lost, the crew being rescued.

Two weeks later Admiral Vian's powerful carrier force, now the nucleus of the British Pacific Fleet, sailed for Sydney, striking at Palembang on the way. With their departure, only three escort carriers were left in the Indian Ocean: the *Empress, Ameer* and *Shah,* all employed on trade protection duties. In March 1945, however, the 21st Carrier Group – comprising the *Stalker, Attacker, Emperor, Hunter* and *Khedive* – began operations in the Bay of Bengal.

In January 1945 the Hellcats of the *Ameer*'s 804 Squadron flew a series of missions in support of the British landings on Ramree and Cheduba Islands off the coast of Burma, the fighters strafing ahead of the advancing troops. It was not until 1 March, however, that 804's pilots had their first encounter with Japanese aircraft, shooting down two Oscars and a Dinah. At the same time, photo-reconnaissance Hellcats of 888 Squadron, operating from the *Empress,* were ranging over northern Sumatra and bring back a wealth of up-to-date intelligence on potential targets.

Armed with this information, the Avengers of 851 and the Hellcats of 808 Squadrons flew three strikes against targets in Sumatra from the *Emperor* and the *Khedive* during the second and third weeks in April, damaging several enemy vessels off Emmahaven and destroying several more enemy aircraft. Between 30 April and 2 May, Hellcats and Seafires from the *Emperor,* the *Khedive,* the *Hunter* and the *Stalker* flew 180 sorties during Operation Dracula, the amphibious landings in the Rangoon area. There were no air combats, the FAA fighters being engaged in strafing attacks on enemy positions near the beach-head. This was followed on 5 and 6 May by attacks on enemy shipping among the islands off the long southern coast of Burma and on airfields in the Tenasserim area. Avengers and Hellcats from the *Shah* and the *Empress* also hit enemy airfields in the Nicobar and Andaman Islands as a diversion, following these strikes up by an attack on Japanese positions around Tavoy on 7 May. In over a week of operations only two Hellcats had been lost to enemy action, although – predictably – there had been the usual spate of Seafire deck-landing accidents, six of the aircraft being completely written off.

On 15 May the Japanese cruiser *Haguro*, accompanied by three destroyers, made a desperate attempt to break through to the Andaman Islands to reinforce the hard-pressed Japanese garrison there. She was located by the *Emperor*'s Avengers and shadowed until the 26th Destroyer Flotilla caught up with her before dawn on 16 May and sent her to the bottom in a gallant torpedo attack.

During June and July 1945 the escort carriers were involved in mopping-up operations against crumbling Japanese resistance in the Andamans. Several strikes were also carried out against airfields and rolling stock in Sumatra and southern Burma. Many enemy convoys in southern Thailand were also attacked, the incessant strafing of the Corsairs and Hellcats blocking the tortuous roads with burning motor transport and tearing troop concentrations to shreds.

On 26 July seven Japanese aircraft swept low over the sea towards the ships of the 21st Carrier Squadron in the Bay of Bengal. Three were shot down by fighters, but the other four came boring in relentlessly, heedless of the flak that poured up to meet them from all sides. Two of the aircraft were hit and exploded, scattering burning debris over the water. A third slammed into the minesweeper *Vestal*, which blew up and sank, and the fourth narrowly missed the carrier *Ameer*, which was damaged by the explosion. Fortunately the damage was not serious and the *Ameer* was able to return to her base at Akyab.

It was the 21st Carrier Squadron's first and only experience of the Kamikazes – the Japanese suicide pilots. And for the Imperial Japanese Air Force in the Indian Ocean, it had been the last desperate act before the final collapse.

Meanwhile, the British Pacific Fleet, having assembled in Sydney, had finally arrived on 19 March at Ulithi Atoll in the Caroline Islands where – as Task Force 57 – it formed part of the American Fifth Fleet. As well as the four carriers, TF 57 consisted of the *King George V,* the *Howe,* the *Swiftsure,* the *Gambia,* the *Black Prince,* the *Euryalus,* the *Argonaut* and a dozen destroyers.

On 23 March the British warships sailed to take part in Operation Iceberg – the landings on Okinawa. Task Force 57's mission was to strike at six enemy airfields in the Sakishima Gunto island group, which lay to the south-west of Okinawa and the other Ryukyu Islands. If these airfields – which were used as staging-posts between Formosa and Okinawa – could be put out of action, the Japanese would be unable to fly in reinforcements and Okinawa would be isolated.

On 26 March TF 57 had reached its flying-off position about one hundred miles south of Sakishima Gunto and the first strike of forty Avengers was launched. While these attacked airfield installations with their 500-pounders, 1770 Squadron's twelve Fireflies went for the flak positions with their rockets. For two days and nights the aircraft of TF 57 kept up a virtual round-the-clock offensive against the islands. Between the main Avenger strikes – of which there were eight during the two days – the FAA squadrons sent in small formations of bomb-carrying Corsairs and Hellcats to keep the enemy in a state of nerves. However, the strikes did comparatively little damage to the airfields themselves; the runways were made of crushed stone and were easily repaired during lulls in the bombing. Few enemy aircraft were caught and destroyed on the ground, but twenty-eight were shot down by the Corsairs and Hellcats for the loss of nineteen Fleet Air Arm aircraft.

Late on the 28th, the Task Force withdrew for replenishment at sea, the operation being prolonged by unexpected bad weather. The carriers were back on station by the 31st, however, to renew their attacks on the enemy airfields. On 1 April the IJAF appeared over the fleet in strength; first high-level bombers, and then the Kamikazes. Most of the latter were splashed by the Combat Air Patrol before they got within striking

F

distance, but one managed to break through and hit the *Indefatigable* at the base of her island. If she had been an American carrier, the aircraft would have torn through the flight deck and turned the hangars below into a blazing inferno; as it was, there was a delay of about forty-five minutes while the burning wreckage was shovelled over the side – and then the *Indefatigable* carried on almost as if nothing had happened.

During the third series of operations against Sakashima, on 6 April, the Kamikazes attacked again. This time, a burning Zero made a desperate attempt to hit the *Illustrious,* but only succeeded in hitting the carrier's island with its wingtip before plummeting into the sea. During this attack, the Corsairs of 1830 and the Hellcats of 1844 Squadrons accounted for five Aichi D4Y Judys and one Nakajima P1Y Frances.

American Intelligence had indicated that many of the Kamikaze attacks were being launched from Formosa, and Admiral Spruance – the C-in-C US 5th Fleet – asked Task Force 57 to mount a series of strikes on airfields in the northern part of the island. The first attack was carried out in poor weather on 11 April by forty-eight Avengers and forty Corsairs. While the Avengers bombed the port of Kiirun, the fighters strafed airfields in the vicinity. The attacks continued on the 12th, when they were met by Japanese fighers. The Hellcats of 1844 shot down four Oscars, a Zero and a Kawasaki Ki 61 Tony, while the Corsairs of 1834 and 1836 claimed an Oscar, a Zero and a Dinah. The Fireflies of 1770 Squadron were particularly lucky; they ran into a formation of five Mitsubishi Ki 51 Sonia bombers heading for Okinawa on a Kamikaze mission and shot down four of them. Another Kamikaze attack later in the day, this time directed at the British carriers, was torn to shreds by the CAP, four Japanese aircraft being shot down and six more damaged. Eight more enemy aircraft were destroyed during the air strikes the following day.

After this operation, the *Illustrious* was withdrawn from the task force, suffering from an accumulation of mechanical troubles – the result of four years of combat operations. In addition, the pilots of her two Corsair squadrons, 1830 and 1833, had done far more than their normal tour and were long overdue for a rest. The carrier was replaced by the *Formidable,* which immediately went into action with the Task Force during another series of strikes against Sakishima between 16 and 20 April. By this time the fleet had spent over a month at sea on operations; the carriers required replacement aircraft and the tankers and supply ships of the Fleet Train badly needed replenishment. On the night of 20 April the fleet sailed for Leyte in the Philippines, where it stayed until 1 May.

When Task Force 57 returned to operations on 4 May the target was once again the enemy airfields on Sakishima. While Avengers attacked Ishigaki, the 14-inch guns of the *KGV* and the *Howe* pounded the airfields and installations on the neighbouring island of Miyako. At 11.00 hours, shortly before the first strikes returned to the carriers, TF 57 was attacked by a formation of twenty Kamikazes. Almost every FAA fighter squadron was involved in breaking up the attack; the Corsairs of 1834 and 1836 Squadrons shot down a Nakajima C6N Myrt, a Judy and two Zeros, the Seafires of 887 and 894 Squadrons destroyed a Val and four Zeros between them, while the Hellcats of 1839 and 1844 Squadrons accounted for a Nakajima B6N Jill and two Zeros. Only two Kamikazes penetrated the fighter screen and the A/A barrage; the first struck the *Indomitable* aft, slid across the flight deck and went over the side in a cloud of blazing debris, and the second hit the *Formidable* at the base of the island. The damage was quickly patched up and the carrier was fully operational again by the end of the day. Eleven FAA aircraft were destroyed by the Kamikaze on the *Formidable*'s deck; fortunately, most of her aircraft were airborne.

She was not so lucky on 9 May, when more Kamikazes attacked TF 57 at 17.00 hours, just after a strike had landed-on. This time, although a crashing Kamikaze left no more damage than a long scar on the *Formidable*'s armoured deck, eighteen Corsairs and Avengers were destroyed by the sheet of blazing fuel that poured over them. Two Kamikazes also hit the *Victorious;* the first damaged the forward lift and caused quite a sizeable blaze and while this was being tackled by the crew a second

Japanese aircraft struck her and bounced into the sea off her deck, writing off four Corsairs on the way.

The strikes against targets on Sakishima Gunto continued until 25 May, by which time Okinawa was in American hands. The *Formidable* had left the area for Sydney three days earlier, following an accidental hangar fire in which thirty of her aircraft had been destroyed.

In two months at sea, the aircraft of Task Force 57 had flown 5,335 sorties, dropped a thousand tons of bombs and fired a thousand rockets. Nearly two hundred enemy aircraft had been destroyed, ninety-eight of them in air combat. But the Fleet Air Arm's losses had been far from light; seventy-three aircraft had been written off by the Kamikazes and in the *Formidable*'s hangar fire, another sixty-one had been destroyed through accidents – and twenty-six had been shot down by enemy flak and fighters. Eighty-five personnel had been killed, including forty-one aircrew.

Nevertheless, the carriers had survived a series of Kamikaze strikes which, had they been delivered against American carriers, would have proved disastrous. The suicide aircraft had bounced off the armoured decks like flies off an elephant; the British designers had proved their point. Perhaps the Royal Navy's attitude to the fruitless hammer-blows of the Kamikazes is best summed up by the exchange of signals between the *Formidable* and the *Indomitable*, Admiral Vian's flagship, after the former had been hit by a Kamikaze on 4 May.

From the *Formidable*: 'Little Yellow Bastard.'

From the *Indomitable*: 'Are You Referring To Me?'

Towards the end of June the fleet carrier *Implacable* joined the British Pacific Fleet at Manus anchorage, in the Admiralty Islands. The carrier had arrived in the Pacific three weeks earlier, and on 10 June she had carried out a two-day series of strikes against the badly-battered Japanese base at Truk, in the Carolines. Now, fully worked up to operational standards, she replaced the *Indomitable*, which departed for a refit.

The fleet sailed from Manus on 9 July, this time designated

Task Force 37, to join the American Task Force 38 under Admiral J. S. McCain in Japanese waters. The *Indefatigable* did not join TF 37 until a fortnight later, having been held up by mechanical troubles. The first strikes were flown on 17 July, when FAA Corsairs and Fireflies attacked airfield and marshalling yards in the northern part of Honshu, the main Japanese island, while the *King George V* and American warships shelled factories in the Hitachi area near Tokyo. The next FAA attacks were made on the 24th, after the arrival of the *Indefatigable,* with airfields and coastal shipping as the main target. The most important strike was mounted by six Avengers, two Corsairs and two Fireflies against the escort carrier *Kaiyo;* the aircraft left her crippled and in flames.

At dusk the following day, the Japanese sent a formation of torpedo-bombers against TF 37. They were fast, powerful Aichi D7As, known to the Allies as 'Grace' – one of the latest types to see service with the Imperial Japanese Navy. They were intercepted by the Hellcats of 1844 Squadron; two were shot down and a third damaged by Lt W. H. I. Atkinson, bringing this pilot's total score of Japanese aircraft to five, and another was destroyed by Sub-Lt R. F. Mackie.

More strikes were flown against enemy shipping on 28, 29 and 30 July. On this occasion, the Seafires of the *Implacable's* 801 and 880 Squadrons also participated, their range greatly extended by American P-38 auxiliary fuel tanks slung under their bellies. The tanks had been 'liberated' from a USAAF stores depot in New Guinea in exchange for several cases of Scotch.

After the strikes at the end of July, operations were delayed for nine days because of bad weather and the dropping of the first atomic bomb on Hiroshima on 6 July. The attacks were resumed on the 9th, the day when the second atomic bomb obliterated Nagasaki.

This time, the main target was a concentration of shipping in Onagawa Wan. Shortly after sunrise, a strike of four Corsairs of 1841 Squadron was flown off by the *Formidable*. Over Onagawa Wan, in the blue early morning haze, the pilots spotted five enemy destroyers and escorts anchored around the fringes of the bay.

While two of the fighter-bombers strafed enemy anti-aircraft positions and a third provided top cover, the leader – Canadian-born Lieutenant Robert Hampton Gray, who had won the DSC for his part in the *Tirpitz* strikes the year before – dived towards the escort sloop *Amakusa*. Levelling out at a hundred feet above the water, he streaked towards the target at close on four hundred miles an hour, his Corsair the focal point for glowing streams of anti-aircraft fire from thirty guns around the anchorage. Pieces flew off the aircraft, which was almost hidden by fountains of spray whipped up by the storm of shellfire. The distance between the aircraft and the enemy ship closed rapidly. Suddenly, the Corsair was enveloped in a brilliant glare as a shell slammed into the fuel tank in its port wing, sending a sheet of flame streaming in the fighter's wake.

The Corsair's single 1,000-pound bomb hit the warship just aft of the funnel and the *Amakusa* erupted in a vast cloud of flame and smoke. Out of the other side of the oily mushroom a burning comet emerged, a ball of fire that climbed steeply, trailing a thick streamer of smoke. The shattered Corsair reached the top of its arc, then plunged into the water in a cloud of incandescent wreckage.

Gray was later awarded a posthumous Victoria Cross, the second to be won by a Fleet Air Arm pilot.

On 10 August, in a series of strikes that lasted from dawn until dusk, the Fleet Air Arm brought the total of Japanese warships sunk or damaged during the two-day operation to six. Fifty aircraft were also destroyed on the ground for the loss of thirteen FAA machines. With the terms of the Japanese surrender being negotiated, the main body of the British Pacific Fleet returned to Sydney, leaving the *Indefatigable,* the *KGV,* two cruisers and ten destroyers in Japanese waters.

At dawn on 15 August the Avengers of 820 Squadron were intercepted by ten Zeros during an attack on targets in the Tokyo area. The Japanese fighters were immediately overwhelmed by the Seafires of 887 and 894 Squadrons, who shot down eight of the Zeros for the loss of one of their own number. It was the last time that fighters met in combat during World War Two.

Two hours later, all offensive operations against the Japanese home islands were suspended.

14 One Damn' War after Another

The dust of the Second World War had hardly had time to settle when the time-bomb left behind by the retreating Japanese exploded and a series of bitter conflicts evolved out of the post-war chaos in South-East Asia, spreading like tentacles from the struggle between Communists and Nationalists in China. Guerrilla organizations which had fought against the Japanese now turned their weapons on former allies in a bid to establish communist domination in Indo-China, Burma and Malaya.

In the summer of 1948, British forces found themselves committed to large-scale security operations against the Malayan People's Anti-British Army (MPABA). Under the difficult conditions imposed by the mountainous, heavily-forested Malayan terrain, the ground forces could not have operated without air support; in June 1948 this was provided by the Spitfires of Nos. 28 and 60 Squadrons, the Mosquitos and Spitfires of No. 81 Squadron, and the Sunderland flying-boats of Nos. 205 and 209 Squadrons, Royal Air Force. These were joined in August by the Beaufighters of 45 Squadron, and air strikes against communist hideouts became a daily occurrence.

Early in 1949, however, No. 28 Squadron was withdrawn to strengthen the defences of Hong Kong, and soon afterwards additional reinforcements – including Seafires – arrived at the colony aboard the maintenance carrier *Unicorn*. The transfer of 28 Squadron left the RAF's strike forces in Malaya badly depleted, and it was not until August 1949 that the light fleet carrier *Ocean* arrived at Seletar docks with two more squadrons, Nos. 33 and 80.

So far, Fleet Air Arm aircraft had not taken part in Operation Firedog, as the strikes against the Malayan terrorists was known.

In May 1949, however, the light fleet carrier *Triumph* sailed to join the Royal Navy's forces in the Far East, and in December of that year she was detached to assist the RAF in the Malayan operations. On 19 December 1949 her Seafires and Fireflies of 800 and 827 Squadrons joined RAF Beaufighters and Tempests in rocket and strafing attacks on terrorist bases near Kluang – the first of several similar strikes. The *Triumph* was one of eight 13,000-ton light fleet carriers commissioned during 1945 and 1946. The first four – the *Venerable* (1851 and 814 Squadrons), the *Colossus* (1846 and 827 Squadrons), the *Glory* (1831 and 837 Squadrons) and the *Vengeance* (1850 and 812 Squadrons) had joined the Pacific Fleet at the end of the war, but all except the *Venerable* – whose aircraft had destroyed a number of Japanese MTBs off Hong Kong in September 1945 – had arrived too late to see service. The *Colossus* later went to the French Navy and became the *Arromanches;* the *Venerable* became the Dutch *Karel Doorman* in 1948; and the *Vengeance,* after being loaned to the Royal Australian Navy, was sold to Brazil in 1956.

The other four were the carriers *Triumph, Ocean, Theseus* and *Warrior;* each was capable of operating up to forty aircraft. The *Ocean,* in fact, had the distinction of being the first carrier in the world to land-on a jet aircraft when a de Havilland Sea Vampire touched down on her flight deck off the Isle of Wight on 3 December 1945, the aircraft being piloted by Lt-Cdr E. M. Brown.

This historic deck landing heralded the start of a new era for the Fleet Air Arm. At the end of the war, the Royal Navy had found itself the proud possessor of several thousand first-line American naval combat aircraft – Corsairs, Hellcats, Avengers – which, under the terms of Lease-Lend, had to be paid for if they were retained. With Britain in the grip of a postwar financial crisis and severe reductions in the strength of the armed forces coming into effect, this was out of the question – and most of them were simply dumped over the side. A few Hellcats and Corsairs equipped the light carrier air groups until the middle of 1948, when they were replaced by Seafire 47s, Sea Furies and Firefly 5s.

The Royal Navy, however, had not been slow to recognize the potentialities of the jet aircraft, and following the first jet deck landing a small batch of Sea Vampires was ordered for jet familiarization flying. But neither the Vampire nor the Meteor – the first two RAF jet fighters – was considered suitable for carrier operations, and in 1946 the Admiralty placed an order for two prototypes of a new jet aircraft – the Supermarine Attacker, which first flew on 26 July that year. In 1949, it was decided to order enough Attackers to equip three FAA squadrons as an interim measure until an even more advanced jet fighter, the Hawker Sea Hawk, came into service. In the event, Nos. 800, 803 and 890 Squadrons commissioned with the Attacker in 1952, and the type remained in first-line service until 1954. After that, it equipped several Reserve squadrons, and it was not until 1957 that the Attacker disappeared from Fleet Air Arm service.

Early in 1950, however, it was the Firefly, Seafire and Sea Fury that formed the standard equipment of the FAA's air groups: and it was with these aircraft that the Fleet Air Arm was soon to be engaged in another conflict.

On 25 June 1950 the North Korean Army struck southwards across the 38th Parallel and the United Nations called upon member countries to go to the aid of the unprepared, hard-pressed South Koreans. Small units of poorly-trained, badly-equipped American base troops were hurriedly flown in from Japan and flung into combat, but the Northern advance swept on unchecked to within fifty miles of the vital south coast port of Pusan, seizing the Southern capital, Seoul.

When the invasion came, a force of British warships which had been in Japanese waters – the carrier *Triumph,* the cruisers *Belfast* and *Jamaica,* the destroyers *Cossack* and *Consort* and the frigates *Black Swan, Alacrity* and *Hart* – sailed immediately for the Yellow Sea. They were on action stations by 30 June, and the Seafire 47s and Firefly FR 1s of the *Triumph*'s air group immediately began operations against the enemy. Five days later, the RN force had been joined by two more British destroyers and seven warships drawn from the Canadian, Australian and New Zealand Navies.

Meanwhile, a second light fleet carrier – HMS *Theseus* – had also been warned for duty in Korean waters. She was in the United Kingdom at the time, and her 17th Carrier Air Group – No. 807 Squadron (Sea Furies) and No. 810 (Fireflies) – was disembarked at Ford for a period of ground-attack training. The Air Group was given only six weeks to get ready; the squadrons were short of fourteen pilots, and ten had to be drawn from training units. The squadrons got in some intensive flying on the way out to Singapore, which the *Theseus* left four days ahead of schedule to take part in defence exercises at Hong Kong. During these exercises, for which the Air Group was based on Kai Tak, 807 Squadron suffered a severe blow when its senior pilot, Lieutenant Green, was accidentally killed.

Early in October, HMS *Triumph* also arrived at Hong Kong. During three months of operations her aircraft had flown 895 sorties mainly in the ground attack role. Her arrival was the signal for the *Theseus*'s departure; the carrier went to action stations off Korea on 9 October, having embarked one Sikorsky S-51 plane guard helicopter at Hong Kong. There was only one serious incident on the way out, when a Firefly bounced over the barrier and destroyed two more.

The *Theseus* formed part of a Task Force under Rear-Admiral Andrews. Her Air Group began operations on the day of her arrival in the Yellow Sea, and between then and the 22nd the aircraft attacked targets at Chinnampo, Haeju, in Hwanghai Province and at Pakchon and Chonju. Several strikes were flown against Chinnampo, which the UN forces – now beginning to drive the North Koreans back – hoped to capture and use as a supply port. During this period, 807 Squadron flew 264 sorties and the Fireflies of 810 flew 120. On the 22nd, the carrier withdrew for a short rest at Iwakuni, Japan, returning early in November to cover minesweeping operations in the Chinnampo estuary. She then returned to Hong Kong to take part in another exercise, having temporarily disembarked six of her Fireflies for bombardment spotting duties.

The next series of strikes was mounted between 6 and 26 December, the aircraft this time concentrating on roads, bridges, airfields and rolling stock – any target whose destruction might help to impede the advance of the Chinese Field Armies which were now pouring into the country, and give the UN forces a badly-needed respite. So far, no enemy aircraft had been encountered by the Fleet Air Arm pilots; in fact, none were to be met at all by the *Theseus*'s aircraft during her period of operations, and the only damage was caused by anti-aircraft fire and technical troubles. The latter gave one of 807 Squadron's pilots, Lieutenant D. P. W. Kelly, a few nasty moments on Christmas Day 1950, shortly after he had set off on a strike in his heavily-laden Sea Fury; the engine began to bang and cough alarmingly and there was nothing for it but to ditch in the icy waters of the Yellow Sea. Kelly wasn't encouraged by the rumour, currently doing the rounds, that it was impossible to ditch a Sea Fury successfully – but he brought it off all right and the aircraft stayed afloat long enough to allow him to scramble out of the cockpit. Fortunately, the ditching had been seen by the crew of the Canadian destroyer *Sioux*, which picked him up minutes later. He was flying again the next day.

During the December series of strikes, the 17th Carrier Air Group flew 630 sorties. Throughout the period, Fireflies equipped with long-range tanks maintained anti-submarine patrols; it was known that the small North Korean Navy had two Russian-built submarines and they were believed to be in the Yellow Sea, but they were not sighted. A combat air patrol was also maintained during daylight, and a staggering total of 3,900 interceptions and visual identifications were made by the Fireflies and Sea Furies. All the aircraft intercepted turned out to be Allied types, mainly B-29s, Neptunes and Sunderlands.

Top cover – up to forty thousand feet – for all strikes launched by the *Theseus* and subsequent carriers operating off Korea was provided by the United States Air Force, with Mustangs, F-84s, F-80s and later Sabres. Strikes were often directed by T-6 or L-4 light spotter aircraft. Armed reconnaissance was the task of 810 Squadron's Fireflies, flying at fifteen hundred feet or less over enemy territory – often a risky business because of intense small-arms fire. The information they and other UN recce aircraft brought back was co-ordinated by the Joint Operations Centre at Taegu, where two US Navy and one Royal Navy liaison officers analyzed potential targets for assignment to the carrier aircraft. The high quality of the reconnaissance, resulting in very accurate and devastating strikes, soon made enemy movements in daylight extremely hazardous. Bridges were among the main objectives; following the earlier strikes, however, reconnaissance showed that the enemy was rebuilding these almost as quickly as the FAA knocked them down, so from then on delayed action bombs were used to make his task more difficult.

Because of the shallow waters off the Korean coast, the *Theseus* had to stand off at a distance of up to seventy miles – a long haul over water, in an aircraft suffering from battle damage. It was here that the plane guard S-51 helicopters proved their worth; they rescued four ditched pilots and also snatched another four from behind the enemy lines.

In January and February 1951, aircraft from the *Theseus* were engaged in spotting for the Allied naval forces bombarding Inchon. Afterwards, the carrier moved from her station on the west coast into the Sea of Japan, where, between 9 and 19 April, in company with the US carrier *Bataan,* her aircraft spotted for warships shelling Wonsan and Songjin. It was the British carrier's final operation in Korean waters, where she had spent a total of six and a half months. During that time, her aircraft had made 3,489 operational sorties, dropping 92, 1,000-pound and 1,474 500-pound bombs, launching 7,317 rocket projectiles and firing over half-a-million rounds of 20-mm ammunition. Many of the operational sorties had been flown in bad weather, particularly in December and January, when snowstorms often swept across the country without warning.

The *Theseus* was relieved by HMS *Glory,* whose aircraft carried on in the pattern laid by the preceding carrier. In the summer of 1951, she flew off eighty-four sorties in a single day, setting up a record that was broken the following year by HMS *Ocean*'s 802 and 825 Squadrons. In one period of seventy-nine days flying, they averaged a daily sortie rate of 76.3, the highest for one day's operations being 123 – which was later equalled by the *Glory* during a second tour in Korean waters.

The *Ocean*'s 802 Squadron set up a new record, too, when one of its Sea Furies shot down a MiG-15 – the first jet aircraft to be destroyed by the Fleet Air Arm. The Fireflies and Sea Furies were never seriously challenged by enemy fighters, and although North Korean and Chinese Yak-9s, La-7s and La-9s began to appear in increasing numbers during 1951, they were always effectively dealt with by the escorting American fighters. Then the MiG-15 appeared in Korean skies. It was an aircraft about which the Allies knew very little at that time, and there was quite a sensation when one fell practically into their lap, in ten feet of water to the north of Chinnampo to be exact, in August 1951. The aircraft was located by an S-51 helicopter from HMS *Glory* and subsequently retrieved by the frigate *Cardigan Bay* and a landing ship, providing the Allies with the opportunity of examining the type in detail for the first time.

There were fears that the Fleet Air Arm's piston-engined aircraft might suffer badly at the hands of the MiG-15, but fortunately this was not the case – mainly because the type was encountered only on rare occasions. Only once before the end of 1952 did some MiG-15s succeed in breaking through the fighter cover to attack a formation of 802 Squadron Sea Furies during a strike; it happened on 9 August 1952, and the Sea Furies came out best in the argument – one MiG being shot down by Lieutenant P. Carmichael and three more damaged by other Furies. Only two of the latter sustained any damage.

Altogether, five fleet carriers – the *Triumph, Theseus, Glory, Ocean* and HMAS *Sydney* – served in Korean waters; the *Glory* spent longer in the war zone than any of the others, carrying out three separate tours off Korea. In a total of 316 days in the combat zone, she flew off 9,500 operational sorties. The total number of combat sorties flown by the five carriers was almost thirty thousand, and in three years of war the Sea Fury and Firefly squadrons lost twenty-two pilots killed – a remarkably light casualty figure, considering the risk involved in striking at heavily-defended targets, and one due in no small measure to the complete air superiority enjoyed by the UN Air Forces.

Throughout the operations, spares and replacements were ferried to the war zone by the maintenance carrier HMS *Unicorn* and, on one occasion, by HMS *Warrior*.

As far as the Fleet Air Arm was concerned, one of the major lessons to emerge from the Korean War was the usefulness of the helicopter for a variety of tasks ranging from air-sea rescue to anti-submarine warfare. The Royal Navy's first operational helicopter squadron, No. 848, was formed at the end of 1952 and hurriedly sent out to Malaya, equipped with Sikorsky S-55s supplied under the Mutual Defence Assistance Programme. Officers and men had no opportunity of training and flying together before leaving, and their experience on the S-55 was severely limited. Nevertheless, during 1953, the Squadron – commanded by Lt-Cdr Sydney H. Suthers – airlifted over ten thousand troops and evacuated two hundred and twenty casualties, as well as transporting two hundred thousand pounds of freight, dropping leaflets and carrying out reconnaissance work in support of the security forces. The S-55s spent more than three thousand hours in the air during the year; the squadron never had to cancel an operation because of unserviceability and none of the helicopters was lost. It was quite a remarkable achievement.

In October 1953 the Fleet Air Arm's first anti-submarine helicopter squadron – No. 706 – was formed at Gosport and moved to Eglinton in Northern Ireland with its Whirlwind 1s. No one, at this stage, seriously believed that Naval policy would, in just a few years' time, envisage the replacement of most of the FAA's fixed-wing aircraft by helicopters – but few would deny that the Royal Navy's helicopters seemed destined to play an increasingly important part in the years to come.

15 Operation Musketeer

Shortly before midnight on 31 October 1956 a stick of 500-pound bombs erupted slap on the intersection of the runways at Almaza airfield, a few miles to the north-east of Cairo. They had been dropped by a Canberra B.2 bomber of No. 10 Squadron, RAF, one of a formation which had taken off from Nicosia in Cyprus fifty minutes earlier. The Egyptians knew nothing of the presence of the aircraft until the first bombs exploded; the Canberras were bombing from forty thousand feet, the dull rumble of their engines lost in the thunder of the bomb-bursts.

During the night, the Canberras of 10 and 12 Squadrons and the Valiants of No. 148, operating out of Malta, attacked a total of twelve Egyptian airfields in the Nile Delta and on the Suez Canal. It was the preliminary to Operation Musketeer – the Anglo-French invasion of Suez and occupation of key points on the Canal.

Forty-eight hours earlier, in the evening of 29 October, Israeli forces had thrust into Sinai and fought their way through the Mitla Pass in the face of stiff Egyptian resistance, spearing westwards to Port Tewfik and then southwards to join up with the Israeli Parachute Brigade at El Tur. Meanwhile, on the afternoon of 30 October, a joint ultimatum had been delivered by Britain and France to the governments of Egypt and Israel, stating that unless hostilities ceased and both sides withdrew ten miles from the Suez Canal an Anglo-French force would occupy key positions to safeguard joint interests. The ultimatum was rejected by Egypt and it was decided to go ahead with the invasion, plans for which had been in force for some time.

On 31 October there were thirty-two RAF bombers, fighter, PR and transport squadrons based on Cyprus and Malta – the biggest concentration of aircraft seen in the eastern Mediterranean since the war. Two French fighter and two transport squadrons were also based on Cyprus, at Akrotiri and Tymbou. With the coming of daylight on 1 November the attacks on the airfields were kept up by RAF Canberras and Venoms, together with French Air Force F-84F Thunderstreaks, all operating out of Cyprus. RAF Meteors and Hunters also took part, but their combat radius was strictly limited and they were not used again after the first day.

By this time, the Fleet Air Arm had also arrived on the scene in the carriers *Eagle*, *Bulwark* and *Albion*, and throughout that day an intensive series of strikes was flown by the Wyverns of 830 and 831 Squadrons, the Sea Hawks of 800, 802, 804, 810, 897 and 899 Squadrons, and the Sea Venoms of Nos. 809, 891, 893, 894 and 895 Squadrons. Post-strike reconnaissance was the task of the Skyraiders of 849, 'A' Flight being embarked in the *Eagle* and 'B' in the *Albion*. A great deal of attention was paid to the airfields on the coast and in the vicinity of Cairo itself – Dekheila, Inchas, Cairo West, Almaza and Bilbeis; the Fleet Air Arm aircraft attacked with rockets, bombs and cannon, knocking out fifty enemy aircraft on the ground. These included five MiG-15s and eight Ilyushin 28 jet bombers.

The following day – after more night raids by the RAF's Canberras and Valiants – the French carrier *Arromanches,* formerly HMS *Colossus,* arrived and the Corsairs of her 14F and 15F fighter squadrons began a series of attacks on Egyptian naval vessels in Alexandria harbour and on various installations in the area. The Fleet Air Arm meanwhile went on hitting the airfields but now switched part of its offensive against supply depots, gun emplacements, communications and military targets around Port Said. At no stage did the naval aircraft meet any opposition from Egyptian fighters; some thirty MiG-15s and twenty Ilyushin 28s had been hurriedly evacuated to Syria and Saudi Arabia on the night of the 31st, before the airfields came under heavy attack, and those that were left were destroyed on the ground during the next three days. Twenty more Ilyushins flew south to Luxor, where they were all promptly destroyed in a surprise attack by French fighters based in Israel.

HMS *Albion* was withdrawn for refuelling on 3 November, leaving the *Eagle* and the *Bulwark* to carry on the offensive. With the date of the actual invasion now fast approaching, the Fleet Air Arm concentrated its attacks on targets around the main landing zone at Port Said. This area was heavily defended, and some of the aircraft suffered severe damage from anti-aircraft fire. It was here that the FAA suffered its first loss of the operation, when one of the *Eagle*'s Wyverns dived into the ground and blew up after receiving a direct hit.

The *Albion* returned to her station on Sunday 4 November, relieving the *Eagle* which also withdrew for replenishment in turn. As the *Albion* and the *Bulwark* continued their attacks on targets in the Port Said area, the United Nations called for a ceasefire – but it was too late. The invasion forces were already committed. Two invasion fleets – one British, consisting of a hundred warships including the light fleet carriers *Ocean* and *Theseus,* which had been hurriedly equipped for assault duties, and one French, comprising thirty ships – were already heading for Egypt from Malta and Cyprus.

At 04.44 hours on Monday 5 November the first wave of transport aircraft – the vanguard of a total of six RAF Hastings and Valetta squadrons, and two FAF Noratlas units – roared away from their airfields in Cyprus and set course southwards over the Mediterranean. Soon after 07.00 hours the British 16th Parachute Brigade and the French 2nd Parachute Regiment – seven hundred and fifty men in all – tumbled from the bellies of their transports and went down on two key points, Gamil airfield and a vital bridge connecting Port Said with the main road leading south.

The troops of the 16th Brigade met stiff resistance, and the Fleet Air Arm was called in to give close support. The *Eagle* was now back on station, and this time it was HMS *Bulwark* that withdrew. During the four days of combat, her air group had been particularly successful, destroying or damaging over a hundred Egyptian aircraft and sinking four MTBs. The score of aircraft destroyed included seven Ilyushin 28s, eight MiG-15s, nine

Harvards, seven Dakotas, six C-46s, a Lancaster, a Meteor and a Hawker Fury.

Meanwhile, the invasion fleets were forging steadily closer to the Egyptian coast, their path swept by the Malta-based Shackletons of 37 Squadron, RAF Coastal Command, and covered by patrols of Hunters and F-84Fs from Cyprus. Throughout the voyage, the fleets had been subjected to considerable annoyance from the American Sixth Fleet, whose warships crossed and re-crossed the track of the invasion force while US Naval aircraft circled overhead, causing a good deal of confusion on the Allied radar screens. American submarines were also detected on the fringes of the convoy, but sheered off prudently when the British and French escorts, not knowing whether the intruders were Russian or not, went to action stations and closed in on them. Fortunately there were no incidents, although some US Navy pilots very nearly got a nasty surprise when they buzzed the French cruiser *Georges Leygues;* the French gunners came within in seconds of opening fire before the aircraft were identified as F-4 Furies.

By Monday night, after further paradrops, both Gamil airfield and the bridge at Port Said were in Allied hands, although it had taken several hours of heavy fighting to secure these two objectives. The Fleet Air Arm and the French Navy flew standing patrols over the combat areas, diving down to strike at pockets of enemy resistance when called in by the ground forces. Once again, the naval aircraft took considerable punishment – particularly the Wyverns, whose size made them very vulnerable to small-arms fire. However, all the aircraft returned safely to their carriers, but some were so badly shot up that they took no further part in the operations.

At dawn on the 6th, the main invasion fleet was within range. On the flight decks of the carriers *Ocean* and *Theseus,* the Whirlwinds of No. 845 Squadron and the Whirlwinds and Sycamores of the Joint Experimental Helicopter Unit were already running up their engines as the men of No. 45 Royal Marine Commando filed aboard. Minutes later they took off and headed for their objectives, while two more Royal Marine Commandos

stormed ashore from landing craft. It was the first large-scale heli-
copter-borne assault in history, and it was over in less than
ninety minutes. After they had landed the Marines, the Whirlwinds and Sycamores turned to casualty evacuation; the first
Marine casualty was being operated on in the *Ocean*'s sick bay
less than an hour after he had eaten breakfast in the same carrier
prior to the assault.

The carrier aircraft were now operating flat out in support
of both the advancing Marines and the paratroops, who were
pushing their way steadily through Port Said to link up with
the new arrivals. In some cases, the Egyptians fought back vali-
antly and had to be winkled out of their strong-points with
tanks or aircraft. The bitterest resistance came from the Admiralty building, where Egyptian sailors succeeded in beating off
several assaults. In the end, a flight of Sea Hawks was called in
and pulverized the building with three-inch rockets.

Ironically, it was on this day – the last day of fighting – that
the Fleet Air Arm suffered its heaviest loss, when a Wyvern and
two Sea Hawks were shot down. The pilots of the Wyvern and
one of the Sea Hawks baled out and were picked up, but the
pilot of the second Sea Hawk was killed. That brought the total
Fleet Air Arm losses for the week of fighting to only four aircraft
– a small price to pay, especially since three of the pilots had
been saved, for a large share in the destruction of two hundred
and sixty enemy aircraft. The French had lost a Corsair and a
Thunderstreak, both their pilots being killed – as were the crews
of two RAF aircraft, a Venom and a photo-reconnaissance Canberra, the latter shot down by a MiG-15 while on a mission to
gather photographic evidence of the build-up of Soviet aircraft
on Syrian airfields.

British and French naval aircraft continued to fly patrols and
reconnaissance missions over Egyptian territory for another week
after the cease-fire, until the arrival of the first United Nations
troops on the 15th. During the operation itself, the Fleet Air
Arm's strike aircraft had made some sixteen hundred sorties; at
the peak period, the number of carrier take-offs and landings had
averaged one every two-and-a-half minutes. Four hundred more

sorties had been made by the helicopters from the *Ocean* and the *Theseus*. By the end of November, the Anglo-French forces in Suez totalled more than twenty thousand men and four thousand vehicles; the last of them was re-embarked on 23 December, leaving the United Nations in somewhat unsteady control of the situation.

In terms of the aims it had been designed to achieve, there was no disputing the fact that the Suez operation had been a failure. It had been intended to safeguard the canal, but had only resulted in the Egyptians blocking it with seventeen thousand tons of sunken ships – although most accounts of the operation, written by its opponents, conveniently forget to mention that the greater part of the block-ships were raised by an Anglo-French salvage force within two months of the invasion. Perhaps the most serious result of the operation, however, was that it opened the door for Soviet expansion in the Middle East.

As an example of military co-operation, however – and international co-operation at that – 'Musketeer' had been a resounding success. The results, nevertheless, were regarded with mixed feelings. The advocates of an independent British nuclear deterrent felt, justifiably, that the Suez incident lent weight to their cause – and one wonders whether, if Britain had possessed an effective nuclear striking force at that time, the Russians would have been quite so ready with their threats to obliterate London and Paris. For both the Royal Air Force and the Fleet Air Arm, the speed and effectiveness with which enemy targets had been demolished had depended not on surprise – the RAF had dropped leaflets warning of the strafing attacks hours before they began – but on the fact that the Egyptian MiGs and Ilyushins had, on Russian advice, not been committed to the battle. If the Allied strike aircraft had met with determined opposition, the outcome might have been very different.

As far as the Fleet Air Arm in particular was concerned, the value of the assault carriers and their complement of troop-carrying helicopters had been ably demonstrated, and this was to play its part in influencing the future naval policy that resulted in the rebuilding of the *Albion* and the *Bulwark* as commando carriers. The naval strategies, however, appeared to have missed the point; the success of the assault helicopters at Suez was largely due to the fact that opposition had been neutralized by successive air strikes. To commit helicopters to an assault on a hostile objective, without air cover and in the face of strong opposition, would have been little short of suicidal, but the Royal Navy was never called upon to do this during the Suez operation – nor has it been forced to make such an attempt since then, at least not so far. If the high casualty rate suffered by American helicopters in Vietnam in recent years – even when supported by helicopter gunships and fighter bombers – is anything to go by, perhaps it is just as well.

16 The Flying Fire Brigade

In July 1958, less than two years after the Suez crisis, the threat of war once again loomed in the Middle East. The Lebanon was torn by internal strife and her territory was being infiltrated by Syrian troops; and on 15 July the pro-Western government of Iraq was overthrown by a military coup and the Iraqi royal family brutally massacred. Both King Hussein of Jordan and President Chamoun of Lebanon immediately asked Britain and the United States to intervene, fearing that their own governments were about to topple in turn.

The response was rapid. On 16 July United States Marines went ashore in the Lebanon and the following day the first units of the British 16th Parachute Brigade, the veterans of Suez, arrived in the Jordanian capital of Amman. Meanwhile, units of the Royal Navy were being hastily re-deployed to counter any emergency, including possible Soviet intervention. The carrier *Eagle* sailed from Malta and took up station to the east of Cyprus, accompanied by the cruiser *Sheffield* and a screen of destroyers and frigates, and her Sea Hawks and Sea Venoms maintained regular patrols within sight of the Lebanese coast. The carrier HMS *Albion* arrived soon afterwards, having ferried No. 42 Royal Marine Commando from Portsmouth to Malta. She relieved the *Eagle* off Cyprus for a spell – during which time her aircraft, principally the Sea Venom FAW 21s of 809 Squadron, took part in rocket and strafing attacks on EOKA hideouts on the island – then she sailed for the Far East.

HMS *Bulwark,* in the meantime, had sailed from Mombasa to Aden with the 1st Battalion the King's Own Regiment. At Aden, she embarked the 1st Battalion of the Cameronians and ferried them up the Red Sea to the Jordanian port of Aqaba. The rapid deployment of troops by the Royal Navy, the US Sixth Fleet and the RAF had the desired effect; by the beginning of November, the tension had eased sufficiently to enable most of the units to be withdrawn. The Royal Navy's first major exercise in the 'Fire Bridgade' technique – the rapid movement of troops and equipment to counter the threat of a possible conflict – had worked extremely well, and set the pattern for future operations of this kind. The carrier *Albion* in particular had provided a classic example of the Navy's mobility; she was at Rosyth when the emergency began, yet within a matter of days she was fully operational off the Lebanese coast – having picked up 42 Royal Marine Commando at Portsmouth and disembarked the men at Malta on the way.

Just three years later, in July 1961, the Royal Navy played a leading part in preventing yet another Middle East crisis when General Kassim's revolutionary Iraqi Government threatened the tiny sheikhdom of Kuwait. On 30 June the British Government confirmed that it intended to honour its obligations to Kuwait, and the Admiralty announced that warships of the Far East Fleet were on their way to the Red Sea. The *Bulwark* was the first to arrive, and her 845 Squadron Whirlwinds immediately began to land Royal Marines. The fleet carriers *Centaur* and *Victorious* were also sent to the area; the latter carried No. 892 Squadron, the first to equip with Sea Vixens, and No. 893 with the same type was embarked in the *Centaur*. The Marines remained until 12 July, by which time the security of Kuwait had been assured by troops flown in by RAF Transport Command.

The next area in which units of the Fleet Air Arm were involved in a large-scale 'police' operation was Malaysia. In 1963, the 1957 defence agreement between Britain and Malaya was expanded to cover all Malaysian territory, including Sarawak and Sabah; and a request for British help came almost immediately after Indonesia had followed up a virulent propaganda campaign with armed infiltration into Sarawak and Sabah and clandestine landings on the coasts of Malaya and Singapore. The primary task of the Royal Navy was to prevent the landing of Indonesian irregulars on Singapore and Borneo – a far from easy task, as it involved maintaining constant patrols along a 1,300-mile coastline. In these operations the Westland Wasp helicopters of No. 829 Squadron played a leading part; operating from frigates, they were used to patrol the coastline during the dangerous dusk hours, and on more than one occasion they assisted in the capture of Indonesian raiding parties.

During the three years of confrontation the commando carriers *Bulwark* and *Albion* were very active, the Wessex HU. Mk. 5s of their 845, 846 and 848 Squadrons carrying out a variety of tasks ranging from patrol work to transport. Originally embarked in the *Albion*, No. 846 became Malaysia's 'resident' FAA helicopter squadron, and in 1963 was awarded the Boyd Trophy for its work in supporting British troops in Borneo. The difficult terrain called for a high degree of skill on the part of the Fleet Air Arm helicopter pilots; their landing-grounds usually consisted of rough wooden platforms erected in clearings hacked out of the forest on some convenient patch of high ground. Inevitably, a number of helicopters were accidentally written off. Although the brunt of the Fleet Air Arm's work in Malaysia fell on the helicopter squadrons, the Royal Navy's fleet carriers in the area took it in turns to maintain a show of strength by patrolling the contested areas with Sea Vixens, Scimitars and Buccaneers. While engaged in these operations, the fixed-wing aircraft were often detached to Changi air base.

Early in 1966 the fleet carrier HMS *Eagle* was on station in Malaysian waters when she was suddenly diverted to the east coast of Africa following developments in the Rhodesian crisis. From the middle of March, her squadrons – Nos. 800 (Buccaneer S.1), 800B (Scimitar Tankers), 802 (Wessex HAS. 1), 849 'D' Flight (Gannet AEW 3) and 899 (Sea Vixen FAW 1) were engaged in maintaining a non-stop patrol off the port of Beira to intercept any tankers carrying oil for the rebel regime. During the seventy-one days the carrier spent on patrol her Scimitars, Buccaneers, Sea Vixens and Gannets flew over one thousand sorties. In two thousand hours' flying, during which they searched an area roughly twice the size of the British Isles, they covered over 600,000 miles. A thousand sorties were also flown by the helicopters, including plane guard duties. A major part of the burden fell on the crews of 849; one Gannet had to be airborne all the time to keep the area under radar surveillance. By the beginning of May, when the carrier was relieved by the *Ark Royal,* her aircraft had located and identified no fewer than seven hundred and fifty ships in the Mozambique Channel area, and her average daily rate of take-offs and landings had doubled.

The oil-watch flying was not without its risks. The carrier was the only base in the area; there was no diversion airfield available in the event of an emergency. With flying going on at a fairly intense rate, the occasional emergency was inevitable – such as that which faced Lieutenant Allan Tarver, a Sea Vixen pilot with the *Ark Royal*'s 890 Squadron, on the morning of 10 May 1966.

Tarver was heading back to the carrier at the end of a patrol when several things happened all at once. The port engine flamed-out, the electrical system packed in completely, and the instruments indicated that fuel was escaping from the Vixen's tanks at a fast rate. Tarver immediately called up the *Ark Royal,* and was advised that a Scimitar tanker had just been catapulted off and was on its way to rendezvous with the Vixen, which by this time had begun to lose height steadily.

At fifteen thousand feet, with the *Ark* still forty miles away, Tarver spotted the Scimitar approaching from ten o'clock. The Scimitar pilot, Lieutenant Robin Munro-Davies, manoeuvred his aircraft into position above and ahead of the Vixen; from the cockpit, Tarver saw the drogue stream towards him from the tanker. Five times, he tried to make contact with the Vixen's probe, but it was impossible to keep the unwieldy aircraft steady enough.

Suddenly, the whine of the Vixen's one remaining engine died away as the fuel tanks ran dry and the aircraft started to go down rapidly. The pilot could now see the carrier on the horizon; there wasn't a hope of reaching her, but he could try and stretch the glide for as long as possible before he and his observer, Lieutenant John Stutchbury, were forced to eject. The closer they were to the *Ark Royal,* the better their chances of being picked up quickly.

The Vixen glided like a brick. At six thousand feet, Tarver ordered the observer to eject. Out of the corner of his eye he saw Stutchbury reach up, grasp the firing handle of the ejection seat, and jerk the blind down over his face.

Nothing happened. Over the intercom, Tarver yelled at the observer to try and bale out manually while he held the aircraft as steady as possible. It wasn't as easy as it sounded; the observer in a Sea Vixen has a pretty uncomfortable position, his seat buried in the starboard side of the fuselage so that his head is just about level with the pilot's backside. It was a tight enough squeeze for the average man: but for John Stutchbury, six feet tall and with amazingly broad shoulders, it was dreadfully cramped. There was no cockpit canopy over the observer, just a hatch in the top of the fuselage; this should have blasted clear when he pulled the handle – but it hadn't.

Stutchbury now pushed the hatch aside and through the per-spex of the canopy Tarver saw it whirl away in the slipstream. A second later, Stutchbury's head and shoulders emerged – and stuck fast in the opening. By this time the Vixen was down to three thousand feet. Tarver shoved the stick hard over, praying that Stutchbury would fall clear as the aircraft rolled over on her back. But the observer still hung there, buffeted by the two hundred-knot slipstream. Again Tarver rolled the aircraft, still with no effect. There was just one more chance: he lowered the flaps, reducing the airspeed to one hundred and thirty knots. The force of the airflow was much less now, and this might just enable the observer to struggle clear. For an instant, it looked as though the plan would work; more of Stutchbury's body slid through the hatch until the observer was lying flat along the top of the fuselage – but something still seemed to be holding him in the cockpit. Tarver leaned over into the observer's compartment, his hand groping for Stutchbury's feet. With all his remaining strength, he fought to push his friend clear. It was no use; the observer now seemed to be unconscious.

There was nothing more that Tarver could do. Even if Stutch-bury got clear of the aircraft now, his parachute would not have time to open. The altimeter showed four hundred feet and the Vixen was teetering on the edge of a stall.

Circling overhead in the Scimitar, Lt Munro-Davies saw Tarver's Vixen flick into a roll to port. When the aircraft was at about sixty degrees, a black shape hurtled from the cockpit: the pilot's ejection seat. That was all Munro-Davies saw before the whole scene dissolved in a fountain of spray as the Vixen hit the water. The Scimitar pilot reported that Tarver could not possibly have survived.

But Tarver was still very much alive. Although stunned by the impact, he managed to claw his way out from under the folds of his half-opened parachute and inflate his rubber dinghy. Twenty minutes later, he was picked up by the *Ark Royal's* plane guard Wessex. His only injury was a strained muscle in his back.

For his courage in trying to save his friend's life, almost sacri-ficing his chances of survival in so doing, Tarver was later awarded the George Medal.

Between 1964 and the end of 1967, Buccaneers, Sea Vixens and Scimitars from the Royal Navy's fleet carriers – in addition to helicopter detachments from the two commando carriers and 814, 820 and 826 Squadrons – were active at intervals over Southern Arabia, the fixed-wing aircraft engaged in surveillance and occasional strike missions in the troubled Radfan area. These operations were carried out under the control of the RAF Tactical Wing at Khormaksar.

In November 1967, following the British Government's deci-sion to bring forward the date of South Arabia's independence, the Royal Navy assembled the biggest task force since the Suez operation of 1956 in the Gulf of Aden to cover the British with-drawal. The task force was split into two groups; the first con-sisted of the commando carrier *Bulwark,* the assault ship *Fearless* and the fleet carrier *Eagle,* whose squadrons were responsible for providing air cover. The second group, consisting of HMS *Albion,* the assault ship *Intrepid* and the carrier *Hermes,* took up station later in the month. The final stages of the withdrawal were covered by the Royal Marines, and the Wessex helicopters of 845 and 848 Squadrons were the last Naval aircraft to leave the area. Fleet Air Arm squadrons involved in the operation were: Nos. 800 (Buccaneer S.2, *Eagle*), 809 (Buccaneer S.2, *Hermes*), 820 (Wessex HAS.1, *Eagle*), 826 (Wessex HAS.1, *Hermes*), 845 (Wessex HU.5, *Bulwark*), 848 (Wessex HU.5, *Albion*), 849 (Gannet AEW 3, *Eagle* and *Hermes*), 892 (Sea Vixen FAW 2, *Hermes*) and 899 (Sea Vixen FAW 2, *Eagle*). Detachments from 845 and 848 Squadrons also operated from the *Fearless* and the *Intrepid*.

During recent years, the Royal Navy has placed great emphasis not only on the mobility of carriers but also on the rapid deployment of individual squadrons, operating from both carriers and shore bases. The Fleet Air Arm's long-range capability was first demonstrated on 4 October 1965, when Buccaneer S.2 XN974 – piloted by Cdr G. Higgs, CO of the Naval Test Squadron at Boscombe Down – flew from Goose Bay, Labrador, to Lossiemouth, covering the 1,950 miles in four hours sixteen minutes without refuelling. It was the first non-stop crossing of the Atlantic ever made by a Fleet Air Arm aircraft, and the Buccaneer still had enough fuel for a further half-hour's flying in its tanks when it landed. The aircraft was one of three which had been undergoing tropical trials at the US Navy base of Pensacola, during which they had made some one hundred take-offs from the carrier USS *Lexington*. Later that same year, another Buccaneer stayed in the air for eight hours forty minutes, being refuelled twice by a Victor BK.1A tanker of the RAF from Marham.

In June the following year a Buccaneer S.2 of 801 Squadron – which was working up with the new type on the *Victorious* in the Irish Sea – made a 2,300-mile non-stop flight to Gibraltar and back, carrying out a simulated low-level attack on the airfield at Gibraltar at the end of the outward leg. The crew of the aircraft were Lt K. B. Cross, RN (pilot) and Lt-Cdr G. Oxley, RN (observer). The *Victorious* and 801 Squadron sailed for the Far East soon afterwards, where the Buccaneers took part in an exercise with the US Navy, together with the American carrier USS *Enterprise,* whose Douglas Skywarriors acted as flight-refuelling tankers for the British aircraft on several occasions.

In 1968 the Fleet Air Arm gave another demonstration of its new mobility when twelve Sea Vixen FAW 2s of 893 Squadron flew non-stop from RNAS Yeovilton to RAF Akrotiri, Cyprus, refuelling from Victor tankers en route. It was the longest flight ever made by the Sea Vixen – some 2,200 miles – and the first time that a naval air squadron had been deployed in this way. Operating from the shore base, the Vixens took part in a ten-day air defence exercise over the island before returning to the United Kingdom. A few months later, in November, a large-scale NATO air-sea exercise – 'Eden Apple' – was staged in the Mediterranean, with the main object of providing a show of strength for the benefit of Soviet naval forces in the area. The Fleet Air Arm squadrons involved again operated from shore bases, to demonstrate the effectiveness (or lack of effectiveness) of shore-based air support for the Royal Navy after most units of the fleet carrier force have been phased out of service in the 1970s. During the exercise, the twelve Buccaneer S.2s of 800 Squadron were based on Luqa, Malta, while the Sea Vixens of 899 Squadron and the six Gannet AEW 3s of 849 'D' Flight operated out of Decimomannu in Sardinia. The Buccaneers co-operated with RAF Canberras in carrying out strikes against targets on land and at sea, while the Vixens maintained a continuous day-and-night combat air patrol in relays of two aircraft over the warships engaged in the exercise. One early warning Gannet was also continuously on station.

By way of a contrast, also in 1968, the fleet carrier *Eagle* demonstrated her continued value as a mobile air base when she took part in the NATO naval exercise 'Silver Tower' in the North Atlantic. It was the first time that a major NATO exercise had been held without an American attack carrier, because of the latters' heavy commitments elsewhere, and on this occasion the *Eagle* formed the spearhead of the striking force, comprising forty-three ships. As the striking force steamed eastward to the south of Iceland, it was systematically overflown by Russian

Bison, Badger and Bear reconnaissance aircraft, all of which were intercepted by the *Eagle*'s Vixens and escorted clear of the area. Most of the interceptions took place well beyond the range of shore-based fighter aircraft – a fact that makes its own pointed comment on the theory, so often disproved by history, that land-based aircraft can provide adequate protection for naval forces. On the other hand, several hits on the *Eagle* were claimed by 'enemy' submarines; whether these claims were valid has not been revealed. Several 'kills' were in turn claimed by the carrier's anti-submarine Wessex helicopters.

While the *Eagle* was engaged in Exercise Silver Tower, HMS *Hermes* – which had begun a new commission the previous May – was in the Far East, and in August 1968 she played her part in a new experiment designed to establish the feasibility of providing rapid air reinforcement for the Far East Fleet without the need for large shore establishments in the area. Four Buccaneer S.2s of 803 Squadron flew from Lossiemouth to join the carrier in the eastern Indian Ocean staging through Nicosia, Masirah and Gan, and refuelling in flight from Victor tankers. After spending a few days on board the *Hermes,* the aircraft returned by the same route. It was another convincing demonstration of the carrier's value in providing a powerful striking force in an area where no shore bases may be available in the future.

It is not often in peacetime that the Fleet Air Arm's pilots get a taste of the 'real thing' – an opportunity to use live weapons against shipping. It happened in March 1967, however, by accident – when the huge tanker *Torrey Canyon* broke her back on Seven Stones Reef, sixteen miles off Land's End, and released a massive oil slick that spread out across the Channel. Somewhat belatedly, the RAF and Royal Navy were ordered to bomb the tanker and set her on fire. Operating from Lossiemouth and using Brawdy as an advance base, eight Buccaneers of Nos. 800 and 736 Squadrons dropped forty-two 1,000-pound high explosive bombs on the tanker – which stubbornly refused to sink or burn – on 28 March alone, following up with more attacks during the succeeding days until the *Torrey Canyon* was finally ablaze. It was all good practice, but as a demonstration of effective striking power – against a stationary target, at that – it was hardly impressive.

No survey of Fleet Air Arm operations over the past decade, however brief, would be complete without mention of one task in which the Royal Navy, and particularly the FAA's helicopter pilots, have excelled: air-sea rescue. One of the most classic examples occurred on 13 September 1958, when the 20,500-ton Liberian tanker *Melika* and the 10,715-ton French tanker *Fernand Gilabert* collided and caught fire in the Gulf of Oman. The carrier *Bulwark*, which was in the area at the time in support of British troop movements to Middle East trouble spots, picked up the tankers' distress call and soon afterwards the stricken ships were sighted by a Skyraider of 849 Squadron. A fire-fighting party was landed on the *Fernand Gilabert* by the *Bulwark*'s helicopters, and some time later the blaze was put out. The carrier then headed for Masira Island, and as soon as she was in range her helicopters flew some badly injured members of the French tanker's crew to the RAF base there, where they were taken to hospital. While other British warships took the *Fernand Gilabert* in tow and headed for Karachi, the *Bulwark* returned to the *Melika* and took her in tow – but the cable parted several times, and eventually it was decided to make for Ras al Hadd on the coast of Oman rather than attempt the long haul to Karachi.

After the *Bulwark* had been refuelled by the fleet auxiliary *Wave Knight,* the crippled tanker was once again taken in tow by the carrier and the frigate HMS *Puma*. This time, the *Bulwark*'s Sea Hawks ran up their engines on the flight deck and the powerful thrust of their jets helped to train the ship on course. A week after the collision, on 20 September, the *Melika* was safely brought to anchor in the shelter of the coast. After repairs by the Royal Navy, the tanker was eventually towed to Naples by the fleet tug *Warden*.

In the United Kingdom, a helicopter of a particular RNAS Station Flight is usually on standby for air-sea rescue duties. Because of its location near the holiday beaches of Cornwall, one of the most active ASR Flights is that of RNAS Culdrose, which is under the control of the Southern Rescue Co-ordination

Centre at Mount Batten, Plymouth. Most of the rescues – which are on the increase every year – involve swimmers, climbers and the crews of small boats who get into difficulties among the treacherous currents of the Cornish coast. Several of the Royal Navy helicopter crews have received awards for bravery for their part in rescue operations during recent years.

The primary function of the Fleet Air Arm and the Royal Navy in these troubled times is to maintain a show of strength, a powerful and mobile deterrent to aggression, in areas where the interests of Britain and her allies are at stake. But few would deny that the Fleet Air Arm's 'sundry duties' such as air-sea rescue have done much to underline the efficiency and raise the prestige of the Navy's aircrews at a critical moment in the Service's history.

17 The Future of British Naval Air Power

On 31 March 1969 No. 892 Squadron of the Fleet Air Arm was commissioned at RNAS Yeovilton. The ceremony marked the end of an era; for unless there is a drastic change in present policy, No. 892 – equipped with Phantom FG.1s – will probably be the last Fleet Air Arm squadron to see operational service with conventional fixed-wing aircraft.

Early in 1970 No. 892 embarked in HMS *Ark Royal* – the only British carrier adapted to operate the Phantom in the full sense, although the *Eagle* has been fitted with more powerful catapults and arrester gear to enable her to receive detachments of Phantoms when necessary. In fact, by 1973 – under the existing policy – the *Ark Royal* and the *Eagle* will be the Royal Navy's only attack carriers, and the *Ark Royal* will reach the mid 1970s as a fully operational unit. The *Hermes* is scheduled to end her operational life in the attack role in 1972-3, and the *Centaur* is already being used as an accommodation ship. That leaves the *Albion* and the *Bulwark,* the two commando carriers.

The idea that shore-based aircraft can provide adequate cover for the Royal Navy's surface units, or for merchant convoys in time of war – which will be the policy from 1972 onwards – is not a new one. It has seldom worked in the past, and there is no reason to suppose that it will work in the future. Even assuming that the Royal Air Force had full use of NATO and Commonwealth bases, air cover could only be provided on anything like the necessary scale in the North Sea, the Mediterranean and the eastern part of the Indian Ocean. There would be dangerous gaps in mid- and south-Atlantic, while the vital routes around the Cape and in the western Indian Ocean would be left

completely naked. The only RAF aircraft of the 1970s with sufficient range to maintain surveillance over these areas is the
Hawker Siddeley Nimrod long-range maritime aircraft, but with
only thirty-eight due to enter service the resources of RAF Strike
Command's Maritime Group are going to be stretched to the
absolute limit – and in any case, the Nimrod squadrons are being
concentrated in the United Kingdom and the Mediterranean.
The Fleet Air Arm is entering the 1970s with four operational
types of fixed-wing aircraft: the Phantom FG.1, the Buccaneer
S.2, the Gannet AEW 3 and the Sea Vixen FAW 2. The latter,
which equips three first-line squadrons, is nearing the end of its
useful life; the Phantoms and Buccaneer will eventually be
turned over to the RAF, which was compelled to accept the Buccaneer as an interim aircraft to fill the gap between the cancelled
TSR 2 long-range strike and reconnaissance aircraft and the
Multi-Role Combat Aircraft at present being studied by Britain,
West Germany and Italy – assuming that this type ever leaves
the drawing-board.

This means that by the late 1970s the Fleet Air Arm will have
been reduced to a helicopter force. The Wessex HU.5 will remain
the standard equipment of the two commando carriers; some of
these helicopters have been converted into 'gunships' by the addition of rocket-launchers and 7.6 2mm machine-guns, but they
are far less effective in this role than, say, the Bell HueyCobra
which has been used with devastating effect in Vietnam. Without
the support of fixed-wing strike aircraft or fast 'gunships', helicopter assault operations are extremely hazardous – as the
Americans have learned the hard way during the Vietnam War

Helicopters have already taken over a large part of the Royal
Navy's anti-submarine work, with Westland Wasps – eventually
to be replaced by the Anglo-French WG-13 – operating from
frigates, and Wessex HAS 3s, now being augmented by the West-
land-built Sikorsky Sea King, operating from converted Tiger-
class cruisers, LSDs or Fast Fleet Replenishment Ships. The Sea
King is also envisaged as a partial replacement for the old Gannets in the Airborne Early Warning role, but the only suitable
ship to operate the AEW helicopters will be the commando car-

rier, which will need at least four Sea Kings to maintain continual surveillance – and which will have to relinquish some of its assault helicopters to accommodate them. AEW is perhaps the most vital role of all, for it means the difference between survival and disaster for a naval force at sea. The function of the AEW aircraft is to detect enemy forces, both sea and air, at extreme range and to direct strike or fighter aircraft on to their targets. With many warships now equipped with surface-to-surface missiles, the AEW role has taken on added importance in recent years – but since its whole concept depends on giving a naval force sufficient warning to enable it to destroy the enemy before he can come within striking distance, it is difficult to see how it can be really effective without the assistance of carrier-based strike aircraft and fighters. The tendency to regard surface-to-air missiles as sufficient defence for a naval force is a dangerous one, for the enemy must be allowed to strike first before they can be used – and quite apart from that, missiles cannot identify a possible target visually.

A possible solution to the naval strike/fighter problem once the carriers have gone would be the introduction of VTOL aircraft like the Hawker Siddeley Harrier now in service with the RAF – but it would need a vessel at least the size of a cruiser to operate just four of these aircraft, taking their support and maintenance requirements into account; and this assumes that the Harrier could be successfully developed for naval operations as a stop-gap measure until a true naval VTOL aircraft and carrier came along. In any case, if a first-generation VTOL combat aircraft like the Harrier was used, it would be cheaper and more effective to keep the existing carriers in commission and operate the aircraft from them, rather than to split them up into small flights divided piecemeal among the fleet. The latter course is rather like saying that half-a-dozen corner shops are more profitable than one branch of Woolworth's! The same argument applies to those who advocate several small carriers in place of a smaller number of large ones; the cost of the smaller carriers would be greater and their overall effectiveness less.

A logical step would be to take a leaf out of the French Navy's book and acquire a number of Anglo-French Jaguar strike fighters for the Fleet Air Arm. This type is due to enter service with the RAF in the mid-seventies, and with the French Navy. It is supersonic and can carry a 10,000-pound warload, and – easily capable of operating from carriers of 23,000 tons or even less – would provide the Fleet Air Arm with a highly efficient multi-role weapon system until well into the 1980s.

To sum up the future of British naval air power is impossible, for one cannot sum up uncertainties. All one can say is this: that in 1980, Britain will be relying on her ocean lifelines for survival just as much as she did in 1880; and to leave those lifelines virtually denuded of the protection of the Royal Navy's most effective weapon, the carrier and its aircraft, will be to invite disaster – especially in the face of the growing naval strength of potential enemies. In an age where military and naval thinking is dictated by the hydrogen bomb, it is too easily forgotten that a nation, particularly an island nation, could be reducd to impotence by a non-nuclear war fought on the high seas.

The lessons of history, apparently, still remain unlearned.

Appendix 1

Fleet Air Arm Squadrons in Major Combat
Operations, 1939–56

Date	Operation	Squadron	Aircraft	Base
Autumn	Atlantic	800	Skua	*Ark Royal*
1939	shipping	801	Skua	*Furious*
	protection/	803	Skua	*Ark Royal*
	Graf Spee	810	Swordfish	*Ark Royal*
	hunt	811	Swordfish	*Courageous*
		814	Swordfish	*Hermes*
		816	Swordfish	*Furious*
		818	Swordfish	*Furious*
		820	Swordfish	*Ark Royal*
		821	Swordfish	*Ark Royal*
		822	Swordfish	*Courageous*
		700	Seafox (one)	*Ajax*
		710	Walrus	Freetown
Spring	Norway	800	Skua	Orkneys &
1940				*Ark Royal*
		801	Skua/	*Furious* &
			Roc	*Ark Royal*
		802	Sea	
			Gladiator	*Glorious*
		803	Skua	*Ark Royal*/
				Orkneys/
				Glorious
		804	Sea	
			Gladiator	*Furious* &
				Glorious
		810	Swordfish	*Ark Royal*
		816	Swordfish	*Furious*
		818	Swordfish	*Furious*
		820	Swordfish	*Ark Royal*
		823	Swordfish	*Glorious*
		825	Swordfish	*Furious*
Summer/	Mediter-	800	Skua	*Ark Royal*
Autumn	ranean	806	Fulmar	*Illustrious*
1940		808	Fulmar	*Ark Royal*
		810	Swordfish	*Ark Royal*
		813	Swordfish/	

Date	Operation	Squadron	Aircraft	Base
			Sea Gladiator	*Eagle*
		815	Swordfish	*Illustrious*
		818	Swordfish	*Ark Royal*
		819	Swordfish	*Illustrious*
		820	Swordfish	*Ark Royal*
		824	Swordfish	*Eagle*
Spring 1941	Eastern Med/ Crete	803	Fulmar	*Formidable*
		805	Fulmar	*Formidable*
		,,	Buffalo	} Crete
			Sea Gladiator	
			Hurricane	
		806	Fulmar	*Formidable*
		815	Swordfish	Crete
		826	Albacore	*Formidable*
		829	Albacore	*Formidable*
May 1941	N. Atlantic/ *Bismarck* hunt	800	Fulmar	*Victorious*
		807	Fulmar	*Ark Royal*
		808	Fulmar	*Ark Royal*
		810	Swordfish	*Ark Royal*
		818	Swordfish	*Ark Royal*
		820	Swordfish	*Ark Royal*
		825	Swordfish	*Victorious*
July 1941	Syrian Campaign	803	Hurricane	Ramat David
		806	Hurricane	Ramat David
		815	Swordfish	Nicosia
		826	Albacore	Nicosia
		829	Albacore	Ramat David
July 1941	Kirkenes and Petsamo	800	Fulmar	*Furious*
		809	Fulmar	*Victorious*

Date	Operation	Squadron	Aircraft	Base
		812	Swordfish	Furious
		817	Albacore	Furious
		827	Albacore	Victorious
		828	Albacore	Victorious
		880A	Sea Hurricane	Furious
Autumn 1941 to Autumn 1942	Russian Convoys	802	Sea Hurricane	Avenger
		809	Fulmar	Victorious
		817	Albacore	Victorious
		820	Albacore	Victorious
		825 Flt.	Swordfish	Avenger
		832	Albacore	Victorious
		883	Sea Hurricane	Avenger
May 1942	'Ironclad' (Diego Suarez)	800	Fulmar	Indomitable
		806	Fulmar	Indomitable
		810	Swordfish	Illustrious
		827	Albacore	Indomitable
		829	Swordfish	Illustrious
		831	Albacore	Indomitable
		880	Sea Hurricane	Indomitable
		881	Martlet II	Illustrious
		882	Martlet	Illustrious
August 1942	'Pedestal' (Malta Convoy)	800	Sea Hurricane	Indomitable
		801	Sea Hurricane	Eagle
		804	Sea Hurricane	Furious
		806	Martlet II	Indomitable
		809	Fulmar	Victorious
		813	Sea Hurricane (two)	Eagle

Date	Operation	Squadron	Aircraft	Base
		813	Swordfish	Gibraltar (Disembarked)
		817	Albacore	*Victorious*
		822	Albacore	*Furious*
		824	Swordfish	*Eagle*
		827	Albacore	*Indomitable*
		831	Albacore	*Indomitable*
		832	Albacore	*Victorious*
		880	Sea Hurricane	*Indomitable*
		884	Fulmar	*Victorious*
		885	Sea Hurricane	*Victorious*
November 1942	'Torch' (North Africa)	880	Sea Hurricane	*Biter*
		801	Seafire	*Furious*
		802	Sea Hurricane	*Avenger*
		804	Sea Hurricane	*Dasher*
		807	Seafire	*Furious*
		809	Fulmar	*Victorious*
		817	Albacore	*Victorious*
		820	Albacore	*Formidable*
		822	Albacore	*Furious*
		832	Albacore	*Victorious*
		833	Swordfish	*Biter*
		880	Seafire	*Argus*
		882	Martlet	*Victorious*
		883	Sea Hurricane	*Avenger*
		884	Fulmar	*Victorious*
		885	Seafire	*Formidable*
		888	Martlet	*Formidable*
		891	Sea Hurricane	*Dasher*

Date	Operation	Squadron	Aircraft	Base
		893	Martlet/ Fulmar	Formidable
July 1943	'Husky' (Sicily)	807	Seafire	Indomitable
		817	Albacore	Indomitable
		820	Albacore	Formidable
		880	Seafire	Indomitable
		885	Seafire	Formidable
		888	Martlet	Formidable
		893	Martlet	Formidable
		899	Seafire	Indomitable
9/12 September 1943	Salerno	807	Seafire	Battler
		808	Seafire	Battler
		809	Seafire	Unicorn
		810	Barracuda	Illustrious
		820	Albacore	Formidable
		834	Seafire	Hunter
		878	Martlet	Illustrious
		879	Seafire	Attacker
		880	Seafire	Stalker
		885	Seafire	Formidable
		886	Seafire	Attacker
		887	Seafire	Unicorn
		888	Martlet	Formidable
		890	Martlet	Illustrious
		893	Martlet	Formidable
		894	Seafire	Illustrious/ Unicorn
		897	Seafire	Unicorn
		899	Seafire	Hunter
Sept. 1941- Sept. 1944	Battle of the Atlantic	800	Hellcat	Emperor
		802	Martlet	Audacity
		804	Hellcat	Emperor
		808A	Seafire	Battler
		811	Swordfish/ Wildcat	Biter

194

Date	Operation	Squadron	Aircraft	Base
		813	Swordfish/Wildcat	Campania
		816	Swordfish/Seafire	Tracker
		818	Swordfish	Unicorn
		819	Swordfish	Archer/Activity
		824	Swordfish	Unicorn/Striker
		825	Swordfish/Sea Hurricane	Vindex
		833	Swordfish/Wildcat	Stalker/Activity
		834	Swordfish/Seafire	Hunter
		835	Swordfish/Sea Hurricane	Nairana/Battler
		842	Swordfish/Seafire/Wildcat	Fencer
		846	Avenger/Wildcat	Tracker
		879	Seafire	Attacker
		881	Wildcat	Pursuer
		882	Wildcat	Searcher
		886	Seafire	Attacker
		887	Seafire	Unicorn
		892	Martlet	Archer
		896	Wildcat	Pursuer
		898	Wildcat	Searcher
		836		Maydown
		840	Swordfish	(N. Ireland) and
		860		MAC-Ships

Date	Operation	Squadron	Aircraft	Base
August 1944	'Dragoon'	800	Hellcat	Emperor
Sept.-Oct.	(S. France)	807	Seafire	Hunter
1944	and the	809	Seafire	Stalker
	Aegean	879	Seafire	Attacker
		881	Wildcat	Pursuer
		882	Wildcat	Searcher
		899	Seafire	Khedive
3 April,	'Tungsten'	800	Hellcat	Emperor
17 July and	'Mascot'	801	Seafire	Furious
22-29 Aug.	and 'Good-	804	Hellcat	Emperor
1944	wood'	820	Barracuda	Indefatigable
	(Tirpitz	826	Barracuda	Indefatigable/
	strikes)			Formidable
		827	Barracuda	Victorious/
				Formidable/
				Furious
		828	Barracuda	Formidable
		829	Barracuda	Victorious
		830	Barracuda	Furious/
				Formidable
		831	Barracuda	Furious
		842	Swordfish	Fencer/
				Furious
		846	Avenger/	Trumpeter
			Wildcat	
		852	Avenger/	Nabob
			Wildcat	
		880	Seafire	Furious
		881	Wildcat V	Pursuer
		882	Wildcat V	Searcher
		887	Seafire	Indefatigable
		894	Seafire	Indefatigable
		896	Wildcat V	Pursuer
		898	Wildcat V	Searcher
		1770	Firefly	Indefatigable
		1834	Corsair	Victorious
		1836	Corsair	Victorious

Date	Operation	Squadron	Aircraft	Base
		1840	Hellcat	*Furious/ Indefatigable*
		1841	Corsair	*Formidable*
		1842	Corsair	*Formidable*
October 1944 to May 1945	Norway (shipping strikes)	746A	Firefly	*Searcher*
		801	Seafire	*Implacable*
		813	Swordfish	*Campania*
		821	Barracuda/ Wildcat	*Puncher*
		828	Barracuda	*Implacable*
		835	Swordfish/ Wildcat	*Nairana*
		841	Barracuda	*Implacable*
		842	Wildcat	*Campania/ Fencer*
		846	Avenger/ Wildcat	*Premier/ Trumpeter*
		852	Avenger/ Wildcat	*Fencer/ Trumpeter*
		853	Avenger/ Wildcat	*Queen*
		856	Avenger/ Wildcat	*Premier*
		880	Seafire	*Implacable*
		881	Wildcat	*Premier/ Pursuer/ Trumpeter*
		882	Wildcat	*Searcher*
		887	Seafire	*Implacable*
		894	Seafire	*Implacable*
		1771	Firefly	*Implacable*
March 1944 to May 1945	Russian convoys	811	Swordfish/ Wildcat	*Vindex*
		813	Swordfish/ Wildcat	*Campania/ Vindex*
		816	Swordfish/ Wildcat	*Chaser*

Date	Operation	Squadron	Aircraft	Base
		819	Swordfish/ Wildcat	Activity
		824	Swordfish/ Wildcat	Striker
		825	Swordfish/ Wildcat	Vindex
		835	Swordfish/ Wildcat	Nairana
		842	Swordfish/ Wildcat	Fencer
		846	Avenger/ Wildcat	Tracker/ Trumpeter
		853	Avenger/ Wildcat	Tracker/ Queen
		856	Avenger	Premier
April 1942	Defence of Ceylon	800	Fulmar	Indomitable
		803	Fulmar	Trin- comalee
		806	Fulmar	Trin- comalee
		814	Swordfish	Hermes
		820	Albacore	Formidable
		827	Albacore	Indomitable
		831	Albacore	Indomitable
		880	Sea Hurri- cane	Indomitable
		888	Martlet	Formidable
1943-1944	Indian Ocean Trade Protection	832	Avenger/ Wildcat	Begum
		834	Swordfish/ Seafire/ Wildcat	Battler
		845	Avenger	Ameer
		851	Avenger/ Wildcat	Shah
		889	Seafire	Atheling
		890	Wildcat	Atheling

Date	Operation	Squadron	Aircraft	Base
May-July 1943	Solomons (Task Group 36.3)	832	Avenger I	*Victorious*
		882	Wildcat IV	*Victorious*
		896	Wildcat	*Victorious*
		898	Wildcat	*Victorious*
April 1944 to 5 January 1945	Indian Ocean (strikes on Andamans, Nicobars and Sumatra)	810	Barracuda	*Illustrious*
		815	Barracuda	*Indomitable*
		817	Barracuda	*Indomitable*
		820	Avenger	*Indefatigable*
		822	Barracuda	*Victorious*
		831	Barracuda	*Victorious*
		832	Avenger	*Illustrious*
		845	Avenger	*Illustrious*
		847	Barracuda	*Illustrious*
		849	Avenger	*Victorious*
		854	Avenger	*Illustrious*
		857	Avenger	*Indomitable*
		887	Seafire	*Indefatigable*
		888	Hellcat	*Indefatigable*
		894	Seafire	*Indefatigable*
		1770	Firefly	*Indefatigable*
		1830	Corsair	*Illustrious*
		1833	Corsair	*Illustrious*
		1834	Corsair	*Victorious*
		1836	Corsair	*Victorious*
		1837	Corsair	*Illustrious*
		1839	Hellcat	*Indomitable*
		1844	Hellcat	*Indomitable*
January 1945	Palembang	820	Avenger	*Indefatigable*
		849	Avenger	*Victorious*
		854	Avenger	*Illustrious*
		857	Avenger	*Indomitable*
		887	Seafire	*Indefatigable*
		894	Seafire	*Indefatigable*
		1770	Firefly	*Indefatigable*
		1830	Corsair	*Illustrious*

Date	Operation	Squadron	Aircraft	Base
		1833	Corsair	*Illustrious*
		1834	Corsair	*Victorious*
		1836	Corsair	*Victorious*
		1839	Hellcat	*Indomitable*
		1844	Hellcat	*Indomitable*
		S&R	Walrus (2)	*Victorious*
January 1945	Bay of Bengal; Andamans, Burma & Sumatra strikes	800	Hellcat	*Emperor/ Shah*
		804	Hellcat	*Ameer/ Empress/ Shah*
		807	Seafire	*Hunter*
		808	Hellcat II	*Khedive/ Emperor*
		809	Seafire	*Stalker*
		845	Avenger	*Empress/ Shah*
		851	Avenger II	*Emperor/ Shah*
		879	Seafire	*Attacker*
		888	Hellcat PRII	*Empress/ Emperor/ Ameer*
		896	Hellcat	*Ameer/ Empress*
		1700	Sea Otter (S&R)	*Emperor/ Hunter/ Khedive/ Stalker/ Ameer*
March-April 1945	Sakishima (Task Force 57)	Squadrons and ships the same as for the Palembang strikes, with the addition of:		
		848	Avenger	*Formidable*
		1841	Corsair	*Formidable*
		1842	Corsair	*Formidable*

Date	Operation	Squadron	Aircraft	Base
July-	Strikes on	801	Seafire	*Implacable*
August	Japan	820	Avenger	*Indefatigable*
1945	(TF 37)	828	Avenger	*Implacable*
		848	Avenger	*Formidable*
		849	Avenger	*Victorious*
		880	Seafire	*Implacable*
		887	Seafire	*Indefatigable*
		894	Seafire	*Indefatigable*
		1771	Firefly	*Implacable*
		1772	Firefly	*Indefatigable*
		1834	Corsair	*Victorious*
		1836	Corsair	*Victorious*
		1841	Corsair	*Formidable*
		1842	Corsair	*Formidable*
		1844	Hellcat	*Formidable*

The following squadrons were embarked on carriers of the Fleet Train (Task Force 112):

		Squadron	Aircraft	Base
		885	Hellcat	*Ruler*
		1840	Hellcat	*Speaker*
1950-1953	Korea	800	Seafire 47	*Triumph*
		801	Sea Fury	*Glory*
		802	Sea Fury	*Ocean*
		804	Sea Fury	*Glory*
		805	Sea Fury	*HMAS Sydney*
		807	Sea Fury	*Theseus*
		808	Sea Fury	*HMAS Sydney*
		810	Firefly 5	*Theseus*
		812	Firefly 5	*Glory*
		817	Firefly 5	*HMAS Sydney*
		820	Firefly 5	*Glory*
		825	Firefly 5	*Ocean*
		827	Firefly FR.1	*Triumph*

Date	Operation	Squadron	Aircraft	Base
Oct.-Nov. 1956	'Musketeer' (Suez)	800	Sea Hawk	*Albion*
		802	Sea Hawk	*Albion*
		804	Sea Hawk	*Bulwark*
		809	Sea Venom	*Albion*
		810	Sea Hawk	*Albion*
		830	Wyvern	*Eagle*
		831	Wyvern	*Eagle*
		849 A Flt.	Skyraider	*Eagle*
		849 B Flt.	Skyraider	*Albion*
		845	Whirlwind	*Theseus*
		891	Sea Venom	*Eagle*
		893	Sea Venom	*Eagle*
		894	Sea Venom	*Albion*
		895	Sea Venom	*Albion*
		897	Sea Hawk	*Bulwark*
		899	Sea Hawk	*Eagle*

JEHU (Joint Experimental Helicopter Unit)

	Whirlwind/ Sycamore	*Ocean*

Appendix 2

Aircraft Carriers of the Royal Navy, 1919–69

Name	Type	Com'd	Disposal
Activity	Escort	1943	Reconverted after WW2; broken up in April 1968 in Hong Kong as SS *Nan Chang*.
Africa and *Arrogant*	Fleet carriers	—	Cancelled at end of WW2.
Albion	Fleet carrier, converted to commando carrier in 1961-2	1954	In service 1969.
Ameer	Escort	1943	Returned to USA.
Arbiter	Escort	1945	Served briefly in Pacific (11th ACS) as ferry carrier. Returned to USA.
Archer	Escort	1943	Returned to USA.
Argus	Fleet carrier	1918	Scrapped after WW2.
Ark Royal (1)	Fleet carrier	1938	Torpedoed by the *U-81*, sank 14/11/41 while under tow.
Ark Royal (2)	Fleet carrier	1955	Laid down in 1943 as HMS *Irresistible*. Undergoing special refit in 1969, recommissioned in 1970.
Atheling	Escort (Assault CVE)	1944	Returned to USA.
Attacker	Escort (Assault CVE)	1943	Returned to USA.
Audacity	Escort	1941	Sunk by the *U-741*, 21/12/41.
Avenger	Escort	1942	Sunk by the *U-155*, 15/11/42.

204

Name	Type	Com'd	Disposal
Battler	Escort	1943	Returned to USA.
Begum	Escort	1944	Returned to USA.
Biter	Escort	1942	Transferred to French Navy, 1945, as the *Dixmude*; returned to USA and used as floating barracks, 1960; sunk as target vessel 1965.
Bulwark	Former 'Centaur' class fleet carrier converted to commando carrier 1959-60	1954	In service 1969.
Campania	Escort	1944	Used as HQ ship for Montebello A-bomb test, 1952; subsequently scrapped.
Centaur	Fleet carrier	1953	In service 1969; used mainly as an accommodation ship for carriers refitting.
Chaser	Escort	1943	Returned to USA.
Colossus	Light fleet carrier	1945	Sold to France in 1951 and renamed the *Arromanches*. In service 1969.
Courageous	Fleet carrier	1928	Sunk by the *U-29*, 17/9/39.
Dasher	Escort	1942	Caught fire and blew up, 27/3/43.
Eagle (1)	Fleet carrier	1921	Sunk by the *U-73* on 11/8/42.

Name	Type	Com'd	Disposal
Eagle (2)	Fleet carrier	1952	Laid down October 1942 as HMS *Audacious*. Reconstructed 1959-64; improvements included angled deck. In service in 1969.
Emperor	Escort	1943	Returned to USA.
Empress	Escort	1944	Returned to USA.
Fencer	Escort	1943	Returned to USA.
Formidable	Fleet carrier	1940	Placed in reserve and scrapped in 1953.
Furious	Fleet carrier	1922	Scrapped in 1947.
Gibraltar (*Audacious*-class)	Fleet carrier	—	Cancelled at end of WW2.
Glorious	Fleet carrier	1930	Sunk by the *Scharnhorst* and the *Gneisenau*, 8/6/40.
Glory	Light fleet carrier	1945	Operational in Korean War; scrapped in 1961.
Hercules	Light fleet carrier	1961	Construction suspended in 1946. Completed in 1961 for Indian Navy and renamed the *Vikrant*.
Hermes (1)	Fleet carrier	1922	Sunk by Japanese carrier aircraft, 9 April 1942.
Hermes (2)	Light fleet carrier	1959	Laid down in 1944 as HMS *Elephant*. Refitting in 1969.
Illustrious	Fleet carrier	1940	Scrapped in 1956.
Implacable	Fleet carrier	1944	Scrapped in 1955.
Indefatigable	Fleet carrier	1943	Scrapped in 1956.

Name	Type	Com'd	Disposal
Indomitable	Fleet carrier	1941	Scrapped in 1955.
Khedive	Escort	1944	Returned to USA.
Leviathan	Light fleet carrier	—	Suspended in 1946 and never completed. Towed from Portsmouth to be broken up at Faslane in May 1968.
Magnificent	Light fleet carrier	1946	Lent to Canada 1946-57. Scrapped in 1965.
Majestic	Light fleet carrier	1955	Modified and completed for Royal Australian Navy as HMAS *Melbourne*. In service in 1969.
Malta	Fleet carrier	—	Cancelled in 1945.
Monmouth	Light fleet carrier	—	Cancelled in 1945.
Nabob	Escort	1944	Damaged beyond repair, 1944.
Nairana	Escort	1943	Sold to Royal Netherlands Navy.
New Zealand	Fleet carrier	—	Cancelled in 1945.
Ocean	Light fleet carrier	1945	Fought in Korean War. Scrapped in 1962.
Patroller	Escort (Transport CVE)	1943	Returned to USA.
Perseus	Maintenance carrier	1945	Scrapped in 1958.
Pioneer	Maintenance carrier	1945	Scrapped in 1954.
Powerful	Light fleet carrier	1957	Completed for Royal Canadian Navy as HMCS *Bonaventure*.

Name	Type	Com'd	Disposal
Premier	Escort	1944	Returned to USA.
Pretoria Castle	Escort	1944	Used only for training in home waters and subsequently reconverted.
Puncher	Escort	1944	Returned to USA.
Pursuer	Escort	1944	Returned to USA.
Queen	Escort	1945	Returned to USA.
Rajah	Transport CVE	1945	Returned to USA.
Ranee	Transport CVE	1945	Returned to USA.
Ravager	Training CVE	1944	Returned to USA.
Reaper	Transport CVE	1945	Returned to USA.
Ruler	Escort	1945	Returned to USA.
Searcher	Escort	1944	Returned to USA.
Shah	Escort	1944	Returned to USA.
Slinger	Transport CVE	1944	Returned to USA.
Smiter	Escort	1945	Returned to USA.
Speaker	Escort	1945	Returned to USA.
Stalker	Escort	1943	Returned to USA.
Striker	Escort	1943	Returned to USA.
Terrible	Light fleet carrier	1949	Handed over to Royal Australian Navy and renamed HMAS *Sydney*. In service in 1969.
Thane	Escort	1944	Damaged by the *U-482* and returned to USA.
Theseus	Light fleet carrier	1946	Took part in Korean War. Scrapped in 1962.
Tracker	Escort	1944	Returned to USA.

Name	*Type*	*Com'd*	*Disposal*
Triumph	Light fleet carrier/ heavy repair ship	1946	Took part in Korean War. Converted into a heavy repair ship during late 1950s. In service in 1969, on Far East station.
Trouncer	Transport CVE	1945	Returned to USA.
Trumpeter	Escort	1943	Returned to USA.
Unicorn	Maintenance carrier	1943	Served during Korean War. Scrapped at Dalmuir in 1959.
Venerable	Light fleet carrier	1945	Sold to Royal Netherlands Navy in 1948 and renamed the *Karel Doorman*; resold to Argentina in 1968 and named the *De Mayo*.
Vengeance	Light fleet carrier	1945	Sold to Brazilian Navy in 1956; after modernization, was brought into service in 1960 as the *Minas Gerais*.
Victorious	Fleet carrier	1941	Decommissioned on 13/3/68; towed away to be broken up in 1969.
Vindex	Escort	1944	Reconverted after WW2. Still in merchant service as the *Port Vindex*, owned by the Port Line Ltd.
Warrior	Light fleet carrier	1946	Sold to Argentina in 1958; renamed the *Indepéndencia*.

Appendix 3

Aircraft of the Fleet Air Arm, 1924–69

Abbreviations

F/Str	Strike Fighter
AEW	Airborne Early Warning
ASW	Anti-Submarine Warfare
Comm	Communications
DB	Dive Bomber
FAW	All-Weather Fighter
FGA	Ground-Attack Fighter
GP	General Purpose
MRC	Multi-Role Combat
Sp/R	Spotter-Reconnaissance
S&R	Search and Rescue
TB	Torpedo Bomber
TBR	Torpedo-Bomber-Reconnaissance
TSR	Torpedo-Spotter-Reconnaissance

Manufacturer	Name	Role	Entered Service	Remarks
Avro	Bison	Sp/R	1923	41 delivered.
Beech	Traveller	Comm.	1941	Approx. 90 used by RN 1941-45.
Blackburn	Blackburn	Sp/R	1923	35 delivered to Nos. 420 and 422 Fleet Spotter Flights.
Blackburn	Baffin	TSR	1934	Development of Blackburn Ripon with radial engine.
Blackburn (HS)	Buccaneer S.1 and S.2	Strike	1962	Operational with Nos. 800, 801, 803 and 809 Sqns.
Blackburn	Dart	TB	1923	117 delivered. (Nos. 460-464 Fleet Torpedo Flights).
Blackburn	Firebrand	F/Str	1944	Equipped Nos. 708, 813 and 827 Sqns. Phased out in 1953.
Blackburn	Ripon	TSR	1929	Equipped Nos. 810, 811 and 812 Sqns. (HMS *Courageous, Furious* and *Glorious*) in 1933. Replaced by the Baffin.
Blackburn	Roc	Fighter	1940	136 built. Never operated from carriers. Served

Manufacturer	Name	Role	Entered Service	Remarks
				on shore bases only.
Blackburn	Shark	TSR	1936	Equipped Nos. 810, 820, 821 and 822 Sqns, and No. 705 Catapult Flt.
Blackburn	Skua	DB	1938	First FAA combat monoplane. Served with Nos. 800, 801, 803 and 806 Sqns.
Brewster	Buffalo	Fighter	1941	28 received by FAA. Some used by 805 Sqn in defence of Crete, and with 885 Sqn in Egypt.
Chance Vought	Corsair I to IV	Fighter	1944	1,977 delivered. Equipped Sqn nos: 1830 and 1831, 1833 to 1838, 1841 to 1843, 1845 to 1853.
De Havilland	Sea Hornet	FAW	1946	Equipped Nos. 801, 806 and 809 Sqns and Nos. 728 and 771 Fleet Requirements Units. Also 736, 738 and 759 Training Sqns.

Manufacturer	Name	Role	Entered Service	Remarks
De Havilland	Sea Vampire F.20 and F.21	Fighter	1946	Small batch only built for jet familiarization and experimental carrier flying.
De Havilland	Sea Vampire T.22	Trainer	1953	Standard FAA advanced trainer during 1950s. Identical with RAF's Vampire T.11.
De Havilland	Sea Venom NF 20	Night Fighter	1953	Naval version of Venom NF 2.
De Havilland	Sea Venom FAW 21/22	FAW	1954	Replaced the Sea Hornet. Operated with Nos. 809, 891, 893, 894 and 895 Sqns during Suez Campaign of 1956.
De Havilland (HS)	Sea Vixen	FAW	1959	Equipped Nos. 890, 892 and 893 Sqns and Nos. 766 (Trg.) and 899 (HQ) Sqns.
Douglas	Skyraider AD-4W	AEW	1952	Equipped No. 849 Sqn (four operational Flights embarked on various carriers).

Manufacturer	Name	Role	Entered Service	Remarks
Fairey	Albacore	TSR	1940	Entered service with 826 Sqn, in March 1940. Operated by 15 FAA Sqns. Total of 801 built.
Fairey	Barracuda	TBR	1943	No. 827 Sqn first to equip with type. First saw combat with 810 Sqn at Salerno. Total of 1,718 built.
Fairey	Firefly	Fighter	1943	Became operational with 1770 Sqn during *Tirpitz* attacks in 1944. Last combat ops. flown nine years later, over Korea and Malaya.
Fairey	Fulmar	Fighter	1940	Became operational with 806 Sqn, July 1940. Served with 14 FAA Sqns.
Fairey	Gannet A.S.1, A.S.4/ 5, T.2/5	ASW	1954	Entered service with No. 703 Sqn Service Trials Unit in April 1954. Operational with 826 Sqn, 1955.

Manufacturer	Name	Role	Entered Service	Remarks
Fairey	Gannet AEW 3	AEW		Replaced Sky-raiders with 849 Sqn. Based on RNAS Brawdy; flights detached for sea-going duties when required.
Fairey	Flycatcher	Fighter	1923	Standard Fleet fighter with FAA during late 1920s.
Fairey	Seafox	Sp/R	1937	All-metal two-seat floatplane. Still equipped five Catapult Flights at out-break of WW2.
Fairey	Seal	Sp/R	1930	FAA equivalent of RAF's Fairey Gordon.
Fairey	Swordfish	TSR	1936	Most famous of all FAA types. Became opera-tional with 825 Sqn, July 1936. Last operational mission flown only four hours before German surrender in May 1945. 2,391 Swordfish built.
Fairey	IIID/ IIIF	Sp/R	1924/ 1928	Reconnaissance floatplanes.

Manufacturer	Name	Role	Entered Service	Remarks
				IIIFs replaced all Blackburn Blackburns in 1931.
Gloster	Sea Gladiator	Fighter	1938	Served with Nos. 802, 804, 805, 813 and 885 Sqns. Total of 98 built or converted for FAA.
Grumman	Avenger	TBR	1943	Total of 1,958 Avengers of all marks supplied to FAA before end of WW2.
Grumman	Gosling (Widgeon)	Comm.	1944	Fifteen supplied to RN and used mainly in East Indies. Serials FP455-469.
Grumman	Martlet (Wildcat)	Fighter	1940	Total of 1,191 (all marks) supplied to FAA.
Grumman	Hellcat	Fighter	1943	Biggest kill ratio (19 to 1) of any fighter in WW2. Total of 1,182 supplied to FAA.
Hawker (HS)	Hunter T.8	Trainer	1958	Identical with the Hunter T.7, with the addition of airfield arrester hooks.

Manufacturer	Name	Role	Entered Service	Remarks
Hawker (HS)	Hunter GA 11	Weapon trainer	1962	Fifty converted from Hunter Mk. 4. Used as shore-based ground attack trainers.
Hawker	Nimrod	Fighter	1931	Equipped Nos. 800, 801 and 802 Sqns. Naval version of Hawker Fury biplane.
Hawker	Osprey	Sp/R	1932	Naval version of Hawker Hart.
Hawker	Sea Fury	Fighter	1948	Equipped Nos. 801, 802, 803, 804, 805, 807, 808 and 883 Sqns; also seven RNVR squadrons.
Hawker/ Armstrong Whitworth	Sea Hawk	Fighter (GA)	1953	Operated by Nos. 800, 802, 804, 810, 897 and 899 Sqns during Suez Campaign. All but 35 Sea Hawks built by Armstrong Whitworth.
Hawker	Sea Hurricane	Fighter	1941	Equipped Nos. 800, 801, 802, 804, 806, 824, 835, 877, 880,

Manufacturer	Name	Role	Entered Service	Remarks
				881, 883, 885 and 895 Sqns. Total of 800 built or converted.
Hunting (Percival)	Sea Prince	Trainer and Comm.	1951	Sea Prince T.1 used as radio, radar and ASW trainer; C.1 and C.2 served as light transport and comm. aircraft.
McDonnell-Douglas	Phantom F-4K	MRC	1968	First and only FAA operational Phantom Sqn is No. 892. Fifty F-4Ks on order. Will be handed over to RAF when FAA loses fixed-wing squadrons.
Parnall	Plover	Fighter	1923	Only six Plovers entered service with Nos. 403 and 404 Fleet Fighter Flts; Fairey Flycatcher selected in preference.

Manufacturer	Name	Role	Entered Service	Remarks
Short	Seamew AS1	ASW	1955	24 delivered to RN at Lossiemouth. Carrier trials carried out on HMS *Bulwark* and *Warrior*. Type generally unsuitable; served only a few months.
Short	Sturgeon	GT/TT	1950	Equipped No. 728 Sqn and the Fleet Requirements Unit at Hal Far, Malta.
Stinson	Reliant	Comm.	1943	Used in small numbers, mainly in the East Indies.
Supermarine	Attacker	Fighter	1951	FAA's first operational jet. Equipped Nos. 736, 800, 803 and 890 Sqns, and replaced Sea Furies with several Reserve squadrons.
Supermarine	Seafang	Fighter	1946	Naval version of Supermarine Spiteful. Eighteen only delivered to FAA handling unit; 7 never flew.

Manufacturer	Name	Role	Entered Service	Remarks
Supermarine	Seafire	Fighter	1942 (Seafire I)	Entered service with 807 Sqn, June 1942. First 166 converted from Spitfires. 1,982 Seafires (all Mks.) built during WW2. Last variant, Seafire FR47, used by 800 Sqn during Korean War.
Supermarine	Sea Otter	S&R	1944	Standard equipment with several Search and Rescue Flights, 1944-51, mainly in Far East.
Vickers-Supermarine (HS)	Scimitar	F/Str.	1957	Developed from Supermarine 525. Entered service with 803 and 807 Sqns, followed by 800 and 804 Sqns. Last of 76 aircraft delivered in 1960; type now phased out.
Supermarine	Seagull	GP/R	1926	Only a small number built; equipped No. 440 Flt.

Manufacturer	Name	Role	Entered Service	Remarks
Supermarine	Walrus	S&R	1937	Equipped Nos. 700, 711, 712 and 714 Fleet Spotter Sqns. Originally used as a Fleet reconnaissance aircraft, became better known for its air-sea rescue work.
Vought-Sikorsky	Chesapeake	DB/R	1941	50 aircraft, originally intended for France, allocated to RN in 1941. Only Chesapeake Sqn was No. 811 at Lee-on-Solent; type not suited to escort carrier work and used for training.
Vought-Sikorsky	Kingfisher	Trainer/Sp/R	1942	100 delivered to RN: saw service as trainers with FAA in West Indies, and as catapult-launched recce aircraft on armed merchant cruisers.
Vultee	Vengeance TT.IV	TT	1943	Used by the FAA in small numbers for target-tow-

Manufacturer	Name	Role	Entered Service	Remarks
				ing. Adapted from the Vengeance IV dive-bomber.
Westland	Lysander III	Target-tug	1941	20 supplied to 755 FAA Sqn at Worthy Down. Used until early 1943.
Westland	Walrus	Sp/R	1923	30 built from DH 9A spare parts. Equipped Nos. 420 and 421 Flights at Gosport.
Westland	Wyvern	F/Str	1953	Went into service with 813 Sqn, May 1953, followed by 827, 830 and 891 Sqns. Used by last two Squadrons in Suez operations.

HELICOPTERS

Manufacturer	Name	Role	Entered Service	Remarks
Hiller	HT.1/2	Training	1953 (HT.1) 1963 (HT.2)	Equips No. 705 Sqn at RNAS Culdrose. 24 HT-2s supplied.
Sikorsky	Hoverfly II	Comm/ Training	1946	First helicopter in British service. 15 supplied (705 Sqn).

Manufacturer	Name	Role	Entered Service	Remarks
Westland	Dragonfly (S-51)	S&R/ Comm/ plane guard	1950	Entered service with 705 Sqn.
Westland	Sea King	ASW	1969	First Sea King squadron in FAA, No. 700S, commissioned August 1969.
Westland	Wasp	ASW/ GP	1963	Entered service with 829 Sqn. Wasps deployed singly aboard 14 Tribal and Leander class frigates.
Westland	Wessex	ASW · (HAS 1&3) Commando transport (HU 5)		Equips Nos. 706, 737, 771, 814, 819, 820 and 826 Sqns (HAS 1 and 3) and Nos. 707, 845 and 848 Sqns (HU 5).
Westland	WG 13	ASW	—	Anglo-French anti-submarine helicopter for use on board frigates.
Westland	Whirlwind	GP/ S&R	1952 (HAR Mk 1)	Entered service with 848 Sqn; used extensively in Malaya during 1953. Whirlwind Mk 5 and

Manufacturer	Name	Role	Entered Service	Remarks
				HAS Mk 7 (anti-subversion) entered service in 1957. Gnome-engined HAS 7 became HAR Mk 9. Production phased out early 1968.

Index

226